Read stories by your favorite players, coaches, and sportswriters!

- Playing basketball with **Barack Obama** on the campaign trail
- **Pat Riley**—Miami Heat President; former coach of the Los Angeles Lakers and Miami Heat
- **Grant Hill**—current NBA player with the Phoenix Suns
- **Dolph Schayes**—former NBA great; one of the top 50 players in NBA history
- **Gregg Popovich**—head coach of the San Antonio Spurs
- **Caron Butler**—current NBA All-Star for the Washington Wizards
- **Chris Paul**—current NBA All-Star and USA Basketball Olympian
- **Greg Kite**—former NBA player
- **Skip Caray**—former well-known sports broadcaster
- **Bob Love**—former NBA All-Star
- **Ed O'Bannon**—Collegiate Basketball Player of the Year in 1995 for UCLA
- **Jim Les**—former NBA player and current college coach (Bradley University)
- **Jim Jones, Jr.** on how basketball gave him back his family name
- **Matt Doherty**—former UNC player and head coach; current head coach at SMU
- **Ann Meyers Drysdale**—first woman to play in the NBA; current GM of the Phoenix Mercury (WNBA)
- **Charlie Villanueva**—current NBA player
- **Chuck Daly**—Basketball Hall of Fame coach; won two championships with the Detroit Pistons; coached the 1992 Dream Team
- **Donn Nelson**—General Manager of the Dallas Mavericks

- **Sheila Johnson**—President of the Washington Mystics (WNBA)
- **Ron Hunter**—head coach at IUPUI
- **Sam Smith**—well-known sports writer/basketball columnist
- **Adonal Foyle**—current NBA player
- **John Gabriel**—NBA scout and former Orlando Magic General Manager
- **John Feinstein**—bestselling sports author

Praise for
Inside Basketball

Pat Williams utilizes his vast basketball experiences to capture the essence of the game he loves. Pat has many hoop friends that have played a vital role in providing these wonderful inspirational and motivational stories. It's awesome, baby!

~Dick Vitale, Broadcaster, ESPN

I enjoyed this book! ~Billy Packer, Broadcaster

Pat Williams has been involved in professional basketball for forty years, and there may not be a person in the history of the game who has seen and experienced as much as he has. Pat's gift is his vision and his ability to describe life in its details, which is what makes him a great NBA executive. It's also what inspired his book. In *Chicken Soup for the Soul: Inside Basketball*, Pat shares countless inspirational and beautiful stories from his career that prove basketball is much more than a game. It is life. And life is in the details — the stories, the relationships, the adversity, the challenges, the failures and successes — that make the game so human and so compelling. That's what this book is all about.

~Steve Kerr, President of Basketball Operations
and General Manager, Phoenix Suns

A great collection of wonderful messages.

~Jim Boeheim, Head Basketball Coach, Syracuse University

This offer of *Chicken Soup for the Soul* basketball stories is long overdue. I have enjoyed reading every one of them, and you will, too.

~Jerry Sloan, Head Coach, Utah Jazz

This batch of *Chicken Soup for the Soul* stories is guaranteed to delight basketball fans of all ages. Dive in and see what I mean.

~*Maurice Cheeks, Former Head Coach, Philadelphia 76ers*

I have used Pat Williams' books for guidance and inspiration since I was playing basketball in college. Pat is a great coach of the game of life. I look forward to using what I have learned from him as I embark on my head coaching career.

~*Pat Knight, Head Basketball Coach, Texas Tech University*

Pat Williams is very inspiring, and I loved reading this book concerning life and basketball. Pat has a unique way of combining the two. I recommend this book to anyone who wants to be inspired and educated. Pat is one of the best at expressing the magic of our wonderful game.

~*Jim Calhoun, Head Basketball Coach, University of Connecticut*

Pat Williams has assembled an all-star lineup. The result? One story after another which entertain, enlighten and encourage. What a resource for coaches, speakers and—above all—moms and dads.

~*Ernie Johnson, Jr., Studio Host, The NBA on TNT*

These 101 basketball stories are guaranteed to give you goose bumps, stir your heart or bring a tear to your eye. I couldn't stop reading.

~*Donnie Walsh, President, New York Knicks*

What a wonderful reading experience. These inspiring basketball stories will give you a big lift.

~*Adrian Dantley, Former Notre Dame and NBA Great*

I really enjoyed reading this book. It's loaded with stories that pack an enormous emotional wallop.

~*Lute Olson, Former Head Basketball Coach, University of Arizona*

101 Great Hoop Stories
from Players, Coaches, and Fans

Jack Canfield
Mark Victor Hansen
Pat Williams

CSS

Chicken Soup for the Soul Publishing, LLC
Cos Cob, CT

Chicken Soup for the Soul: Inside Basketball;
101 Great Hoop Stories from Players, Coaches, and Fans
by Jack Canfield, Mark Victor Hansen, Pat Williams

Published by Chicken Soup for the Soul Publishing, LLC   www.chickensoup.com

The publisher gratefully acknowledges the many publishers and individuals who
granted Chicken Soup for the Soul permission to reprint the cited material.

*Front cover photo courtesy of Getty Images/Taxi/ Jim Cummins. Back cover photo courtesy of Pat
Williams. Interior photos courtesy of iStockPhoto.com/© Stuart Miles/stuartmiless99, and Jupiter
Images/Photos.com*

Cover and Interior Design & Layout by Pneuma Books, LLC
For more info on Pneuma Books, visit www.pneumabooks.com

Distributed to the booktrade by Simon & Schuster. SAN: 200-2442

Publisher's Cataloging-in-Publication Data
(Prepared by The Donohue Group)

Chicken soup for the soul : inside basketball : 101 great hoop stories from
     players, coaches, and fans / [compiled by] Jack Canfield, Mark Victor Hansen
     [and] Pat Williams.

        p. ; cm.

     ISBN-13: 978-1-935096-29-0
     ISBN-10: 1-935096-29-X

1. Basketball--Literary collections. 2. Basketball--Anecdotes. I. Canfield, Jack, 1944-
II. Hansen, Mark Victor. III. Williams, Pat, 1940- IV. Title: Inside basketball

PN6071.B32 C45 2008
810.8/02/0357   2008941348

PRINTED IN THE UNITED STATES OF AMERICA
on acid∞free paper
16 15 14 13 12 10 09 08   01 02 03 04 05 06 07 08

*This book is dedicated to the late Irv Kosloff and
Dr. Jack Ramsay, who gave a young minor league baseball
executive a shot at the Philadelphia 76ers front office in 1968.
Fast break to forty years later, where this hopefully older and
wiser executive hopes that his mentors are pleased and
proud of that hiring decision.*

~Pat Williams~
Orlando Magic
February, 2009

Contents

❶
~Bouncing Back~

❷
~Assisting Others~

❸

~Scoring Triumphantly~

❹

~Keeping the Faith with Perseverance~

❺

~Energy and Effort Lead to Excellence~

❻

~Teamwork: Working for a Common Goal~

❼

~Beating the Odds: Overcoming Difficulties~

❽

~Achieving Greatness~

❾

~Leadership: The Coaches' Corner~

❿

~Living Large On and Off the Court~

⑪

~Overtime Points~

⑫

~A Final Word from Pat Williams and Family~

Foreword

Basketball is so much more than a game. It means more than wins and losses, Xs and Os, packed arenas and championship trophies. If it were merely a game, I would not be Coach K. I would be investing my life in other meaningful pursuits. Basketball, however, has certain intrinsic elements that forge my passion for what I do for a living and a life.

Consider taking a collection of individuals and molding them into a team, mentoring, developing friendships, earning trust, communicating clearly, setting goals, taking responsibility, nurturing disciplines, being confident and creative, honing skills through hours of practice and hard work, handling crises, having pride, courage and passion that lead to individual and corporate heroics (and, at Duke University, high graduation rates).

I am a firm believer in the philosophy that the importance of basketball is not in the making of shots, but is in the people who make those shots. For this reason I am pleased to write the foreword for *Chicken Soup for the Soul: Inside Basketball.*

My friend, Pat Williams, has spent forty years as an executive in the National Basketball Association, and has experienced the realities that transcend this sport. Executives, coaches, players, trainers, ball boys, ticket-takers, and team mascots in his vast network have responded to his request for their favorite basketball stories.

I am confident that you will be moved by these contributions that echo the character-building traits and actions described above. Read, be inspired, and enjoy wins on and off the court.

~Mike Krzyzewski
Duke University Blue Devils Head Coach
February, 2009

A note from Pat Williams: Mike Krzyzewski was the head coach of the 2008 United States gold medal-winning Olympic Basketball team. He is enshrined in the Basketball Hall of Fame. Coach K is a graduate of West Point, where he played for Bobby Knight and he returned to coach there for five years, is a 12-time *National Coach of the Year*, was named *Time* magazine and CNN's *America's Coach*, and has been head coach of the Duke University Blue Devils since 1980.

Introduction

Collecting the ingredients for these servings of *Chicken Soup for the Soul: Inside Basketball* has been a most satisfying "culinary" delight. As portions poured in from contributors, ladle by ladle, spoonful after spoonful, I fed on rich, inspiring offerings from these "courtly chefs." Each story is seasoned with zest and is brimming with the best this life offers. Enjoy a taste-filled feeding as you keep on reading.

For forty years I have been a veteran of the "cage wars" in the National Basketball Association, with tours in Philadelphia, Atlanta, Chicago, and Orlando. At each stop along the way I have cultivated friendships with executives, coaches, players, trainers, ball boys, ushers, ticket-takers, concession stand operators, and fans. In seeking contributors for this book, over 15,000 individuals in the NBA, collegiate and high school ranks have been contacted, and you now hold in your hands "the All-Star team" of those submissions. The responses have served as an affirmation of my love affair and involvement in Dr. Naismith's wonderful game.

Since this is a "hoops" book, I have organized the stories around a basketball acronym:

Bouncing Back
Assisting Others
Scoring Triumphantly
Keeping the Faith with Perseverance
Energy and Effort Lead to Excellence
Teamwork: Working for a Common Goal
Beating the Odds: Overcoming Difficulties
Achieving Greatness
Leadership: The Coaches' Corner
Living Large On and Off the Court

It is my hope that this book will contribute to your daily victories and a champion's heart and character.

~Pat Williams
Orlando Magic Senior Vice President
February, 2009

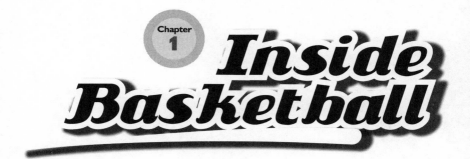

Chapter
1

Inside Basketball

Bouncing Back

Fire is the test of gold, adversity of strong men.

~Seneca

Keeping Up with the Joneses

In each family a story is playing itself out,
and each family's story embodies its hope and despair.
~Auguste Napier

I wouldn't be talking to you if it weren't for basketball. It spared my life. The words may seem like an empty cliché, but they are true. Basketball kept me alive, and now my son, Rob, and basketball are helping restore honor to my family name.

I never will forget the day. It was November 18, 1978. I had moved from the San Francisco area a few years earlier with my dad as he set up his ministry, Peoples Temple, in the nation of Guyana. The town we lived in was called Jonestown.

My life was built around basketball. I loved the sport and was in the capital city of Georgetown, Guyana, playing in a tournament on that infamous day. I was absolutely overwhelmed when I got a horrifying message from my father over the ham radio.

My father was explaining to me that California congressman Leo Ryan was in Jonestown investigating my father's ministry and that we would be blamed for people wanting to leave because of the injustices against Peoples Temple. He said that people were going to lay their lives down, that they were going to commit revolutionary suicide. It still echoes in my head how I argued with my father, "Why are we doing this? Isn't there another way?"

Hours later I learned that Congressman Ryan had been murdered and over 900 people had consumed a cyanide-laced beverage resulting in their deaths. My dad had a bullet through his head. I had lost everyone I loved—my parents, my wife, and my unborn child. My world was rocked forever. That experience was one that I wouldn't wish upon anybody because everything that I had lived for over my eighteen years was gone.

I returned home to my roots in the San Francisco area after this senseless tragedy, but I was haunted by those memories for years. I had many regrets, much remorse, and was besieged with survivor guilt as I wrestled with the questions, "How did I escape? Why was I one of the chosen few?" The reason, of course, is that I was away playing basketball.

For many years, my solution to my mental anguish was to totally divorce myself from the sport that I loved. I blamed basketball. If I wasn't selfishly away playing basketball, maybe I could have made a difference. So I had no contact with the game at all.

As I put my life back together, I eventually married and our union was blessed with children. One of our sons, Rob, was gifted with some exceptional athletic talents. As he grew older, it was obvious that he had a bright future as a basketball player. I began to work with him one-on-one and started coaching some of his youth teams. In addition to contributing some value to his life, the love I had for basketball was rekindled after a long absence from the sport. My enthusiasm returned, and I found myself elated to be a part of the sport again—through my son.

As Rob advanced through his high school career, he became a highly recruited college prospect. He grew into the best high school basketball player in the Bay Area—a 6'6" 230-pound forward with strength, quickness, and a well-rounded floor game. After evaluating all of his options, Rob decided to accept a scholarship at the University of San Diego to play collegiate basketball. As a freshman, he averaged nine points and six rebounds per game, and was named to the West Coast Conference All-Freshman team for the 2007-08 season.

When I first saw an article in the paper about my son's high school basketball team—"Jones leads Riordan to the top"—I paused reflectively. Anytime our family name had been in the news—Jones leading anybody—it was associated with leading individuals to a very negative outcome. It made my heart swell with pride to know a Jones was leading a group of people in a very positive direction. I am so proud of Rob's accomplishments on the floor, but I'm more proud of the fine young man he is turning out to be.

For years, I tried to escape the stigma of being Jim Jones, Jr. I was never able to do that. I was known in basketball gyms as the son of the infamous Jim Jones. Now I'm known as the father of Rob Jones. That amazing transition has left me with an extremely good feeling.

The wonderful game of basketball helped make it happen.

~Jim Jones, Jr., Pacifica, CA

Johnston Waxes Courage and Inspiration

One cannot control the length of his life,
but he can have something to say about its width and depth.
~Charles Colson

Ray Johnston was "living the dream." The former University of Alabama point guard was dating Miss Texas, modeling for Kinko's ads, and playing on the Maverick's summer league team trying to make it in the NBA. In the summer of 2004, however, Ray lapsed into a coma after contracting a rare and aggressive form of leukemia.

Ray was in a coma for over two months and "coded" three times. Over the next three years he survived two relapses of cancer, kidney failure, heart fibrillation, seizures, blood clots, pneumonia, the loss of his spleen and seven toes as well as his ability to dunk on the fast break. Ray's dream life had turned into a nightmare.

Odds were that Ray was not going to survive the leukemia—the doctors gave him one hundred days to live. The outlook was bleak but the support was tremendous. There was an outpouring from the Dallas community, specifically the Dallas Mavericks' organization. Everyone—from owner Mark Cuban and general manager Donnie Nelson to players and equipment managers—became emotionally invested in Ray's recovery. Ray was welcomed with open arms at Dallas games and in the locker room. In January, 2007, Ray underwent a bone marrow transplant. After at least three brushes with death, Ray appears to be beating the odds.

After Johnston's miraculous "reprieve" it would be natural to think that he would seek to "eat, drink, and be merry." Nothing could be further from the truth. Instead, Ray Johnston is giving back to the Dallas community by investing his time in the lives of high school basketball players.

Ray Johnston now heads the Heroes Organization basketball program. Realizing that most of the at-risk, inner city teens in his basketball program will not ascend to the NBA ranks, Ray created a "Prepare for College Fair." With the help of the Dallas community—Southern Methodist University, Brookhaven College, volunteers and corporate sponsors—Ray leads a hands-on seminar instructing the student-athletes on how to take the SAT, apply for college and practice for job interviews.

While most of these kids have many obstacles to overcome to succeed, they don't have far to look for inspiration in overcoming life's bad bounces. Ray Johnston is still living the dream.

~T.O. Souryal, MD,
Head Team Physician of the Dallas Mavericks

Fast Break: Fear Fouls Out

*You gain strength, courage, and confidence by every experience
in which you stop to look fear in the face.
You must do the things you think you cannot do.*
~Eleanor Roosevelt

As the head coach at Westfield State College, I was lucky to recruit a youngster named Rick Martin who hailed from Taunton, Massachusetts. I had arrived here following a stint as an assistant coach at Colgate University. At Colgate, we were successful in convincing a young man named Adonal Foyle to travel a divergent path and spurn offers from nearly every big time college program in America.

In Rick Martin, I thought we had found the Division III version of Adonal, and someone who would truly be a difference maker as we began to grow our program. I can remember going home on the night of October 15, 2002, and thinking that our program was about to climb to heights never seen here before, much like our time at Colgate. We have always prided ourselves on recruiting good people and this young man and his family are cut from the finest cloth.

On the second day of practice, in his first year of participation, Rick Martin suddenly dropped to the floor and subsequently passed away in my arms in front of the entire team. Meeting the family at the hospital was the hardest thing I have ever done as player or coach and I can still feel the October rain pouring down from the heavens as I approached Dana Martin to tell her that her son had died. Tears from heaven poured onto all of us as we stood and cried with the family. We realized then that none of us would ever look at life in the same way again. Rick had an undetected heart ailment that took his life, but I truly believe that he had developed more heart in his nineteen years than most of us do in a lifetime.

The beginning of the year was most difficult on the team and our administration even considered canceling the season to allow time for healing. The team collectively fought that idea, and, within two days of Rick's passing, they had gone around campus with water cooler jugs and raised more than $4,000 to help defray the cost of the funeral for the family.

The losses mounted as we struggled to reclaim our collective spirit to compete and to regain the competitive nature that had helped us all become college players. The team headed home after a tough loss and on the bus ride there were some heated exchanges among the players. My biggest concern that we might turn on ourselves out of fear was becoming a reality.

I met with the captains and queried them about the team's demeanor. Although I was extremely unhappy with the way we were honoring Rick's memory, I found myself being happy that we all returned to our families at the end of the day. The abilities I had as a coach to motivate, instill confidence and keep our esprit de corps at a high level completely abandoned me. In a desperate attempt to motivate them, I screamed at my captains and asked them what they were waiting for. The answer they gave was a hard one for a head coach to swallow: "We're waiting for you, coach."

The next day's practice was more like the kind we were used to having. Fear was cast aside and I began to reconnect with the people I value most—my family and players. The familiar squeak of rubber on wood came back to our gym. I knew it had weighed on these young men but I never understood how much this trauma had impacted my ability to do my job properly.

We won our first game after many losses, and, instead of

celebrating, our locker room was filled with tears. I knew this was the spark we needed, and as a devout Bruce Springsteen fan I began to reach back into his song catalog and pull out things that connected with our situation. "Can't start a fire without a spark," hung on our locker room door. I could feel a lift in my spirits and began to realize that my players were, in fact, waiting for their old coach to show up.

The wins kept coming, and the feeling of the team kept changing with every win. The season ended with thirteen consecutive victories, which is a school record that still stands. The Rick Martin Scholarship was established by our team and today boasts over $20,000 in assets.

The Martin Family has been with us always, and Dana comes once every year to see the team play and somehow keep our spirits high. As a father, I am in awe of her strength and resolve and I will always remember the class and dignity with which the family handled that dark day. As a coach, you never hope to pay this high of a price for education, but this has transformed all of us for the better and impacted the way I approach every day as father, coach and teacher.

The truth is that sometimes you get to coach them for four years and sometimes you only get one day. Make the most of the time you have and stare your fears in the face.

~Richard Sutter, Men's Head Basketball Coach,
Westfield State College, Westfield, MA

A Lighter Shade of Pail

Learn to do common things uncommonly well;
we must always keep in mind that anything that helps fill the dinner pail
is valuable.
~George Washington Carver

I worked in the front office of the Philadelphia 76ers when they made their championship run during the 1982-83 season. We had been on the cusp of a title before, but it wasn't until we traded for Moses Malone in the off-season that we had a complete championship team. Without him, we would not have been able to win the NBA crown that year.

Moses was the missing link. He was a terrific center as well as a great teammate—a huge presence inside, a rebounding force, and someone who did all the "little things." He is what I would call a "lunch pail" player. He wasn't the most glamorous or the best athlete or the smoothest player on the court, but he was the quintessential worker. Seemingly, Moses led the league in every category that year—including sweat. He worked so hard that buckets of sweat poured off him, and ball boys spent the entire night on the floor with towels keeping the court dry.

Moses was relentless in pursuing the ball—rebounds, blocks, loose balls—and he always put in a full night's work every time he stepped on the floor. Moses led the league in pursuing every rebound and diving on the floor for loose balls. He gave everything he had that year to help the 76ers win the championship.

After sweeping the Los Angeles Lakers in the NBA Finals, the team returned home to a huge crowd when they landed at the Philadelphia International Airport. The victory parade took place the next day. Nearly two million people lined the streets of Philadelphia, and there was a special salute for Moses as the team neared the Academy of Music on Broad Street.

There was some construction work going on in that area as the parade passed by right around lunch time. There were about thirty workers up on the scaffolding eating their lunches as the parade reached that point. As Moses' float moved in front of the construction site, each one of those workers lifted up his lunch pail as if on cue and saluted the 76ers' hard-working center. When Moses waved back, I got a big lump in my throat just watching that heartfelt exchange. That was a real tribute from a bunch of blue-collar guys to a blue-collar basketball player.

Moses was a "grinder," especially when times got tough for the 76ers. I have thought about Moses a lot over the years, especially during difficult days in my life. He has taught me about persevering, never letting up and continuing to bang the boards of life going after every loose ball.

~Clayton Sheldon,
former Philadelphia 76ers Assistant Director of Group Sales

The Return of the Little Girl Who Loved the Game

We are judged by what we finish, not by what we start.
~H. Jackson Brown, Jr.

I met Marsha Kinder when I first came to Bridgewater College (Virginia) in the fall of 1996. At the time, she was a sophomore basketball player for our local high school, Turner Ashby. Marsha's father, Dr. Tom Kinder, was the athletic director at B.C. (Bridgewater College). Everyone knew who Marsha was—she was the local star. My first impression when I saw her play was, "What a hard worker!" She was all over the court, shooting threes, playing defense, doing whatever her team asked of her.

At that time, Virginia high schools' girls 2A and 1A played basketball in the fall. I can remember when we would be at our practice during the winter and I would look up onto the upper level and there she'd be, Marsha with a ball in her hand... watching, listening, and learning about the game she loved so much. For two years we watched as she grew and matured into an outstanding basketball player.

As her senior year approached, everyone speculated about where Marsha would go to school. Those of us who knew her (and a lot on our staff had literally watched her grow up) wondered why she looked so thin. There had been times when we would come in late from a game and there she'd be in our gym working out, drenched in sweat. Was she pushing herself too hard? She exerted herself so much, but was she healthy?

She missed some games her senior year because of a stress fracture in her foot. She was so frail other players would just push her around. Yet, she was such an exceptional basketball player that she earned a scholarship to attend West Virginia University. The whole community was proud of her.

In the fall of 2000, Marsha was a freshman basketball player at WVU. By this time her eating disorder had become intense and had taken a toll on her body. She suffered stress fractures in her shins and was forced to red shirt (be inactive for a season). In January 2001, she left WVU and checked into the Ridgeview Institute Eating Disorder Treatment Center for three months. Feeling like she was "cured" she returned to WVU that summer with hopes of being an elite Division I athlete.

Tragedy struck in the fall of 2001 when her father suddenly died of a heart attack. It was a shock to everyone. Dr. Kinder, who ate right, exercised every day, and treated his body well, was no longer there. Everyone in the department had a tough time with it but it was especially difficult for Marsha. She and her father had spent countless hours in the gym at Bridgewater College's campus working on perfecting her game. Not long after her father's death, Marsha's mother, Debra, fell off a wall at their home. She suffered a concussion. In January 2002, Marsha transferred to James Madison University to be closer to home. She walked on the women's team in the fall of 2002, but, after seven years of anorexia, her body was "falling apart."

That same year Debra was diagnosed with breast cancer. It was another blow to the young girl who dreamed of being an elite athlete. Feeling as though she could not control the circumstances around her, her anorexia escalated. After surgery and chemotherapy, Debra was doing fine but her daughter was facing a battle of her own.

Marsha played one year at JMU, but her body was weak from the lack of nourishment. Inside she was still a little girl who had a love for the game but that love, along with her health, was rapidly diminishing. In January 2004, she checked herself into the Remuda

Ranch Eating Disorder Treatment Center in Arizona. When she left home at the end of January to enter treatment, her resting heart rate was so low she was close to death. After three months, she returned home a healthier, happier Marsha.

One day Marsha stopped by to visit Bridgewater College head coach Jean Willi. Jean had been a member of the Bridgewater College staff since 1983 and had seen Marsha grow up. The more they talked, the more Marsha became interested in playing for B.C. After checking with our NCAA compliance coordinator we learned that Marsha had two years of eligibility left to play.

She enrolled in the fall of 2004 with the hopes of rekindling her love for the game. Marsha started six games and played in twenty-three averaging 7.8 points per game in a season where the Eagles finished 22-6. She wasn't totally healthy, but she was getting there.

Marsha entered the 2005-06 season with a mission. The team's only senior, she embraced a leadership role that exemplified the kind of person Marsha is—a loving and caring one. I think a lot of that had to do with the fact that she had matured after facing many challenges in a short span of time. She had a knack for making everyone around her feel important, and no matter what their role was it was significant for our team's success.

"All" she did that year was average 17.7 points per game, lead B.C. to the NCAA Division II tournament Sweet 16, and a 24-7 record (tying the school's record for wins in a season), and sharp-shooting 42.5 percent from beyond the three-point arc.

Somewhere during that year Marsha became that little girl again who fell in love with the game at age five. She learned to have FUN while doing something she loves.

After basketball, Marsha finished her master's degree in counseling at Baylor University. She married in May 2007, and her future is bright. Her hope is to help people like herself overcome the disease that almost took her life.

~Cyndi Justice, Assistant Women's Basketball Coach,
Bridgewater College (VA)

Just Call Me "Lefty"

I'd give my right arm to be ambidextrous.
~Groucho Marx

uring a game against the Boston Celtics in 1952, I was upended driving to the basket. The strategy is called "bridging" and is considered to be a "not-so-nice" tactic because the offensive player is defenseless. I crashed to the floor, landing on my head and outstretched right hand. One might think that hitting the cranium would be the most damaging result; however, that was not the case with me.

The head wound required ten stitches to close, but my right wrist, after X-rays, showed an incomplete fracture of a small bone that required a cast to immobilize it. (By the way, immediately after the incident, a brawl broke out between the teams. The Syracuse Nationals did not take dirty play lightly!)

Was the season over for me? Was my young career in jeopardy? With more than half a season to go, I wanted to continue playing. The healing process was projected for eight weeks. The orthopedic surgeon crafted a lightweight cast, leaving the fingers and half a palm free. A rubberized product was affixed to the cast and was wrapped in an Ace bandage, giving my right wrist the appearance of a loaf of bread.

I was permitted to play with the cast as long as I didn't use it as a weapon. What a break for me! I learned to play left-handed by studying and mimicking southpaws. I copied their moves (eating and opening doors with my left hand). I evolved into a left-hander, averaging fifteen points per game as a southpaw.

When my right hand healed I was able to play injury-free. I had matured into a stronger player for I had become a double threat. My left/right capabilities made my drives to the basket nearly unstoppable, and I found myself taking more trips to the foul line (about eight to ten per game).

I had a local machine shop fabricate a 14-inch rim that was fastened inside the regulation 18-inch rim. As a result of daily practice on the smaller rim, my free throw percentage increased from seventy-five to ninety percent. I had a high arcing soft shot, and my confidence soared because I was shooting at the "larger" regulation rim.

In 1963, the Nationals moved from Syracuse to Philadelphia and became the 76ers. When Wilt Chamberlain was traded to the Philadelphia 76ers in 1964, I tried to help him with his foul shooting woes. We had contests, and my shots would only count if I swished them. He would sometimes hit eighty percent in practice, but, much to his frustration, he never beat me. Practice may not make perfect, but hard, meaningful work surely pays off!

~Dolph Schayes, NBA Hall-of-Famer

Super Glue

We all want character, but not the trials that produce it.
You can't build character in a cocoon.
~Pat Williams

ich Young had offers to play college basketball out of Farrell High School in Pennsylvania; that wasn't the problem. A 6'5", 205-pound gritty defender, Rich showed signs of his ability to play at the next level right off the bat. The bright lights of NCAA basketball simply had no allure for the soft-spoken guard.

Instead, Rich opted for a higher calling, one that was very close to his heart: he wanted to serve his country in the Marines along with his brother, Brandon.

While most college freshmen were learning how to use their dorm's coin-operated washing machine, Rich was cutting his teeth at the infamous "Ambush Alley" as his patrol exchanged fire with insurgents in Baghdad. During his four-year tour of duty, Rich "visited" such lavish tourist destinations as Kenya, Kosovo, and Iraq. Fire fights, starving children and chemical warfare were just a few of the threats that Rich encountered during his enlistment. So, cut him a break when the thought of making a game-winning free-throw or guarding an opponent's toughest player doesn't make him flinch.

All of that experience is what made Rich such a valuable basketball asset upon his arrival back in the States. After a couple of years at Eastern Oklahoma State College, the coaching staff at the University of North Texas took one look at Rich and recruited him to play basketball in 2005. With passion and intensity, he powered the North Texas defensive effort that saw the Mean Green win a school-record twenty-three games, earning the program's first Sun Belt Conference title and its first trip to the NCAA Tournament since 1988.

"The Glue," as his teammates called him, was at the center of it all. He became the first player in school history—and the only player in the Sun Belt in 2006-07—to record at least fifty assists, thirty blocks and thirty steals in the same season.

He also reluctantly stepped into the media spotlight. A shy, quiet personality, Rich isn't one to toot his own horn. Still, his story was featured all over the country, from *The New York Times, ESPN*, and the *Associated Press* to the *CBS Evening News with Katie Couric*.

Rich Young always found a way to answer the call whenever North Texas needed a rebound, steal, or defensive stop. Head coach Johnny Jones was accustomed to "The Glue" delivering the goods. He knew that whatever he asked of the former U.S. Marine sergeant, Rich was trained and equipped for any challenge.

The four-year tour of duty with the Marines that preceded his collegiate basketball career gave Rich a mental toughness that served him well both on and off the court. At age twenty-six, Young helped lead UNT to its best season in twenty-five years.

"It was hard to be in Iraq and be away from home, period," Young has said. "You know that you can die any day from a bomb, a bullet or some kind of chemical. That is always on your mind."

Being down seventeen is nothing after you have been to Iraq.

~Stephen Howard, Sports Information Director,
University of North Texas

8

Rebounding from a Bad Bounce

Every day is a gift to be unwrapped. That's why it's called "the present."
~Abigail Van Buren

In 1999, I was a freshman basketball player at the College of Saint Benedict in Saint Joseph, Minnesota. The College of Saint Benedict was an established Division III program that was returning four of five starters from the previous year's National Championship runner-up team. As a freshman, I knew it would be hard to get playing time, but I looked forward to the challenge.

Fortunately, after a few weeks I did begin to see a lot of playing time. The head coach and I were getting along well, I was making new friends on and off the basketball court, and I was dating a great guy.

Due to an unfortunate injury to one of the seniors, I was soon in the starting lineup. With talented teammates around me and increased playing time, I had a terrific freshman season and was well on my way to all-conference honors. But, with two games left in the regular season, an accident changed my life forever.

On an early Sunday morning I was taking a shower when I fainted. I had fainted a few times before so this feeling was not new; however, this time I wasn't able to sit down quickly enough and banged my forehead against the shower wall. The impact left a cross imprint directly in the center of my forehead. When I came to minutes later, I picked myself up slowly and reached for my towel. Then I fainted again.

When I woke up the second time my neck was resting on a three-inch ledge that separated the shower from the changing area. I sat up and my neck flopped backwards. It felt like there was nothing left to hold up my head. Not knowing what was going on, I held my head up with my hands, wrapped a towel around myself and went to find help. I opened and knocked on many doors looking for help while my hands never left my head or towel. Finally, I found a friend's room and was able to lie down until help arrived.

After I got to the hospital by ambulance, a nurse told me, "Be very careful not to move. If you do, there is a strong possibility that you may become paralyzed." One of my first thoughts was if I would ever play basketball again. After taking an X-ray, the doctors discovered that I broke the tip of my spine and C1 vertebra, which is at the base of the skull. The vertebra shattered and was fractions of a millimeter from going into my spinal cord.

Many people who have breaks similar to this don't survive and those who do are quadriplegic. I was very fortunate—especially since I was walking around trying to find help.

I was put into a halo, which is a ten-pound apparatus that is screwed into the skull in four places and bolted around the chest in a sheepskin vest. Once on, movement of the head and neck is not possible. While I was scared at first, I quickly became accustomed to the halo. By the end of the evening I was able to get out of bed and walk to the end of the hallway with the aid of my family and friends. The doctors told me that I was the first person they'd ever seen walk with a halo on the first day. I knew the next twelve weeks were going to be full of challenges and I could either face them with a positive attitude or let them ruin my life.

My everyday activities were now a challenge to me. I needed help with all of them; family and friends had to sleep over in case I needed help at night. I couldn't shower or wash my own hair. My mother made special clothes to fit over my head or around the vest. I couldn't carry a backpack. Worst of all, I was "the girl with the halo" on campus.

Luckily, I had the total support of my family, friends, teammates, and coach helping me along, one day at a time. Even though I received many stares, I tried not take offense but rather took it as an opportunity to meet new people and explain to them what happened. I quickly learned that people were staring out of curiosity and not to ridicule me.

The doctors told me they weren't sure if I'd be able to play basketball again. The C1 vertebra controls range of motion and it all depended on how the vertebra healed. My goal was to do whatever possible to play basketball again. It was such a large part of my life. I had to get back on the court.

Twelve weeks went by slowly with no word if basketball was in my future. When the doctors finally took off the halo, I was excited to learn that I could be back on the basketball court in just two more months.

My first game was a summer league game and I was nervous. Would I be the same player? Could my neck break again? Every question was asked over and over again in my mind. Within minutes of stepping onto the court, I was on a fast break and I missed my first lay-up because I was afraid of contact. The doctors reassured me that after a break the bones heal harder than normal, so my vertebrae were actually stronger than before. It was from that missed lay-up that I decided if I was going to play I was going to go all out.

From that day on, every time I stepped on the court I imagined it could be my last game. I realized how lucky I was to be able to play. I spent a lot of time on the floor diving after loose balls with a smile of appreciation on my face. I am thankful that things turned out the way they did and I was given a second chance not only to enjoy the game of basketball but also life.

My career at the College of St. Benedict's could not have turned out better. During the four years I was on the team, we captured two conference championships and advanced to the national tournament twice. I was also fortunate to receive the individual honors of DIII

All-American, Conference Player of the Year, three-time team MVP and became the program's second all-time leading scorer.

This experience brought me closer to my family and friends. My mom, dad, and sister are also closer because of this injury. As for the great guy who I began dating a few months prior to the accident, he is now my husband. We all learned not to take things for granted and how quickly lives can change. Even though this was a very hard experience, I would not change a minute of it. It taught me that with a positive outlook, any challenge or obstacle can be overcome. I am proud to say that I live everyday to the fullest with the attitude of not knowing what tomorrow may bring.

~Michelle (Barlau) Goodman,
former player at College of Saint Benedict (MN)

Nary a Dry Eye

Ultimately, love is everything. When we love something it is of value to us, we spend time with it, time enjoying it and taking care of it.
~M. Scott Peck

I have to have the best job in the world.

Ever since I graduated from Duke University, I have traveled the country writing about sports. Initially, I was covering sports for newspapers, but over the last twenty-five years I have branched out into the world of sports books.

The best part of my job is the athletes and coaches I have come to know personally and write about in depth. I've covered golf, baseball and football in addition to basketball. I guess it's no great secret that I'm a basketball junkie at heart.

Many of the basketball personalities I have covered have left a deep imprint on my life, but none more than the legendary John Wooden. Coach Wooden's UCLA teams won ten NCAA titles in twelve years (from 1964-75), including seven in a row — records that will never be broken. Coach Wooden was extraordinarily good at what he did on the floor, but I admire him even more as a human being.

Coach Wooden and his wife, Nell, had a remarkable marriage. She died many years ago, and Coach Wooden has never gotten over that. The condominium they shared in Encino, California, remains exactly the same as Nell left it. Coach has never altered her side of the bed and writes her a letter every month and adds it to the stack on her bed.

In the closing years of Nell's life, she was wheelchair-bound but still able to attend the Final Four weekend. One evening in the main hotel, the lobby was packed with a large gathering of coaches, wives and other basketball aficionados. At about ten P.M., Coach Wooden decided it was time to head up to their room and go to bed. He started pushing Nell's wheelchair towards the elevator, when this large crowd of people in the lobby—almost on cue—stepped back and formed an open pathway to make room for Coach and his wife. The pathway led all the way to the elevator, and everyone in that lobby began applauding as the Woodens departed for the evening. There were not many dry eyes, including mine, as that unbelievable event took place. It was a sight I will never forget, as those assembled paid tribute to the legendary Coach and his loving faithfulness to his lifetime partner.

After Nell's death, Coach was devastated. He went many years without attending the Final Four weekend. Eventually, he returned. One morning I was having breakfast in the hotel restaurant when Coach Wooden walked in to an enthusiastic round of cheers. As he walked by my table, I introduced myself and said, "Coach Wooden, I'm John Feinstein."

Coach Wooden replied, "Oh yes, John, I know you. Tell me, what book are you working on?"

I answered, "I'm writing a book about Red Auerbach and sharing many of the basketball stories that Red told me over the years. Red can really tell'em, and we're having a good time together on this project."

Coach said, "That's wonderful. Red is such a nice young man."

I couldn't help but laugh. At the time of that exchange, Coach Wooden was ninety-three and Red Auerbach was eighty-six!

I guess it's safe to say that life, as well as basketball, is all about your perspective.

~John Feinstein, Best-Selling Sports Author

Chapter 2

Inside Basketball

Assisting Others

When God measures a man,
He puts the tape around his heart—not his head.

~Author Unknown

Mo's Timely Assist

The smallest act of kindness is worth more than the grandest intention.
~Oscar Wilde

Maurice Cheeks spent fifteen years as an NBA point guard, making everybody else look good. Never one to seek the spotlight, he dutifully put others in a position to succeed, most notably superstars like Julius Erving, Moses Malone and Charles Barkley, teammates during his time quarterbacking the Philadelphia 76ers.

Little changed when Cheeks became a head coach, as he showed on April 25, 2003. In his second year as the Portland Trail Blazers' boss, his team was about to face the Dallas Mavericks in the third game of a best-of-seven playoff series, a series the Blazers trailed 2-0.

The national anthem was to be sung that day in Portland by Natalie Gilbert, a 13-year-old from Lake Oswego, Oregon. One problem: No sooner did she begin than she stumbled, forgetting the words.

She stopped. The crowd hooted. Mortified, she looked around for her parents.

And then Maurice Cheeks, who had been watching from his spot in front of the Blazers' bench, appeared at Natalie's side. He put his arm around her, offered a reassuring word or two, and began singing. He waved to the crowd, encouraging everyone to join in.

Before long Natalie had regained her voice, and with some

20,000 others providing accompaniment, sang as stirring a rendition of the anthem as has ever been heard.

And Cheeks? Well, no one was surprised. He was just making someone look good, same as always.

Maurice told me he remembered thinking, "I cannot let her stand there by herself. I didn't know if I knew the words or anything; I just started walking. Even my assistant coaches, when it was all said and done, were like, 'We didn't know where you were going.' I didn't know what I was doing. I just reacted.

"When I first showed up, I think she was surprised. I was scared myself. I've been standing next to people who sung the words so many times, but to stand up in front of people and sing it, I'd forget them, too. The crowd got me through it."

After the game, none of the reporters talked about Cheeks' team being down 3-0 (after a 115-103 loss). They only talked about him singing the anthem. Even Mavs assistant coach Del Harris was more interested in talking about the pregame than the game. He walked into Cheeks' office after the game and said, "Forget the game. What you did was so amazing." Cheeks didn't realize the impact of what he had done until Harris said that.

"I'm not an e-mail person, so I didn't even know how many e-mails people sent me about helping Natalie; our public-relations people kept forwarding them. It was unbelievable. There were things that almost put me in tears. I had no idea it would rise to the level it became.

"There have been people who recognized me for doing that and not playing or coaching in the NBA. I didn't know it would have that much impact, and I didn't do it for that reason."

Maurice Cheeks was just doing what he always does: dishing out another assist.

~Gordie Jones, former Sportswriter
for the *Allentown Morning Call*

Mark Madsen Walks the Walk

That we are alive today is proof positive that
God has something for us to do today.
~Anna R.B. Lindsay

n July 9th through the 13th, 2007, our two sons Cody (thirteen) and Blake (eight) attended the Mark "Mad Dog" Madsen Timberwolves Basketball Camp in Eden Prairie, Minnesota. This camp was wonderful! Mark incorporates education, nutrition, and fair play along with building basketball skills. Mark and his coaches were friendly and professional and just fun to watch as they worked with all the campers. During the second day of camp, Cody and Blake asked me if they could attend Mark's camp again next summer.

I had an opportunity to talk with Mark a few times. He was very impressed with both our boys and stated to me that he thought they were very good basketball players, were polite, had positive attitudes, and hustled. Mark went on to talk about Cody and told me that Cody was an incredible ball player. He also told me Cody was quick, had a fantastic shot, and he really liked how Cody would push the ball up the floor on every possession.

When Cody was four years old he was diagnosed with a hearing loss. Since that day he has worn wrap-around hearing aids. Mark approached me on the fourth day of camp and started asking me some questions about Cody's hearing. We talked for a few minuets about Cody and then Mark went on coaching the camp.

Just before noon, Mark came up to me and said that he would like to do something for Cody. He asked if we would be interested in going to Starkey. He explained that this was a company that made state-of-the-art hearing aids. These hearing aids were fitted to go inside the ear. I explained to Mark that we could not afford those kinds of hearing aids. Mark said it would be no expense to us; he wanted to see if they would work for Cody and if we did not like them there would be no obligation for us to do this.

I talked it over with Cody and he said he would like to try these new hearing aids. I told Mark that we would meet him after camp was finished for the day. I asked him, "Why would you want to do this?" He told me that he was so impressed with Cody's athletic ability and that he was such a good kid that he wanted to do something for him.

After camp was over for the day we followed Mark to Starkey and he introduced us to Heather. Heather took us inside and they took Cody right away into a sound booth. They did a hearing test and then Mark introduced us to Bill Austin. Mr. Austin personally made the molds for Cody's new hearing aids. He checked on Cody's progress several times while we were there. His entire staff was wonderful. Within two hours, Cody had state-of-the-art hearing aids. I could not believe what Mark had done for Cody. When we left the building I had tears in my eyes. What a wonderful person Mark Madsen is to want to do something for a kid who he had just met three days earlier.

We often hear about how professional athletes get into trouble. But when they do great deeds for others you very rarely hear about them. Mark Madsen is a great person—someone who is passionate about what he does and what he believes. He walks the walk and talks the talk.

~Nancy and Duane Martinz, Custer, SD

"He's the MVP"

If I only had a little humility, I'd be perfect.
~Donald Trump

Danny Gathings is a player I coached at High Point University. Danny, a native of Winston-Salem, North Carolina, transferred to High Point from Virginia Tech. During his time with us, he experienced more growth as an individual than any player I have ever coached.

Danny was phenomenal his junior year. He led the team in scoring and rebounding, was named the Big South Player of the Year, was the first player in High Point history to be named Honorable Mention All-America by the Associated Press, and led the team to the Big South Tournament finals. Although we lost in the finals to Liberty University, Danny was named Big South Tournament MVP.

Danny's game had grown up. He was about to, too.

On April 14, 2004, I stood with Danny at a convocation service in the Liberty Vines Center of Liberty University. Rival Liberty guard Larry Blair was being honored. Blair had hit seven three-pointers in the championship game in which Liberty beat us. Danny was there to honor him.

With the Liberty faculty and student body looking on, Danny held the 2004 Big South Tournament MVP plaque that he had been awarded a few months earlier. He then turned and handed the award to Larry Blair. Danny believed that Larry was more deserving of the award than he. He had looked at the stats sheet and realized that Larry had better numbers.

When Danny relinquished the honor, the Liberty students responded with a standing ovation. I was stunned and moved by the crowd's spontaneous appreciation of Danny's humility and sportsmanship. A rival crowd cheering, commending, and praising one of my players? I consider it a once-in-a-lifetime experience for a coach.

As Danny transferred the plaque to Larry, he told me, "This is something I need to do. Larry deserves this award more than I do. I am happy to give it to him and honor his efforts that helped his team win the championship. Hopefully, I'll deserve it next year." Needless to say, I was choked up.

Danny Gathings' act of humility earned him the NCAA sportsmanship award that year, and he has been recognized by several other organizations.

Danny is one of the finest young men I have met, on or off the court. When he first arrived at High Point, he was a student some expected to fail because of his background. Yet, by the time he finished his course work, he was a responsible role model for young people — particularly those who find themselves in difficult environments and circumstances.

Because of his character and humility, Danny Gathings is now an MVP to so many more people.

~Bart Lundy, Head Coach,
High Point University, High Point, NC

13

For Taking a Stand, Take a Seat

Courage is not the absence of fear, but the mastery of it.
~Mark Twain

Dallas Mavericks season ticket holder, Neal Hawks, has an eye for great real estate deals. He is also on the lookout for ways that he can encourage seriously wounded soldiers who have returned from Iraq and Afghanistan. That's why he came up with the idea of "Seats for Soldiers."

"These men and women have put their lives on the line so that we can enjoy the lives and freedoms we have here. Many of them have returned to the United States as amputees and burn victims. This is just one way to say 'thank you'," explains Hawks. In 2004, Hawks read an article about returning soldiers who needed surgery and rehabilitation. Not only did he donate his eight front row seats, he even paid the airfare for the veterans to be flown from San Antonio's Brooks Army Medical Center. Then Hawks enlarged his vision. He did missionary work to bring other courtside season ticket holders on board.

Mavericks' owner, Mark Cuban, who donates his five courtside seats for Seats for Soldiers Night, is ecstatic about this show of community support. At the most recent fête, 145 courtside seats were filled with soldiers. "Seats for Soldiers has been a true source of pride for the Dallas Mavericks and the community. We should never take our freedoms for granted and must remember that there is a cost. Heroes such as these defend our abilities to enjoy our lives," Cuban notes.

American Airlines now donates the flights from San Antonio to Dallas. Abacus, a Dallas restaurant, donates pre-game dinners to the soldiers. At game time, the guests of honor receive a standing ovation from 20,000 appreciative fans.

Seats for Soldiers is a special salute to those who have served. It's our way of saying thank you to our country's true heroes.

~Donn Nelson, Executive, Dallas Mavericks

14

The Doctor Makes a House Call

Practice courtesy. You never know when it might become popular again.
~Fred Allen

In more than thirty-five years covering sports, primarily the 76ers and the NBA, for the *Philadelphia Daily News*, I don't think I've asked for three autographs. To me, professionally, it's just not the right thing to do. But I can think of one memorable exception.

My parents, Molly and Al, were preparing to celebrate their fiftieth wedding anniversary. Family and friends had various things planned to commemorate the moment, but I wanted something additional, something unique, a gift they couldn't get from anyone else.

I had a photo of me presenting a special award to Julius Erving, the legendary Dr. J, the captain of the Sixers. I had chronicled more than a decade of his Hall of Fame career, from practices to games to personal appearances to charitable endeavors. I always believed that, if I went to every game he played, I would see at least one new thing every time.

And after virtually all of those games, he was the most accessible player with whom I had ever dealt.

I took the 8x10 glossy to Doc and asked if he would sign it for my parents. I told him why. It was okay to ask for this autograph. I knew he'd do it.

I'll never forget his response. He said no. I left disappointed, not really understanding.

It wasn't until a couple of days later that I learned I had completely misunderstood. He said he had wanted the time to think of a proper, meaningful message.

He took the glossy, and signed the front. On the back, he wrote a beautiful personal note to Molly and Al, congratulating them and wishing them a happy life together. I frequently think about that, a signature moment, no pun intended.

On their anniversary, I presented the signed glossy to them. I had a frame, but I kept the photo and the frame separate so that they could read the message on the back. My mom had that photo hanging on a wall in the den of her apartment until the day she died.

Thanks, Doc.

~Phil Jasner, *Philadelphia Daily News* Sportswriter

An Outstanding Feat

Go as far as you can see and when you get there,
you will always be able to see farther.
~Zig Ziglar

I had an amazing experience on the night of January 24, 2008. I coached my college team, IUPUI, to a victory over Oakland University of Michigan. I must say, I looked sharp in my black shirt, cream-colored vest and slacks, but there was one thing missing. I coached without shoes or socks on.

I was trying to raise awareness for needy children in Africa. So, in conjunction with an organization called Samaritan's Feet, I set a goal of collecting 40,000 pairs of shoes. I decided on the number 40,000 in honor of the fortieth anniversary of the death of Dr. Martin Luther King, Jr.

I learned about Samaritan's Feet after a mutual friend had given my phone number to Emmanuel "Manny" Ohonme, a native of Nigeria and founder of Samaritan's Feet. Ohonme received his first pair of shoes at the age of nine from an American missionary. He eventually earned a scholarship to play basketball at Lake Region State College in North Dakota.

Samaritan's Feet came up with the idea of me coaching without shoes. They told me the idea, and, at first, I laughed because I thought they were surely joking. They weren't. Then I remembered a recruiting trip to Lagos, Nigeria in 2004 where I saw examples of extreme poverty. The call from Ohonme and prayer were enough to persuade me to go shoeless for a night.

I told my team about the mission, and it moved freshman Christian Siakam, who is from Cameroon. He said a lot of college athletes get free pairs of shoes and take such perks for granted. There are so many kids in Africa, including people in Siakam's family, who don't have shoes. It hit home with him. I knew we were doing the right thing when I saw the look on his face.

When we started this cause, I thought our goal of 40,000 shoes was going to be tough. When I was told before the game that we already had collected 100,000 pairs, I almost broke down in tears. Thousands of those shoes were donated from Converse, Wal-Mart, Nine West, and the Department of Homeland Security. As a result of our "campaign," nearly $20,000 and 110,000 pairs of shoes were donated to Samaritan's Feet. The shoes were given to needy children in the United States and around the world.

This has turned into a full-time job for me. I never did this for the publicity. I'll be honest with you; I'm going to be doing this for the rest of my life. This is not something I'm going to stop doing next year. I will continue to do this as long as I live, whether I'm coaching or not. It's overwhelming. I haven't had a day go by when people haven't dropped off shoes at my house.

Time will tell whether I coach another game barefoot, but I promise I'll get a fresh pedicure just like I did this time. By the way, we won the game that night. Maybe I should coach all of my games barefoot!

~Ron Hunter, Head Coach,
Indiana University-Purdue University Indianapolis

16

The Admiral's Charitable Armada

If you want the world to heed, put your creed into your deed.
~Croft M. Pentz

At 6'11", David Robinson really stands tall even before he commits intentional acts of kindness. Known as "The Admiral," the Annapolis graduate has served his nation, team, and communities, dare we say "admirably"?

Robinson is not on shore leave when it comes to community service. Along with his wife, Valerie, David founded the Carver Academy, committing $11 million to the inner-city San Antonio school that educates pre-school through sixth graders. He is active with the Make-a-Wish Foundation, the NBA's All-Star Reading Team, testifies about his Christian faith with the Fellowship of Christian Athletes, and lends his voice to numerous public service announcements. As a player, he sponsored Mr. Robinson's Neighborhood of Achievers with fifty San Antonio Spurs season tickets.

The 2008 NBA All-Star Game Weekend found the Admiral and his "crew" working to build two homes in New Orleans. The crew included a JP Morgan Chase team working with Habitat for Humanity. Sixty Chase employees and NBA volunteers worked on the homes, and Chase and Robinson contributed $170,000 to absorb construction costs. Two families who helped with the build are now benefiting as they live in their new homes.

Robinson's charitable actions prompted the NBA to rename its monthly Community Assist Awards as the "David Robinson Plaque" which is inscribed, "Following the standard set by NBA legend David Robinson, who improved the community piece-by-piece."

It was a true privilege to have coached David Robinson. He was a fierce competitor, practiced hard, and didn't "take off" plays. Supportive of his coaches, he was a true team player, and, as evidenced above, David Robinson cares about his community. I consider him to be a once-in-a-lifetime player and a tremendous, compassionate human being.

This Admiral has a knack for getting all (helping) hands on deck.

~Gregg Popovich, Head Coach, San Antonio Spurs

A Pastor Praises Penny

*A person should be like a watch—
open-faced, busy hands, well-regulated, and full of good works.*
~Roy B. Zuck, The Speaker's Quotebook

Each year I serve as committee chairman for a golf tournament known as "The Pastors' Masters," that raises money for Faith Lutheran Church, formerly located in Pine Hills, FL. The funds go toward youth programs for our kids and the kids of surrounding communities. We strive to use the proceeds from this event in the best ways possible. For example, every other year there is a national Christian youth gathering for kids from all over the United States. Registration is $275 per participant. Our golf tournament proceeds subsidize the cost, reducing the participant's cost to $50.

The tournament is held each year at MetroWest Country Club. In 1997, we raised a record $4,700. Former NBA star Penny Hardaway, coincidentally, was playing the course that day. He had teed off prior to our event, and it didn't take long before everyone was aware that he was out on the course. This, of course, created a growing buzz, particularly among our youth volunteers. We exhorted the kids to restrain themselves and to respect Penny's privacy.

Then it happened.

One of our foursomes was waiting to tee off (four dads and their "caddies" [children]) as Penny and his group came off the green from a distant hole. Although it was definitely out of his way to the next hole, Penny spied the kids and spontaneously detoured his cart to spend some minutes talking with our youth. Our group was stunned and the impact he made on both adults and children was immeasurable. One of the fathers talked my ear off, telling me that his daughter had received the thrill of her young life. What an act of caring and class!

Some basketball players make news for all the wrong reasons—arrests, suspensions, etc.—but it's stories like this one that don't make the news. It's moments like this that make you a basketball fan for life.

~John David Morris,
member at Faith Lutheran Church, Winter Garden, FL

18

The Un-Spartan Spartan

I never met an unhappy giver.
~George Matthew Adams

etired NBA great, Steve Smith, is a proud Spartan and graduate of Michigan State University (1987-1991). But when it comes to giving, Smith is about as un-Spartan as a person can be.

After graduating from Detroit's Pershing High School, Steve enrolled at MSU, became the Spartans' all-time leading scorer, and was a first-team all-American. During his NBA career, Smith played for the Miami Heat, Atlanta Hawks, Portland Trail Blazers, San Antonio Spurs (the NBA champions in 2003) and the Charlotte Bobcats.

Wherever he landed in his NBA journeys, he had as much impact in the community off the court as he did on it, and when you look at his game achievements that translates to an amazing impact.

In addition to tallying big numbers on the hardwood, Steve Smith established a record (at the time) for the largest single donation from an athlete to a university. He gave $2.5 million to MSU to help build the Clara Bell Smith Student-Athlete Academic Center. The center is named in honor of his mother who died during Steve's NBA rookie year. "I have had great coaches," he said at the dedication, "but none greater than my mother. I have had great role models, but none greater than my mother. I have had great teammates and fans, but none greater than Clara Bell Smith."

Smith has mirrored the role-model qualities his mother exhibited, actively working with inner-city groups. He has donated an additional $600,000 to endow the Steve Smith/Pershing High School/Michigan State University Scholarship for Academic Achievement. The award goes to high-achieving Pershing graduates who attend MSU. His three annual golf fund-raisers have added an additional $500,000 to his charitable endeavors.

Steve Smith freely distributes of his self, service, and substance. He has balanced an award-winning basketball career as a collegiate all-American, gold medal Olympian, and NBA champion with his all-star habit of giving. He was awarded the J. Walter Kennedy Citizenship Award and the Joe Dumars Sportsmanship Award. He also serves on MSU's alumni board and the national board of Reading is Fundamental.

Steve Smith, the "un-Spartan Spartan," is a shining example of a life "well-gived."

~Joe O'Toole, former Athletic Trainer, Atlanta Hawks

Flip-Flopping in the Philippines

*Happy is the man who has learned to hold the things of this world
with a loose hand.*
~Warren Wiersbe

During the summer of 1987, between my junior and senior years of college, I was a player/athletic trainer on a mission trip to the Philippines. I was part of a basketball team made up of college players that traveled around the northern part of the island of Luzon playing fifty games in forty-eight days. During halftime we would put on a short program of basketball skills and share our personal testimony. Our team director, Tom Randall, would put on a juggling show and ride his unicycles while I played "Sweet Georgia Brown" on my trumpet.

Tom was amazingly skilled at riding the unicycles and doing basketball tricks (one of the unicycles was normal-sized and the other was tall enough so Tom could dunk while sitting on it). For the grand finale of the halftime show Tom would pick a child from the crowd, put him on his shoulders and ride around the court on the unicycle with Tom pretending to be out of control. Of course Tom was in complete control the entire time—even if every once in a while the child would get so scared he couldn't keep from screaming. Tom would end the show and the kid would be the envy of the town.

After the juggling-and-unicycle show, one of us would give a short testimony which would include our personal story of coming to Christ and accepting him as our Savior. When the program ended and the second half started, the players who were not playing in the game would roam the crowd and sign up the fans for a free non-denominational correspondence Bible course. It was always interesting when the coach wanted to make a substitution. One player would come off the court and another would step onto the court from wherever he was in the crowd, hand off the sign-up materials, and get ready for the ball to be put in play.

In one particular city, we began our warm-up for the game (if you know anything about summer in the Philippines "warming up" was usually not a problem; staying cool was a problem). As we went through the lay-up line, I watched the opposing team go through their warm-ups. I saw that one of the players was wearing flip-flops. This, however, was not unusual as we played many of our games in very poor rural areas and flip-flops were the only footwear many of the people could afford. Amazingly, many Filipinos were very skilled at playing basketball in flip-flops.

What happened next has never left my memory.

The player with the flip-flops turned to the player in line behind him, took off one of his flip-flops and gave it to his friend. His friend took the single flip-flop and put it on his foot. Until that point the player who received the flip-flop was going through the lay-up line barefoot.

As I stood there in my Nikes I couldn't help but be a little ashamed. I put little value in the shoes on my feet, yet one of our opponents recognized that his teammate didn't have anything on his feet and was willing to share his flip-flops so his friend would have at least one to wear. It was an incredible act of giving. I learned that summer that, sometimes, those with the least can teach you the most.

~Tom Smith, Head Athletic Trainer, Orlando Magic

20

The Heart of Jordan

Nobody cares how much you know until they know how much you care.
~Theodore Roosevelt

It was the only time I saw Michael Jordan cry. The toughest guy in the room, on the basketball floor, perhaps the greatest competitor American team sports has ever known.

It was before a game with the Atlanta Hawks before Jordan became just "Michael." He was big already, but still not quite the greatest. The Bulls had yet to win a championship, and some questioned whether they ever would. They were preparing for a game against the Hawks, which always provided a special scoring and high-flyers' duel between Jordan and Dominique Wilkins. It was Easter Sunday, one of those big TV games, and Jordan was sitting quietly in front of his locker watching some tape on the Hawks.

Pre-games were much more informal back then, and there was a pretty little girl there, maybe seven or eight, wearing her pink Easter dress. She was there to see Jordan. The folks from one of the groups that support sick children had arranged a brief meeting with the Bulls and Jordan always accommodated the youngsters. He loved the kids, talking with them as if they were adults, always joking and friendly. But this time it was too much.

The little girl was a portrait. She stood before Jordan transfixed as he joked and talked with her, trying to get a response. She smiled and her eyes sparkled. She said little, but Jordan began to melt in her gaze. After a few minutes, some more talk and an autograph, she was led away, looking back at Jordan and smiling, eyes wide with wonder. Jordan knew she had been ill.

He began to cry.

"How do they expect me to play a game after this?" he asked.

But Michael would as only he could. The legend was only just beginning. A few weeks later, Jordan would make that much shown "shot" against Cleveland to upset the favored Cavs and push the eventual champion Detroit Pistons to a six-game conference finals, the Bulls first appearance in the conference finals in fourteen years. The Bulls would lose that Sunday game in Atlanta, but just barely, as Jordan recorded a triple double with forty points, twelve assists and ten rebounds in forty-three brilliant minutes.

Michael Jordan possessed a big heart both on and off the basketball court.

~Sam Smith, former NBA Writer, *Chicago Tribune*

21

A Clutch Win

Enthusiasm releases the drive to carry you over obstacles
and adds significance to all you do.
~Norman Vincent Peale

Several years ago I received a request from a loyal season ticket holder to make an appearance at a children's hospital for her son. I had visited several hospitals before for people of all ages, but usually to see many individuals and not just one patient. This would generally consist of going room to room and visiting briefly with patients, signing autographs, taking pictures, and trying to spread a little joy through humor and a direct connection to Houston Rockets basketball. I would usually see up to twenty patients, visiting with each for only a few minutes.

This particular Rockets fan wanted me to spend an hour with her six-year-old son who happened to be in a full-body cast up to his neck and was obviously immobilized. I didn't want to ask too many questions about the boy's condition, but I got the feeling that there was something more critical going on than just a few broken bones and that recovery might be somewhat in question. I was apprehensive to say the least. Given the potential circumstances, I really wanted to do a good job, but I still had no idea how I was going to carry a full hour in a little hospital room with an audience of two. At that point in my career I was usually a "part of things" or the "side show." I was not used to being the featured entertainment in crowds of any size. I was scared I'd let this child as well as his mother down.

She obviously needed a boost and to see her son happy, even if just for a little while.

I showed up at the hospital, found my way to the child's floor and, after finding a private, unoccupied room, made my transformation into Clutch in secret. As I was approaching the room, I clearly remember thinking, "There is no way I'm going to be able to make an hour in this room fun and entertaining for a child in a full body cast. I'm in a big bulky costume in which I don't speak and have limited vision." It can be hard to navigate small spaces, especially ones with sensitive medical equipment.

As I entered the door I could see the mother in the corner of the room near the foot of the bed, but not the child yet. I could see the look of hopefulness that this would bring joy to her son, mixed with desperation.

As soon as I stepped far enough into the room to see the boy's face, I was met with a loud joyous eruption of, "CLUTCHHHHHHHHHHH!" In an instant, his expression went from calm and placid to a look of sheer ecstatic disbelief. His eyes were bulging. He was grinning ear to ear. He couldn't believe what he was seeing. I mean he went nuts. I'm not going to be able to do justice in words with just how over-the-top-happy he became. He immediately started a conversation with Clutch as if they were life long friends and Clutch was "real."

"Clutch, I can't believe you are here. What are you doing here? Are you here to see me? Don't you have a Rockets game? Shouldn't you be at the arena? Holy Moly! This is awesome. Mom, Clutch is here! Clutch is here!"

He started to cry tears of joy and amazement. His mother started to cry. I started to cry. I was in a costume. No one knew it, but I was crying too because of how excited and happy this boy was. That is the only time after more than 3,000 events I have ever cried in costume and that includes some amazing wins, disappointing losses, jersey retirements, and a ton of events for charities and kids.

The next hour was the quickest hour of my life. I didn't have to do any entertaining. He entertained me. Even though he couldn't move, he captivated me with one Clutch or Rockets story after the other. He regaled me with all of his favorite Clutch antics and skits. He would ask me a question as to whether I remembered something I did and then tell me all about it. "Remember the time you shook your butt at the other team's huddle? Remember the time you acted like you were sleeping when they announced the other team? Remember the time you shot Silly String on that Jazz fan? Remember the time you ate that guy's popcorn?" The stories just kept coming. Each one was told a little bit more excitedly than the one before. I think that youthful exuberance might be one of the most powerful forces on the planet.

Usually mascots act big and over-exaggerate motions. That night it wasn't necessary. Just little tweaks of my head and small hand gestures were enough to communicate effectively with him. He understood almost everything I was miming as if we were having a regular conversation. I can remember that I actually started to really feel like "Clutch" and not just a guy in a costume portraying him. It was one of the few times that I didn't even realize how hot and sweaty I was and completely lost track of time. He asked me to sign his cast, his Clutch photos, his basketball, his foam finger, his shirt, and just about everything else he could get his hands on.

When it was time to leave I couldn't believe a whole hour had passed. His mother had to pull me away and tell him he needed to rest and that Clutch had to go back to his cave at the arena. After saying my goodbyes to him and receiving his thanks and well wishes for the team, his mother spoke to me just outside the door to his room. I felt naked as a mascot because she was speaking right through the guise of the costume and directly to me in the suit. Though choking back tears, she thanked me and told me that I would never know just how much this meant to her. I will carry that night and feeling that it gave me forever.

I walked out of the hospital that evening feeling like I was flying and loving this job for what I treasure most about it: bringing joy to others! The NBA has a slogan, "I love this game!" Well, "I love this job!"

~Robert Boudwin, the Houston Rockets' Mascot, CLUTCH
"The Rockets Bear," 1995- Present

Chapter 3

Inside Basketball

Scoring Triumphantly

The last shot may give us victory.

~Admiral Duchayla

22

My Bruin Banner

We make our decisions and then our decisions turn around and make us.
~R. W. Boreham

*I*was primed to spend five beautiful, sunny California days on
the campus of the greatest collegiate basketball program ever.
For the second year in a row, I was coaching at the UCLA
Bruin Basketball Summer Camp. The program is an overnight camp
so we sleep in the dorms and have non-stop basketball from 7 A.M. -
11 P.M. For five days, I would be a surrogate Bruin.

The first day of camp we created teams and kept those teams for
the remainder of the week. Every day we ran practices with our teams
and then played in games against the other high school teams. I was
fortunate to get some great kids who were competitive, played hard,
and were eager to please to gain my approval. We won every game
all week and ended up in the championship game on the last day
of camp. The last game is played in Pauley Pavilion on the Nell and
John Wooden court in front of the whole camp and all the parents.

Before the game started, I paused to look at all the championship
banners and to think of all the greats who had played there. Now I
was getting to coach in a championship game in "Basketball's Mecca."
It was just a summer camp game, but the UCLA legacy of excellence
made this a true championship game for me.

The score was close the whole game. Since every camper pays
over $500 for this camp, we are given a substitution pattern we are
supposed to follow so everyone gets equal playing time. It came down

to our last substitution, and the coach of the other team still had not taken out his best player. He was flat-out cheating. One of the other coaches noticed what he was doing and came over to my huddle and said, "Steve, if he is going to cheat, then you can, too. Keep your best guy on the floor."

I said, "No, I don't need to cheat. That's not me."

The final four minutes started and my best player was sitting right next to me. He had heard what the coach had told me and he was willing to go back in. I quickly explained to him that it would not be the right thing to do and that it is important to always do the right thing. The other team took the lead, but I still had my peace of mind and character intact. I looked down at the university's blue ink logo that spelled out Wooden on the court and I was reminded how Coach Wooden talked about having faith that things will work out as they should as long as we do what we should.

The final buzzer sounded and my team won by two points. We did it! We had won and we won the right way. I could envision them raising our banner to the rafters to add to the lofty Bruin collection.

Since there had been so many high school players in camp, it was broken up into two sections, so one more championship game followed ours. One of the coaches in that game was the coach who had come up to me during my game telling me to keep my best players in. I knew he was just trying to defend me as he was upset about what the other coach was doing. Once his game started I didn't think anything of our conversation. His team won the game by one point in overtime. UCLA coach, Ben Howland, gave a speech to all the parents and awards were handed out and camp was over. Many of the parents of my players came and had me pose for pictures with their sons. I felt like I was famous. My team just won a championship game in Pauley Pavilion and now I was posing for pictures. Could it get any better?

A little later that same coach who won his game came up to me and said he wanted to thank me. I asked why. He said that during his game he was tempted to cheat and keep his best player in during overtime. However, the fact that I had chosen not to inspired him and gave him the strength to do the right thing as well. I was blown away. I was just being me; I was not consciously trying to influence another coach. I was twenty-one years old and my example had been a positive influence on a man in his late forties who had been coaching for more years than I had been alive. It was a brief moment shared between two people that no one else knew about. It was my most profound moment of camp.

This moment served to reinforce my beliefs that staying true to myself, never compromising my character, and choosing to always do the right thing was still important and necessary, not just for my well-being, but for that of my fellow human beings as well. It taught me just how powerful positive examples are to leadership and how people are always watching, "taking notes." We never know when the choices we make will have an effect on the choices of those around us and, exponentially, those we have never dreamed of. Remember, it does not matter how old you are, you can still be a formidable leader.

They might not be raising a banner at UCLA for my team's accomplishments at summer camp, but my fellow coach and I experienced a championship thrill like the players represented by the banners in the rafters; not because both our teams went undefeated, but because of the choices we made.

Choices create the champions. You never know when you might change a life. It can happen on a hot summer's day inside a basketball gym through the quick decision you make while you have your team in a huddle. I am proud of what my team did that week at camp. I am pleased that I could mirror UCLA's basketball tradition for the five days I got to be a Bruin. I think Coach Wooden would approve, too, of the manner in which I conducted myself on his court. Every time I return to UCLA to watch a game or observe a practice, I always look up in the rafters, imagine my banner hanging up there, and am reminded of the lives that were elevated along with it.

~Steven Schultz, Boys' Head Basketball Coach,
Fountain Valley High School, Fountain Valley, CA

23

The J-Mac Attack

Some pursue happiness. Others create it.
~Ann Landers

ll the students in the bleachers rose to their feet, cheering wildly and jumping up and down. All I could do was sit down and start crying.

Never had I felt such emotion in my career. It wasn't a buzzer-beating basket; it wasn't a heave from half court; in fact, it wasn't even a play. All I had done was turn toward the player with uniform number 52, point my index finger at him, and say "J-Mac."

Up bounced seventeen-year-old Jason McElwain. My team manager's dream finally came true on February 15, 2006, the last home game of his senior year. Jason—or J-Mac, a tag I had hung on him early in his sophomore year—was about to see his first varsity action ever.

He was small, skinny, autistic, and learning-disabled. He'd been cut three straight years from his teams. But he lived and breathed basketball, and was so dedicated that I had planned for months to give him a special treat on Senior Night—suiting him up in uniform, and perhaps even finding him some playing time.

Jason had taken substantial grief over the years because of his disability. Go to any high school and the kid who's a little different gets singled out for ridicule. In Jason's case, he was an easy target with his unusually loud voice, tendency to laugh at inappropriate times, and habit of repeating things he heard other people say.

Basketball was his salvation, a constant bright light. It kept him enthusiastic and filled his mind with pleasant thoughts. He was a bona fide hoops junkie—loved watching the game on television, loved Kobe Bryant, memorized Final Four rosters, scouted our high school opponents, you name it. Above all, he burned with passion for Greece Athena, the high school for which I'm head coach and he proudly served as manager. I saw how, gradually, the kids on the team started to develop an appreciation for Jason's infectious attitude. As much as some of his autistic tendencies would drive them nuts, he was one of us.

I held to my promise and gave Jason his uniform for our regular-season finale against Spencerport. We moved out to a big lead in that game, and with just over four minutes remaining I felt, "I think it's the right time now." All the players started clapping for Jason as he checked in, and shrieking fans began furiously waving placards with blown-up photos of J-Mac attached. Some students also held oversized letters, forming a row to spell "J M A C." That just blew me away. I got so choked up that I had to sit down, even though I never sit down during games.

Jason's varsity career began with an air-ball and missed short jumper. All I could do was put my head in my hands and say "Please God, let him make just one basket."

Fortunately, God is a basketball fan.

It began with Jason rattling home a three-point basket, creating complete bedlam. From there he went on a hot streak beyond imagination, unless you've seen the game video that's still available on the Internet.

With his teammates looking to feed him the ball at every opportunity, Jason launched thirteen shots in all and made seven—including six three-pointers. That's twenty points in half a quarter, making him the game's high scorer as we won 79-43.

I remember very little about those crazy moments because I was in too much shock. I do recall that in the game's final seconds, Jason's mother, Debbie, came up to me with tears in her eyes, gave me a kiss and thanked me for giving her son this opportunity.

For a grand finale, J-Mac swished in his last shot at the buzzer from NBA range. Then he was mobbed by hundreds of joyous teammates and fans who stormed our court, hoisting him on their shoulders.

News of his feat spread like wildfire and, before you knew it, Jason and I were being pelted with countless media requests and movie offers. It was almost a bit of a side note that our Greece Athena team went on to win the Section Five championship, the first in my twenty-five-year coaching career.

Since then J-Mac and I have made numerous radio and TV appearances, my public-speaking schedule continues to take me all over the country, and a major motion picture is in the works on Jason's life. We've both met celebrities ranging from President Bush to Oprah Winfrey. Some of the top figures in sports — from Billy Donovan to John Calipari, from Dick Vitale to Jim Nantz — have told me how awed and moved they were by J-Mac's accomplishment. In fact, Coach Donovan predicts that thirty years from now, the general public will remember that better than his University of Florida teams having won back-to-back national championships in 2006 and 2007.

I've especially enjoyed feedback from strangers — the hundreds and hundreds of letters, e-mails and phone calls with heartwarming messages. Many have come from folks who have a loved one affected by autism or some other disability, saying how the J-Mac story provided such a vital dose of hope.

I've retold the story probably thousands of times by now, and don't think I'll ever get tired of it. I just feel like I was so blessed to be a part of something that special, that powerful. It almost defies being put into perspective.

Maybe the best way is to view it as a part of God's plan. I absolutely believe this was a miracle — maybe not like Moses parting the Red Sea, but God was definitely smiling on us. You wonder why terrible things happen like September eleventh and Hurricane Katrina. I think God's message with J-Mac is that he just wanted to give people a breath of hope.

There's also a strong message in there about goal-setting and perseverance. What people don't realize is how hard Jason worked for that one opportunity, all the hours and hours he spent working on his game.

Finally, this tale offers a huge life lesson about teamwork. Consider that on his big night J-Mac's teammates kept feeding him the ball, even though I hadn't instructed them to do so. Meanwhile, Jason will tell you to this day that his top thrill was not scoring twenty points in a game, but that our team won a sectional title.

I had always thought winning sectionals would be my own end of the rainbow. But now, it will always be the evening that J-Mac made history. Knowing I played a part in somebody's dream coming true — that's about the most satisfying accomplishment I could ever imagine.

~Jim Johnson with Mike Latona, Greece Athena High School
Physical Education Teacher and Boys' Varsity Basketball Coach,
Rochester, NY

Just Ask

Prayer is asking for rain, and faith is carrying an umbrella.
~Barbara Johnson

In 1995, I was an assistant coach at Arkansas State University, finishing up a bad year and planning to move my wife and three small children to another college basketball job. One afternoon before we were to leave Jonesboro, Arkansas, the president and athletic director of ASU walked into my office and asked if I would be the interim head coach for one year while they conducted a search for a "big name coach." They informed me that I would be head coach for one year at my current salary of $27,000. I would have one assistant and they would reassign the outgoing head coach.

The administration went on to inform me (as if I didn't already know) that we were last in the Sun Belt Conference, had three returning players and were drawing an average of 400 fans to a $10 million arena that seats 10,500. Everyone has an ego, it is just mine isn't very big. So, it hurt my feelings, but I nearly knocked my desk over to tell them, "I'll take it!"

After nine games we were 1-8, just barely beating a Division II team. I could hear the whispers all over town: "Nice guy; he just can't coach." It was a bad feeling. The next game was the first one of the Sun Belt Conference.

Although the season started poorly, I was really looking forward to going to Little Rock to play our first SBC game. We were to play UALR, coached by Wimp Sanderson and led by their star player,

Derek Fisher. I was extremely excited. My parents, high school coach and countless friends would be there to watch. At halftime it was 67-20 in favor of UALR. It was awful. I didn't know what to say at the break, if I said anything at all.

The second half we recovered slightly and finished with a thirty-eight point loss. I tried to keep the players in the locker room for an extended amount of time so that most of the fans would be gone. I dismissed the team to board the bus and the first people I saw were my mom and dad. My mom greeted me with her precious smile and open arms, "You did so well!"

As tears welled up I blurted, "Mom, we were beaten by forty points." Believe me, it was a long ride back to Jonesboro.

The next day was a Sunday and my wife Cathy, our three small children, and I headed to church. Once again I felt the stares and whispers. After church, I hugged Cathy and went off to work to prepare for a meeting followed by practice. I arrived at my office, shut the door and tears began to flow. As I sat there numbly, my phone rang and it was my older brother, Houston, who was at that time the head football coach at Murray State University.

"Dickey, how's it going?" he asked.

"Terrible," I replied. "Houston, I just can't do this! I'm not cut out for this! My players are pitiful, my coaches are pitiful and I am pitiful. People are laughing at me. I'm done, H. I don't want any part of this."

Houston said, "Hold on! Just hold on! Do you have your Bible there with you in the office?"

I said, "What? Yeah, maybe it's around here somewhere." I fumbled around and found it on the shelf behind my desk and dusted it off. "I have it," I said moodily.

Houston said, "Matthew 7:7."

"What? Matthew 7:7?" I flipped through the pages and found the reference.

"Read it," Houston instructed.

"Ask and you shall receive, seek and you shall find..."

"Keep reading it!"

I began to read it over and over. "H, thanks," I said. "I've got to go and get ready for Western Kentucky."

That evening at five, my staff hobbled in. "Hey, guys, want to know something? We are going to win on Thursday!"

"What?" my assistant Charles Cunningham said. "We haven't beaten Western Kentucky in the history of the school."

"That's okay. We will this week," I claimed.

As we hit the practice floor at seven P.M., our players sauntered onto the court. I blew the whistle and said, "Gather around, guys." As they slowly assembled I announced, "Hey, guys, we're going to win this Thursday. Anybody ever heard of Matthew 7:7? 'Ask and you shall receive, seek and you shall find...' Anybody?" Not one player raised his hand. They didn't want to hear it.

I told them, "It's all we have. Are you in or not?"

I heard a soft voice say, "Must be some kind of nut."

"That's okay. We are asking and asking fast."

That Thursday we beat Western Kentucky and two days later we beat Louisiana Tech, a team we hadn't beaten in four years. That was then, this is now.

After thirteen years as head basketball coach at Arkansas State University, I retired. My oldest son, Logan, played for me as a freshman in my last year. My wife and encourager, Cathy, and I have been married for over twenty-three years. My teams have recorded 189 wins, and rank second in victories in the Sun Belt Conference, behind Gene Bartow.

And it all started with Matthew 7:7!

~Dickey Nutt, former Head Coach, Arkansas State University

25

My All-Star Break

The weak can never forgive. Forgiveness is the attribute of the strong.
~Mahatma Gandhi

In the NBA, one of the most sacred times of the year is the All-Star break. This is a period of four to five days during the season when there are no NBA games being played and the coaches and players have time off. All season long everyone looks forward to this break. Some players and coaches even take mini-vacations to exotic destinations and resorts to maximize their time off. In my seventeen years of coaching in the NBA, this is the story of my all-time favorite All-Star Break.

During the 1999-2000 season the Portland Trail Blazers were playing fantastic basketball! We were one of the top teams in the NBA and were picked by many to win the Western Conference and contend for the NBA title. In the midst of what should have been one of the happiest points of my life, I was at one of my lowest.

Even though my team was winning games and having success, I was struggling personally. I guess winning games doesn't mean a whole lot if you have nobody to share it with. Statistics say that the divorce rate in America is just over fifty percent and in professional sports, the rate is around eighty percent. I had just become part of that statistic.

My wife and I had decided to part ways after seven years. The divorce was final the previous year and we had not spoken or seen each other in almost a year. I had lost contact with her and most of her family, except for her grandmother. She was one of the kindest and most godly persons I had ever met in my life. She had always treated me like a son and we had a very special relationship. She was in her eighties and lived in a small town about an hour outside Sacramento. She had become a big basketball fan and loved watching the Trail Blazers play on TV. Every time we came to Sacramento to play the Kings, I would make a special trip to see her.

As we approached the All-Star break, I had made plans to fly to Salt Lake City to visit with my family and friends for a few days. I was excited about my break and was ready to go home. Our team was beginning a road trip right before the break and our first stop was in Cleveland. Our team plane had just landed in Cleveland when I turned on my phone to check my messages. I was stunned to hear the voice of my former mother-in-law. She had called to tell me that her mother had passed away. She said her family wanted me to know, and that she knew how much grandma had meant to me. The funeral services were set for the following Monday in her small town, and although she knew it would be next to impossible for me to make it with our schedule, she wanted me to know that I was welcome to attend the service.

I was filled with mixed emotions about what I should do. Part of me wanted to go to the funeral and pay my respects, but another part of me had not yet forgiven my former wife and told me not to go and face her. I had struggled to find a way to forgive, but it was very difficult for me. I looked for some sort of spiritual guidance to help me, but I found that attending church at home on a regular basis was next to impossible. My NBA schedule was hectic because of games, practice or travel. I attended NBA chapel services before every game home and away, and prayed with many of the pastors to help me find a way to forgive and move on.

After a lot of prayer, I decided to go to the service and asked God for His help to make it happen. I prayed that if it were His will for me to go, the travel plans would somehow work out. I checked for flights to Sacramento on that Monday morning from Portland and was amazed that there were flights available to and from Sacramento.

It was going to be a tight schedule, but it could be done. We had practice scheduled that Monday at 4:00 P.M. I could catch an 8:00 A.M. flight to Sacramento, rent a car and drive an hour to make the 11:00 A.M. service. The return flight was at 2:00 P.M. and I would be back in Portland for the 4:00 P.M. practice. I would be able to stay at the service for about an hour, and then I would have to get back on the road to catch my return flight to Portland. I decided to do it.

That Monday morning I caught the 8:00 A.M. flight from Portland to Sacramento, arrived at 9:15 A.M., picked up the rental car and drove to the service. A million thoughts raced through my mind as I made the drive. With each passing mile I recalled all the times I had made this drive with my former wife. I arrived in town about forty-five minutes before the service and took a long drive through town. I knew that this was the last time I would ever be there. I thought about all the good times I had spent here and how much I would miss Grandma.

The funeral service started at 11:00 A.M., and I wanted to make sure that I was the last person in the church. I really did not want to have to face anyone. My plan was to just sit in the back row, blend in with the crowd, stay for an hour, then get back on the road to catch my return flight. God had different plans for me though.

As the service began, I sat in the middle of the back row and didn't see my former wife or her family. Suddenly from a side door in walked her family and her. They sat in the front row and then the pastor walked up to the podium. He introduced my former wife and then she went up on stage and began to sing a song. I just sat in the back row all choked up. After she finished singing, the pastor began the service.

He talked about Grandma and what a wonderful person she was. He told stories of how she had been such a source of inspiration and love to so many people, and how kind she was to everyone she met. He mentioned how she loved to play dominoes with her friends and how she loved to watch NBA basketball games whenever the Portland Trail Blazers played. He said that her grandson was one of the coaches, and how proud she was of him. When I heard all this, my eyes filled with tears. The pastor then began to pass the microphone around and people in the congregation shared stories of how Grandma had touched their lives.

Before I realized it, over an hour had passed and I began to worry that I wouldn't make my flight back to Portland. After several people shared their stories, the pastor started to close the service and I prepared to make my quick exit. Then, the pastor asked the family to stand up in the front row and for the congregation to stand up, starting with the back row, and come forward in a single file line to pay their respects to the family. All of a sudden I was standing and making my way towards my former wife and her family. I tried to get out of line, but there was no way out. People from in front and behind me just kept the line moving toward the front. God had put me here for a reason and I had to trust Him. My heart sank and I prayed for strength.

Time seemed to stand still as I walked in line. I thought about Grandma, how she would have wanted me to have been there and do the right thing. I thought about her love and how forgiving she was. That was the way she had lived and what she had witnessed to everyone she came in contact with. My eyes got teary as I stepped closer and saw her picture. My legs were weak, but I could actually feel God carrying me every step of the way.

Suddenly it didn't matter who was to blame or why things had happened the way they did in our past. I realized that it was time for me to forgive and stop carrying the burden that I had. I couldn't be forgiven unless I forgave too. As I approached the front, I turned and saw my former wife and family, and gave them all a hug. We spoke briefly and I told them I had to get back on the road to catch my flight. They were all very appreciative of me coming.

As I was making my way out of the church, my former wife called out to me. I turned around and she walked towards me. She told me it meant a lot to her that I had come. We walked outside the church towards my car and I told her how much I would miss coming to this place and seeing Grandma. Standing outside the church in the parking lot, I looked my former wife in the eyes and told her how sorry I was for everything. Her eyes started to tear up and she said that she was sorry, too. I gave her a hug and began my journey home. As I drove back to Sacramento, I felt that a huge weight had been lifted off me and that Grandma was smiling in heaven.

As I got in my car, I looked at my watch and realized that there was no possible way for me to make my way back to Sacramento and catch my return flight. I still had to turn in the rental car and go through security. I started to worry and then thought, "God is my travel agent today. He made this trip possible from start to finish and I'm just going to trust Him."

To this day I don't know how I made it back to Sacramento in time to turn in my car and catch my flight on time, but I did! I landed in Portland and raced back to our practice facility. I hurried and changed my clothes and got ready for practice. I began to stretch out the team for practice and I heard players talking about how they had spent their All-Star break. I just smiled and knew that my All-Star break was the best, thanks to God!

~Bob Medina, Strength and Conditioning Coach,
Portland Trail Blazers

26

Ultimate Friendship

When a friend is in trouble, don't annoy him by asking if there is anything you can do. Think up something appropriate and do it.
~E.W. Howe

ike a kid in a candy store, that was me at the Naismith Memorial Basketball Hall of Fame on Friday, September 10, 2004. At the time, I was the director of athletics at Saint Francis University, a small, private college in Loretto, Pennsylvania, attending the Hall of Fame enshrinement of Maurice Stokes, an All-American when he played at Saint Francis.

As soon as I entered the Hall of Fame's hospitality room, there was Oscar Robertson standing by the doorway; Chuck Daly was nearby, fixing a cup of tea; Earl Lloyd, the first African-American in the NBA, was getting some hors d'oeuvres; James Worthy, Robert Parrish, and Moses Malone were joking with each other in one corner of the room; Bill Walton was sitting at one end of the room, Julius Erving at the other; Pat Summit was chatting with Ray Meyer, while Bob Cousy talked with David Stern.

To me, however, the biggest star in the room was Jack Twyman. A 1983 inductee to the Hall of Fame, Jack was there to make the acceptance speech on behalf of Maurice, for whom Jack lobbied for years to be inducted into the Hall. Jack has described Maurice as a bigger and stronger Magic Johnson and believed Maurice would have been one of the greatest to play the game if he had been able to enjoy a full career.

Maurice, however, was not able to play a full career. He led Saint Francis to the NIT in 1954 and 1955, being voted the tournament MVP in 1955, the only player ever named MVP from the fourth place team. He averaged 26.2 points per game and was named an All-American in 1955. He became that year's first draft pick of the Rochester Royals and went on to win Rookie of the Year honors his first year and earn All-Star honors in each of his first three — and only three — years in the NBA. He averaged 16.4 points, 17.3 rebounds, and 5.3 assists per game over that three-year period.

In 1958, during the last regular season game of the year for the Royals — who moved to Cincinnati in 1957 — Maurice fell, hit his head on the floor and was knocked unconscious. He was revived by smelling salts, but three days later he collapsed on the plane back to Cincinnati from a playoff game in Detroit. The accident sent him into a coma for six weeks and left him paralyzed, beginning a twelve-year battle with encephalitis.

Once the playoffs ended, all of Maurice's teammates headed back to their hometowns, except for Jack. He was the only player on the Royals who made his home in Cincinnati. Jack and Maurice were both from Pittsburgh and knew each other well, but were not particularly close friends. Yet it was Jack who stepped in to help and later became Maurice's legal guardian.

Jack was only twenty-four at the time, but he assumed responsibility for Maurice and worked on creative ways to finance Maurice's health care, such as establishing a summer all-star basketball game at Kutsher's Country Club in New York.

Maurice maintained a positive approach to life throughout his twelve-plus years of hospitalization, including his grueling physical therapy regimen. In fact, Jack often remarked that whenever he was feeling down, Maurice would lift his spirits. According to Jack, "I never, ever saw him feel sorry for himself. I never, ever in twelve years saw him have a bad day, never not have a smile on his face, not be more interested in you than he was in himself. He never pitied the situation he was in."

And while Jack says Maurice gave him back tenfold what he

gave him, what Jack did by taking care of Maurice throughout his hospitalization until his premature passing in 1970, shows Jack to be one of the best friends that a person could ever hope to have.

Jack's Hall of Fame acceptance speech on behalf of Maurice Stokes told the story of Maurice the man. He brought tears to the eyes of everyone at the event and the national television audience as he made them aware of what made Maurice special. In the process, while this was not his intention, the speech also made it clear that Jack is a special man.

At a breakfast reception the morning after Maurice's induction into the Hall of Fame, Jack presented Saint Francis University with Maurice's Hall of Fame award, blazer, and ring for display in the school's Maurice Stokes Athletics Center. A display case with the items was unveiled at the athletics center on November 19, 2004, as part of a special recognition event for Maurice.

While this display celebrates the life of Maurice Stokes, it also celebrates the life of Jack Twyman—two great men who will always be intertwined in the true meaning of courage, caring, and brotherhood.

~Jeff Eisen, Mount Olive (NC) College Director of Athletics

Sleeping with Integrity

Integrity is not a conditional word. It doesn't blow in the wind or change with
the weather. It is your inner image of yourself, and if you look in there and
see a man who won't cheat, then you know he never will.
~John D. MacDonald

One of the darkest periods in North Carolina State basketball came in the early 1990s after the firing of Coach Jim
Valvano. Les Robinson, a former N.C. State player, replaced
Valvano and, after a successful 1990-91 campaign, the Wolfpack hit
the skids and suffered through back-to-back 19-loss seasons.

I was the radio play-by-play announcer for N.C. State during
those tough years and the job wasn't much fun, but Robinson's task
was more difficult than anyone could imagine.

In January 1993, after a blow-out loss at Georgia Tech that
dropped the Wolfpack to 0-6 in the Atlantic Coast Conference, the
team returned to Raleigh immediately after the game. During the
flight, I can remember looking over my shoulder. In the back of the
plane was Robinson in a deep sleep in the last row of seats.

I'd never seen anything like that in the pressure-packed world of
big time college basketball. A coach who wasn't a basket case after a
loss? I'm not sure why, but for some reason, I was never able to forget
that moment. I'm glad I didn't.

As I would learn a while later, Les Robinson's job involved a lot more than just coaching basketball. It was really about executing a very important two-fold mission. Les was given marching orders to improve the graduation rate of the N.C. State basketball program—which had dropped to an embarrassing level—and to repair severely damaged relations with the academic community on campus.

Standing in the way of success were some major challenges. NCAA sanctions restricted recruiting while the university imposed more stringent academic standards on the men's basketball program than on any of the school's other sports.

Robinson had little choice but to recruit student-athletes who were more students than athletes. As the academic record improved, the basketball record took a tumble. Wolfpack fans became critical. The media piled on. Robinson became the butt of jokes. Talk radio hosts renamed the play-in game of the ACC Tournament the "Les Robinson Invitational."

Les never lost his focus. He handled the situation with integrity, class, humor and tremendous humility. It was almost impossible not to like Les Robinson.

As my mind flashes back to that plane ride in January 1993, I realize now that Les could sleep on the ride home and was completely at peace because he knew he was doing exactly what he was ordered to do. He refused to get caught up in all the other stuff. Yes, the Wolfpack lost that night and the criticism hurt, but that wasn't the real issue.

Before resigning in 1996, Robinson successfully completed his mission and restored academic integrity to the Wolfpack men's basketball program, but he never coached again. In six seasons, his record at State was 78-98. Unfortunately, that record is the only thing a lot of people remember.

When I think of Les Robinson, I have a much different memory. I see a servant who focused on the mission, ignored adversity and persevered with class until the job was done.

That flight in 1993 taught me a life lesson. Rest and peace are by-products of obedience. Thanks Les, for showing me what a good night's sleep is really all about.

~Gary Hahn, Broadcaster, Wolfpack Sports Network

A Magic Moment

Practice random acts of kindness and senseless acts of beauty.
~Anne Herbert

During the 1994-95 season, my wife, three children and I had the opportunity to attend the Celtics-Magic game at the Fleet Center in Boston, sitting in courtside seats directly across from the Magic bench. This was particularly fortunate because my nine-year-old daughter, Kelly, lived and died with Shaq, Penny, Horace Grant and the rest of the team. Kelly wore her Magic sweatshirt, her Magic hat and her official Magic game jersey for the special occasion.

During pre-game warm-ups, my little Kelly was getting a piece of gum for herself. Just then, Horace Grant looked over to her. Kelly then held up a piece of gum for Horace. He came over and said he would love a piece of gum. That was the beginning of a two-hour friendship between Horace and Kelly—noticed by a lot of fans seated around us but never to be forgotten by this family!

During the game, Horace would turn and give Kelly a wink and a smile, or he would give the ball to Kelly and Kelly would toss it to the ref to be put back in play. He made Kelly feel like she was the sixth Magic player on the court! With about two minutes left in the game, a time out was called. Horace left the bench, walked over to Kelly and presented her with an autographed towel—a souvenir for life!

It was a small gesture from Horace—something he probably did several times a year—but it meant so much to Kelly. Horace Grant created the memory of a lifetime for a little girl he didn't even know, and gained a fan for life... a family of fans.

~Tom Monahan, Nashua, NH

Taking the Time, Keeping the Hope

There is a time to let things happen and a time to make things happen.
~Hugh Prather

I have the privilege of working for the San Antonio Spurs. One of my job responsibilities involves working at the games as a representative of our organization for not only the families of the players but special guests as well. Prior to one of our recent games I coordinated a visit for a friend of my boss: a meeting with Jermaine O'Neal, then of the Indiana Pacers. On this particular night the weather was overcast and rainy—a perfect night to stay at home—so as I drove to the arena I quietly pined for my couch and a good book in lieu of the game. I can't tell you how glad I am that I didn't stay home.

Upon my arrival I received a call from Chris, the father of Daniel, who had made the meeting request. As I escorted the family down to the court Chris began to tell me about Daniel: he had been diagnosed with T-cell leukemia at the very tender age of seven, which sent the San Antonio-based Edelens to a children's hospital in Indianapolis for chemotherapy and treatment. He fought the disease for three years and, during that time, saw several lives claimed from the very illness that he was trying to overcome.

One day while lying in the hospital, Daniel, who wore an inspirational bracelet, asked his father if he thought he'd ever have his own bracelet to wear. Chris asked Daniel what he would have his bracelet say, and he replied, "The only thing I would say is 'Be Hopeful—Daniel.'" Daniel, his family and friends now wear the bracelet proudly to remind them of the power hope has had in their lives.

During Daniel's stay at the hospital in Indiana, Jermaine O'Neal came in to meet the kids. Daniel and Jermaine would be introduced and an incredible relationship would bloom. O'Neal made it a point to visit Daniel, not only on team visits but on his own time as well. During the visits he would share words of encouragement, cheer and, most importantly, demonstrated a special care for Daniel during his most trying times. He even personally delivered a team autographed ball to Daniel for Christmas!

Since those visits, Daniel completed chemotherapy and his cancer is in remission. When Daniel and his family celebrated his victory over cancer, O'Neal, who wasn't able to attend the ceremonies in person, took the time to videotape a special message to Daniel who he has now declared "his hero." Jermaine and the Pacers come to San Antonio for Spurs match-ups every season, and each trip, Jermaine has made it a point to see Daniel prior to the game. He's even worn Daniel's hope bracelet during one of his games.

This latest visit is the one I was fortunate enough to witness. Jermaine appeared on court for warm-ups and spent some time talking to Daniel, but, this time, it would be Jermaine who was asking Daniel for help. O'Neal had missed several games during the past season due to a knee injury and he knew if anyone would be a source of energy and inspiration, it would be his friend Daniel. Jermaine asked if it would be okay if Daniel could call once in a while and help him in overcoming his knee injury.

I'm sure the best is yet to come for not only Jermaine and Daniel. The real message, however, is to remember what is most important: taking time for one another and keeping the hope.

~Stephanie Sidney, Executive Assistant to R.C. Buford,
San Antonio Spurs

Just Call Me Lucky

Faith gives us the courage to face the present confidently
and the future expectantly.
~Chuck Swindoll

My name is Damon Blust AKA Lucky. Why do they call me Lucky? Well, I'm the official mascot for the Boston Celtics and my character's name is "Lucky the Leprechaun." I'm thirty-two years old and looking forward to my fifth season as the face of the Boston Celtics, and boy has it been an amazing ride!

The road to the Celtics mascot started long before I ever realized it. I didn't aspire to be a professional mascot until I was in my early twenties and after a long, competitive gymnastics career. Ironically, basketball is the only mainstream sport I didn't play during my youth, yet, sure enough, it's the sport that helps me pay my bills today. More importantly, basketball is the sport that fills my life with joy and allows me to fill the lives of others with joy as well.

Being the mascot for the Boston Celtics has offered so many memorable experiences for me over the past four years. I've been showcased on ESPN's *SportsCenter* several times, traveled overseas to represent the NBA, and performed at the 2005 and 2006 NBA All-Star games. I've had many moments that stand out as the result of being Lucky, but none stand out nearly as much as the memories I have as a result of being an unmasked mascot. Unlike traditional mascots that wear masks and don't have voices, I don't wear a mask so I'm able to communicate verbally, not just through goofy expressions you see most mascots use to communicate. Don't get me wrong, I use plenty of goofy expressions, too! Being the first unmasked mascot in professional sports has added to my lifetime of memories and personal growth in more ways than one.

After my first two seasons had gone by and I settled into my new role as Lucky, I had some of the most amazing experiences of my life. Experiences that make any other achievement in my life, aside from becoming a father, pale in comparison. Working in the NBA gave me the opportunity to not only put smiles on the faces of Celtics fans but also put smiles on the faces of children through my God-given talents and abilities that I've been blessed with. Time and time again I could've suffered devastating injuries as a child or a young adult that could've prevented me from having the ability to work as a performing acrobat, but I got lucky. Thankfully my guardian angel has always been by my side! If it weren't for all this good fortune or being lucky, I would've missed out on the most memorable, amazingly heartfelt moment I've ever had... a moment that will raise the hair on my arms, as it does to this day, and I'm sure it will for life.

It was 2006 and one of the most influential people in the history of the NBA, Red Auerbach, had passed away just before the start of the season. In memory of Red, I wanted to do something extraordinary for him. During a time out at a Celtics game, I planned on performing an acrobatic slam dunk off my mini trampoline that had never been performed in an NBA arena: the Flip 60. The stunt required me to do a full twisting front somersault thirteen feet in the air to a slam dunk. After making the dunk my plan was to carry a sign onto the court dedicating the dunk to Red. I made the dunk and carried the sign to center court! The crowd erupted and showed their appreciation for Red, and for the stunt I dedicated to him, with a deafening applause. I was so proud of what I had accomplished, but that stunt soon became the second most special experience for me that night.

Shortly after I performed the stunt I was approached by a young boy named David. David asked me if he could say something to the fans on the PA system. At first I thought this was just some boy being silly and asking for something he knew wasn't going to happen. You know, boys being boys. At that very moment something came over me and rather than politely explaining that I couldn't accommodate his request I asked, "If I could arrange that, what would you like to say?"

David replied, "I have brain cancer and I'd like to ask the fans to pray for me!" My world stopped at that very moment as I could see the genuine sincerity beaming from this seventeen-year-old boy who appeared to be much younger from his struggles with cancer. As much as I wanted to walk David to the microphone I knew I couldn't make it happen. I explained that not even Lucky could get him on the microphone even though I wanted to, but I had an idea that might suffice. I remembered that Reverend Gray, the Celtics chaplain, was sitting courtside that night so I told David I'd be happy to take him down to the reverend for a moment of prayer as I felt that was the least I could do to help. David agreed so off we went.

I explained David's request to Reverend Gray. Without hesitation he, David and I held hands courtside during the fourth quarter as the Celtics were battling back from a huge early deficit. Reverend Gray prayed, and as he prayed—for at least four minutes—the cheers from the crowd got louder and louder. Reverend Gray continued to raise his voice to compete with the noise level in the Garden.

After a beautiful prayer from Reverend Gray, I walked David back toward his seat. I told David he had an amazing energy about him and I just knew he could get through this tough time. David looked back at me and said with a confident smile, "I know, Lucky; I've already overcome six brain tumors!"

For weeks I told everyone who would listen about my incredible encounter with David. I bragged about the courage and strength of this seventeen-year-old boy! That night I realized there is nothing more important than taking time to listen to our children, nothing more important than showing love, care and concern! As proud as I was to give Red a dunk that had never been performed—a dunk that put me in the history books—the Flip 60 took a back seat to what really mattered that night: giving a child hope!

By the way, I saw David at the end of the season and he was doing great! Wow, I love my life! I love being Lucky!

~Damon Blust, AKA Lucky the Leprechaun,
Official Mascot of the Boston Celtics

31

Apology Accepted and Expected

Who so neglects learning in his youth,
loses the past and is dead for the future.
~Euripides

During the NCCAA (National Christian College Athletic Association) Division I Men's Basketball Championship in 2001, the semifinal was a great contest between the number one and number four seeds. The number one seed had basically been crowned champion before the tournament even began due to the seemingly insurmountable record and talent pool they had. However, with 1:15 to play the number four seed held a one point lead.

Their defense had been relentless, and, as the number one seed attempted to push the ball up court, a steal occurred and a breakaway lay-up appeared obvious. Just before leaving the floor to lay it in, the point guard who had stolen the ball made a decision to add emphasis to the bucket and went to dunk the ball instead of opting for the mundane lay-up. His attempt slammed off the back of the rim, a scramble ensued for the rebound and the unfortunate point guard was whistled for a foul with 1:05 left in the game. His frustration was demonstrated by his next poor decision to use the proverbial "F bomb" to describe his emotional state (remember that this was the National Christian Collegiate Athletic Association championship).

What transpired next was the epitome of coaching. The

disappointed coach called a time out, instructed his assistant coach to gather the players and began walking toward his point guard. They met about ten feet from the rest of the team and placing both hands on his player, the coach simply said, "You know better."

The now dejected player sheepishly stated, "I know coach, I should have laid it in." The coach assisted the player with raising his chin to ensure eye contact and very quietly said, "I am not talking about basketball."

In an instant, the player remembered all the devotionals, all the team meetings where life lessons were taught and remembered the institution that graced the front of his jersey. Mostly he remembered that his coach had taught him that the ultimate Coach expected better. The player stepped away from the coach, made his way to his teammates and apologized to them for failing to conduct himself in the way he knew he should.

After the game, this young man sought me out and apologized for embarrassing the NCCAA. I told him that the very reason the NCCAA existed was to allow young men and women who sometimes fail to be taught and molded by men and women called to coach.

Sometimes failing teaches you the most.

~Dan Wood, NCCAA Executive Director

32

Chicken Soup for the Soul

Two Points: Giving Back to Zac

The true meaning of life is not in its duration, but its donation.
~Dr. Peter Marshall

The national anthem was over. The starting line-ups were announced. A large crowd packed the small high school gymnasium on a cold evening in western Pennsylvania. The five starters for the visiting Cambridge Springs Blue Devils made their way to the center circle in blue and white uniforms. The hometown Lakeview Sailors trotted out dressed in red and black. Only a handful of people knew what was about to happen.

It was during pre-game warm-ups that the idea came to me. I presented it to my captains and they loved it. I discussed it with Lakeview's head coach and he agreed with the plan. I then pulled a couple of the Lakeview players aside and whispered to them.

The referee tossed the ball into the air. The boy jumping center for Cambridge never moved and neither did his teammates. The tip went to the Sailors' point guard who immediately tossed it to Nate Miller. This was Nate's one and only time to be in the starting line-up. Luke Eidenmuller gave up his starting position so that his good buddy could score a very special basket. The visiting Blue Devils stepped aside as Nate shot an uncontested lay-up. The confused crowd cheered as the scoreboard operator put two points up for the home team. These were the first points ever recorded on the brand new scoreboard, a memorial scoreboard for 2nd Lieutenant Zachariah Robert Miller, Nate's late brother.

• • •

The painful phone call came early in the morning. There are no words in the English language strong enough to explain how I felt as my mother's best friend told me to sit down and then explained that Zac Miller was dead. I would later find out that the twenty-two-year-old was overcome with heat exhaustion while completing voluntary military training.

Zac Miller is arguably the best person to ever graduate from Lakeview High School. He was valedictorian with a perfect 4.0 grade point average. He was captain of the football, basketball, and track teams and was student council president. Zac received a full scholarship to West Point where he graduated with honors and was named West Point's top graduate in mathematics, computer science and the basic sciences. He received the prestigious Robert E. Lee award and was selected as a Truman and Rhodes Scholar. Zac was enrolled and ready to attend classes at Oxford University.

• • •

I had the privilege of knowing Zac Miller. Our families were extremely close. Zac's parents, Keith and Rosalyn Miller, were like parents to me. They lived in the apartment above us as I was growing up. Keith and "Roz" babysat me on numerous occasions. They were like family and still are to this day. Keith was my sixth-grade teacher and coached me in various sports. The Millers attended all of my birthday parties and were present at my graduation and wedding. Their older son Zac was near and dear to me and my family. I was fortunate to watch him grow and mature into an incredible young man.

I'm proud to say that I also attended the Lakeview schools from third grade through graduation. I played basketball all through high school. A short time after graduating from college, I returned to

Lakeview as a physical education teacher and girl's basketball coach. Throughout my lifetime, many fond memories were created as I spent thousands of hours in the Lakeview High School gymnasium as a player, PE teacher, and coach.

Right before Zac's untimely death, I left Lakeview and the girl's basketball program to accept the boy's basketball position at nearby Cambridge Springs High School. I was in my first year of coaching at Cambridge Springs when Zac passed away. Roz called and told me about the memorial scoreboard. She told me that the dedication would take place the night I brought my team to Lakeview. She was waiting to put the new scoreboard up until I could be there for the ceremony. It was already going to be an emotional game for me. I was anxious about returning to my old school as a visiting coach. Numerous thoughts and memories flooded my mind.

I decided to sit my team down the night before we played Lakeview and explain what was going to happen the next evening. I even brought in the cheerleaders so they would understand what they were going to witness. I wanted to make sure they knew who Zac Miller was and what he and his family meant to me. I told the room full of teenagers all about Zac and his accomplishments, including his perfect SAT score.

I showed them his graduation picture from West Point where he was shaking hands with President George W. Bush. I told them about Zac's life, his funeral and the 21-gun salute. I did my best to inform them about the greatest young man I ever knew.

As I walked into the gym, the atmosphere was overwhelming. The scoreboard looked incredible. I bumped into several former students and players. Many of my old neighbors and friends were in attendance. My high school coach, Jeff Engstrom, greeted me first. Then I saw Keith and Roz. I wondered what it must be like to be in their situation. Then I noticed Nate Miller, Zac's only brother. He would be suiting up for the varsity game in one hour. I wondered what he was feeling.

The dedication ceremony was emotional. I couldn't take my eyes off the Millers. Nate held back tears standing between his parents as Coach Engstrom read all about Zac's accomplishments.

I've been playing and coaching basketball all my life. I've witnessed thousands of games and maybe close to a million points being scored. I remember buzzer-beaters that helped my team win and a last second shot that cost my team a state championship. I recall one of my players shooting into the wrong hoop during a seventh grade game. I vividly remember my son Caleb's very first basket. But the two points I remember most are the two points that were recorded by Nate Miller on the memorial scoreboard for his older brother, 2nd Lieutenant Zachariah Robert Miller. As Nate's shot dropped through the hoop, I looked at his mother sitting directly across the court from our bench. The smile she gave me was priceless.

When the new scoreboard's final buzzer sounded, I was disappointed with my team's score; however, I was extremely satisfied with their effort. The old cliché was never truer, "It's not whether you win or lose but how you play the game."

~Ted Jones, former Basketball Coach,
Cambridge Springs High School, PA

33

Every Day Is Father's Day

My father didn't tell me how to live. He lived and let me watch him do it.
~Clarence B. Kelland

The plane lifted skyward from the mountains of western North Carolina. On board was the happiest, most confident and secretly amazed group of people in the world that day. This group was the University of North Carolina Asheville women's basketball team, their staff and supporters. I'm their coach, and we were on the way to the "Big Dance," the 2007 NCAA Women's Basketball Tournament in Austin, Texas. Having won the Big South Conference tournament, we were realizing a dream that I had planted in these young women's heads and hearts when I arrived in Asheville in 2002.

Aloft, I had the time to reflect on the years of preparation and perseverance that had brought us to this moment—not so much the team's but my own. College coaches have but four years with a student athlete to build that team, hone their skills, convince them to dream and, more than dream, to believe that what they dream can really happen. That's my job, and what I love most about it is to see a young woman finally believe in herself and her teammates enough to reach out and grab that dream for her own.

Much of what I give my teams in the way of confidence building and believing in oneself was given to me by countless teachers, coaches, friends, and family, but I want to tell how one person, above all, gave me unwavering, unconditional support, and that was my dad. In twenty-some years of coaching, I have seen everything from parents. From crippling parental pressure to complete lack of interest, parents can be the barrier to their daughters' satisfying athletic careers. What I wish for them is to have a dad like mine.

First of all, he was always there. I remember the high school game when I cramped up and fell to the floor, and he rushed out onto the court and was told by the referees to leave. He refused and told them that when he was sure I was all right, he would leave. He was there when James Madison University was playing Old Dominion and I took a charge from Nancy Lieberman and split my elbow open. He took me to the hospital and safely back to my dorm that night. He was also there during my college career when I sat on the bench and didn't get the playing time I had earlier enjoyed.

He was there when, as an assistant coach at JMU, we knocked off number one-ranked Penn State. The game film shows him jumping out of the bleachers and rushing the court to grab me in his arms and twirl me around the floor. Somehow he got an official badge and came back to the locker room to celebrate.

He was there for my first head coaching job at Shepherd University, quietly eating popcorn and occasionally pointing out a bad call for the referees. Win or lose, he was there.

He was there for my press conference when UNCA called me to coach a team that had won but one game the year before. Many nights he drove five hours to my game and, against Mom's wishes, turned around and drove home again that night. If he saw me down or disheartened that first year as we struggled to build a team, his favorite phrase and his only suggestion for my coaching methods was to yell, "Suck it up, Bets!" In his dairy-farming vernacular that meant, "Get your head up, Betsy!" And I usually followed his advice.

Dad died in 2004. This strong, seemingly invincible man was stricken with bacterial meningitis, and what was unthinkable had happened. The night of the Big South championship game, as the seconds ticked away on the clock and it seemed that victory was imminent, I looked up into the stands to catch my mother's eyes, but she was gone! "Oh, no," I thought. "Mom couldn't stand the pressure." What I didn't know was that our athletic director had gone into the stands and brought my mother to courtside.

After the game, when I ran into my mother's arms, my first words to her were, "I wish Dad were here to see this."

She said, "Betsy, I think he was here every minute of this journey."

Well, we flew into Austin, this small liberal arts school in western North Carolina that had come so far — from winning three games in 2002-03 to being named the most improved team in NCAA Division I Women's Basketball the next year to winning the conference in 2006-07 — to meet the highly-ranked and highly-skilled team of Louisiana State University. We were humbled in our loss, but as I walked from the court that night, head bowed in defeat, reverberating through my whole being was a voice saying, "Suck it up, Bets!" and I lifted my head.

~Betsy Blose, Head Women's Basketball Coach,
University of North Carolina Asheville

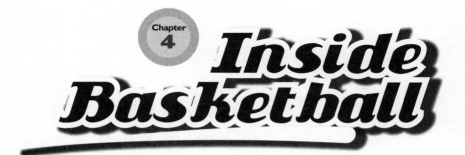

Chapter 4

Inside Basketball

Keeping the Faith
with Perseverance

*I determined to never stop until I had come to the end
and achieved my purpose.*

~David Livingstone

34

Losing to Win

The will to persevere is often the difference between failure and success.
~David Sarnoff

Peter Boutros was a kid who tried his hardest, every time every day, but lacked the needed skills. I had asked Peter if he was new to Fountain Valley High School Basketball because I did not recognize him. Peter informed me that after being cut both his freshman and sophomore year, he decided he would do whatever it took just to have a chance to be a part of the team that year, so he lost fifty pounds.

Even with my empathy for Peter, I had seventeen players who were better than him. I would have to look Peter in the eye and tell him that even after all his efforts he was not going to get a jersey. I gave Peter and the other three players I had to cut the option of being the team manager. The other three players declined, saying it was beneath them. Peter called me and said he would accept on one condition. I liked his boldness; I had never had a player set conditions for him to play for me. Peter said he would be the manager only if he could practice with the team every day. He wanted to do every drill because his goal was to earn a varsity jersey his senior year. I accepted his terms, and for the first time in his life Peter was part of a team.

As a manager, Peter was awful. The stats were never accurate and things were never in the right place. However, Peter was becoming a skilled basketball player and one of the hardest workers in practice.

Soon he had earned the respect of everyone on the team. The beginning of the last week of our season, I had the team meet in the locker room. What took place was one of the most inspiring moments of my life; it is why I teach and why I am a basketball coach.

I had the team sit down and gave them the impression that I was upset. I was holding a bag and said, "Which one of you was so irresponsible to leave your bag in the gym?" Everyone was looking around to see who had done it. I yelled, "Boutros! Never forget your bag again," and I handed it to him. Some of the players had perplexed looks on their faces because Peter did not have one of these bags, only the players did. The players had no idea I was going to do this and I had no idea what they were about to do for this young man, for their teammate, for their brother.

Peter opened the bag and pulled out a jersey — his jersey! Seeing this, the players circled around him. Peter clutched the jersey to his chest and the tears began to roll down his face. Then my players took over. They transformed a magical moment into a miracle moment — a moment which inspired the lives of everyone in the room. In unison they started to chant, "Boutros! Boutros! Boutros!" and they continued for over a minute. Even I got caught up in the enthusiasm and was shouting, "Boutros! Boutros! Boutros!" Then these young men all stood up and began to clap repeatedly. The roar grew louder and louder. They literally gave this kid a standing ovation for over four minutes. I was speechless; I was just in awe, completely engrossed in the moment they were creating.

Peter never stood up and he never let go of his jersey. He sat there on the locker room floor with an indescribable smile and expression of astonishment and exhilaration. As Peter sat there and the tears continued to flow and the applause increased, I wondered what might be going through his mind. Did any of the jokes or harassment he once endured when he was overweight come back to him? Did the dread of being told to go "skins" by a former coach emerge? Did the many embarrassing times of being picked last in physical education classes pop up? Did the ridicule of peers when he dropped a pass, missed a shot, or got beaten on defense flash forward?

Peter went from seeing his name on cut lists to hearing his name echoed over and over again like that of a champion. For the first time in Peter's life he had teammates who made him feel appreciated, important, wanted, needed, valued, respected, cared for, and most powerfully, loved. As Peter said, "Basketball brought me pain for the first fifteen years of my life, but it was all worth it for the one year when it gave me love. Not just love from my teammates, but love for myself. My family grew by eighteen members thanks to this game and thanks to my mentor, and now friend, coach Steven Schultz who opened doors for me that used to be closed."

Giving Peter a jersey was one thing, but getting him in the game was another. We had two games left after Peter got his jersey and these games were probably going to be close, so I did not think I would get him in. My players had other ideas.

There were five minutes left in the fourth quarter and we were only ahead by six points. My best shooter Loren Robb ran past me after a play and said, "Coach, put Boutros in for me." Then our point guard Kevin DeHerrera gave me our sub signal and said, "Peter for me!" These players cared more for their teammate than for their own personal success or winning. They were only doing what we had been teaching them all season, so I thought it was important that I respond accordingly. For the first time in his high school career Peter heard, "Boutros, you're in." Peter played the remaining four minutes and twenty-six seconds of the game and we beat our rival Edison by twelve.

The next game would be our last and would be at home in Berger Gymnasium. The night before, I got a call from Stephan Robb, who was a starter when the season began, but a severe injury kept him out for over a month, and he had just worked his way back to a starting spot two days earlier. Stephan told me that he thought Peter should start tomorrow in his place. I felt like I was in the movie Rudy. This is a great part about being a basketball coach at Fountain Valley High School; I get to be with people who do things on a daily basis that other people make movies about. Basketball truly is a blessing.

The next day both Stephan and Peter started. We lost the game in overtime by one point to the Sunset League champions. What we gained will not be put on a banner in a gym, but cannot be taken from our hearts and souls. Virtue is our victory and family is our prize. Peter and I have a life-long relationship, as I do with the rest of the members of that team. I will never forget the intentness and drive of Peter Boutros and I will always remember the acceptance and love shown by his teammates.

~Steven Schultz, Boys' Head Basketball Coach,
Fountain Valley High School, Fountain Valley, CA

35

Netting an SI Cover

The height of your accomplishments will equal the depth of your convictions.
~William F. Scolavino

Growing up in Lakewood, California, I had two obsessions. One was to be the best basketball player; not the best I could be, but the best in the land. It was far-fetched, but kids do dream. My other obsession was to be on the cover of *Sports Illustrated*. This dream was a little more attainable.

As far back as I can remember, until I went to college, my bedroom was wall-to-wall *Sports Illustrated* covers; of course, only basketball covers. I would lie in bed looking at the faces and expressions of Kareem Abdul-Jabbar, Michael Jordan, Larry Bird, and, my favorite, Magic Johnson. These pictures would talk to me and they would inspire me to get up in the morning.

After winning several division and state championships, I became one of the most sought-after high school recruits in the country. After deciding to attend UCLA, the fanfare was incredible. UCLA had not won an NCAA Championship since the John Wooden Era more than twenty years ago.

I couldn't believe it when I got the call that *Sports Illustrated* wanted to shoot a cover to kick off my freshman season. My dream had come true. I was going to share the cover with UCLA greats Bill Walton, Don McLean and the best player UCLA has ever and will ever produce, Kareem Abdul-Jabbar. The photo was awesome and the experience was unbelievable.

About two weeks after the photo shoot and before the start of the season, I tore ligaments in my left knee while playing pick up basketball with my teammates. I would be playing basketball again after rehabbing my knee, but that wouldn't be until next year. So, *Sports Illustrated* wiped my cover as if it were sweat on the floor. I was devastated.

By my senior year we had a team with a lot of promise. We worked extremely hard from summer workouts to the season, and we earned a trip to the NCAA Championship game. We had excellent leadership from coach Harrick, his staff and a team with three seniors. We went on to win the first NCAA Basketball Championship for UCLA in twenty years with Coach John Wooden in attendance cheering us on!

When we flew back to Los Angeles the next day, Jay Leno invited our team to appear on *The Tonight Show*. While our team was touring the studio, Jay stopped the team and asked, "Where is this guy?" He was holding a copy of *Sports Illustrated* with my picture on the cover cutting down the net! My teammates all turned and pointed to me, pulled me to the front, and Jay extended his hand and said, "Congratulations."

I could not believe what I was looking at. I finally got my *Sports Illustrated* cover. Dreams do come true.

~Ed O'Bannon, former college basketball star and NBA player

36

Nicole Wins the Biggest Contest of Her Life

Few of us are like the Mona Lisa.
She keeps smiling when her back's to the wall.
~Lewis Grizzard

"I knew Nicole was special," said Coach Denise Dillon. "She was so laid back on the court and never got shaken up. She had this calm about her and was always in control when she played and she just let the game come to her."

Sometimes she looked so laid back that it seemed like she wasn't trying hard. And at just that point she would jump a passing lane and tip away the ball for a steal and a break-away lay-up. She lulled her opponents to sleep with that sideways glance up at the basket, then a jab step with a little more conviction, but not enough to sell it to the defender. Then she was gone. With one loping step, like she was skipping over a puddle, she was in the lane, at the basket, making the shot.

I grinned as I noted the time and the basket in the scorebook, thinking to myself, "She's going to be so good."

While Nicole was just the fourth-option-freshman in my first season with the team, everyone knew she had the goods to be special. She had the moves, she had the timing, she made it look easy, and she was only a freshman, full of potential. We all saw the talent that night when she took over the game against the most dominant team in our conference whom we'd never defeated before. She had six steals, grinning the whole time as if she knew something they didn't.

Nicole unwittingly introduced me to the spirit of women's basketball. Are they singing? How can they be ready to play a basketball game when they're singing—is that a three-part harmony? I think that's the Suber twins and Nicole Hester doing their best Destiny's Child impression... on the way to a game. I guess she's just as relaxed off the court as she is on it. We're still winning, so whatever they're doing, it's working.

19-10 in 2004-05.

She's a second-option-sophomore this year and the jump shot is even better. Dropping twenty on Temple, the Owls couldn't stop her. The first of what should be many double-doubles in a tournament in North Carolina. She's not a secret anymore, but it doesn't matter, they're still moving in slow motion when she's on the floor.

15-14 in 2006-07.

When I ran into the team in the weight room this morning, Nicole wasn't working out. She wasn't smiling, just sitting and watching her teammates with a hoodie pulled over her head.

"What's up with you?"

"Oh, nothing, I just had some things removed from my neck, so I can't practice yet."

"But you're okay? You'll be back?"

"Yeah, I think so," she sighed.

We're at pre-game meal before the season-opener against a nearly nationally-ranked Penn State team. It's the same old pasta and chicken. The same dry bread and I drop some sauce on my warm-ups like I always do. But something is different. It's not as loud as it usually is. There is a tension in the room because more people are here, people who don't usually come to pre-game meal. Where is Nicole? Is she playing today? Why hasn't she been practicing?

When Nicole and her parents walked to the front of the room, the grin was gone. She tried to get it out but couldn't. Her father stepped in and explained that everything would be fine. They caught the lymphoma early and Nicole is in good shape, she's a fighter and she has great support from everyone around her. We're going to get through this and she'll be back on the court in no time.

"I'm sorry I couldn't tell you; we just didn't know what it was until now," she managed to get out before being immersed in an ocean of hugs and tears.

I don't know how they focused on basketball that night, but they put up a fight against the Nittany Lions and made a game of it, but didn't win. The contest typified the majority of the season. On the court, the team just kept looking for that other scoring option that would have been Nicole. Off the court the team missed the magnet that held it together.

While the team struggled through the season, it was even tougher to watch the soul of the squad aching without its leader, without a shining talent and a beautiful person in the prime of her life. Nicole faced a challenge tougher than any opponent, one that could not be head-faked or crossed up by a quick first step. Instead of classes and practice, she faced chemotherapy and radiation treatments to kill the cancer before it spread.

As the season dragged on, Nicole came to games when she could make it from home and when her energy level allowed. She surprised the team with an appearance at a road game just before New Year's and the Dragons responded with an inspired effort. The Suber twins, her bandmates, lit it up from outside like they did so often during the trio's freshman year. For forty minutes of basketball, everything was right in the world again.

When Nicole made it to games, even if the team was losing, her presence was a signal that she was winning her battle. She was leading in the biggest contest of her life and was going to beat Hodgkin's lymphoma and get back on the court. After missing the winter term for treatment, Nicole's condition improved as she responded to treatments and she was able to enroll in spring classes and return to campus.

Easing her way back into fitness as her doctors would allow,

Nicole worked hard to get herself back into basketball shape. The medicine that helped fight off the cancer had diminished her lung capacity. But Nicole worked her way through the rehab exercises and conditioning as much as her body allowed, with the goal of rejoining her team for exhibition games in Spain at the end of the summer.

By the end of early preseason practices Nicole was cleared to play in the exhibition contests. She reclaimed her spot in the starting lineup for each of her team's four games in Spain and showed flashes of the player she had been, cutting off passes on defense and knocking down jumpers, despite being limited in playing time.

When the team returned and resumed preseason practices, Nicole was back in full stride. She was absent one week at the beginning of October to have a treatment shunt removed, the last vestige of a nightmarish season. Nicole was declared cancer-free. She was back.

Minutes before tip-off of our final preseason exhibition game, I was running, going through pregame preparations with the scorer's table crew as the teams warmed up on the court. As I went over name pronunciations with the public address announcer, I heard someone singing along with the pregame warm-up tape. I turned around to see Nicole grinning as she grabbed a ball off the rack and dribbled to the lay-up line.

~Britt Faulstick, Drexel University
Associate Director of Sports Information

37

Get Back to the Team: Lessons from a Loving Mom

Adversity causes some to break and others to break records.
~Pat Riley

Wow, what a season for the 2005-06 Georgia Southern University men's basketball team. A 20-10 record, a Southern Conference regular season championship and a bid to the NIT, the Eagles first post-season appearance in thirteen years. Unfortunately, as the head coach, I hardly remember any of it.

On the first day of practice I got "the call" that my healthy mother at the young age of sixty-seven had been diagnosed with cancer of the small intestine. How ironic that a short five months later she would be laid to rest on the same day of our final day of basketball in the NIT.

I left that first day, making the six-hour ride to Florida, knowing that it couldn't be true and was surely a misdiagnosis. Of course, in her typical fashion she insisted that I return immediately for practice, asking how I could possibly miss it. She spoke of how she knew she would be fine and win the fight and how I "better get back there with that team!" That was just her being her, wanting to not be noticed and making sure everyone else was taken care of.

I returned to Statesboro, Georgia, totally distracted with the thought of losing my mother but knowing I had to refocus for a special group of players who had the potential to have a great season. Every off-day or free chance I had, I would go visit her with my wife, Jody, and seven-year-old son, Jaxson, who she totally adored. Her response was always the same: "I'm doing fine. You better get back there and take care of that team."

As the season wore on, the task of concentrating and leading my team became harder and harder as my mother's health continued to decline. It's amazing how so many good traits come out in people during tough times. Every day a few of my players would ask, "How's your mom doing, Coach?" Fans, avid supporters, my staff and our administration would provide words of support as well. I was often told that adversity makes the soul stronger but never dreamed I would have to find out this way.

After each of the twenty wins that season, I would go home and cry, thinking of my mom instead of enjoying the satisfaction of winning. She would always muster up the energy to call and even if she could only speak one word it would be, "Congratulations!" She supported every game I ever played or coached throughout her life and didn't let anything, including cancer, stop her. She passed away right after we were upset in our conference tournament and her funeral was on the same day we played Charlotte in the NIT.

I had convinced myself that I wouldn't go to the game, but instead would stay close to my father who had lost his wife of fifty years. But her constant words of, "You better get back to that team," echoed in my mind. I knew how upset she would be if I didn't go and coach. I caught a flight and arrived two hours before the game and again was stunned by the number of good-hearted people, including our opponents, who gave me strength.

Mom was diagnosed on the first day and passed away on the last day of the season almost as if she planned it that way. Although she was not physically there, she played a huge role in Georgia Southern's most successful season in years.

~Jeff Price, Head Basketball Coach, Georgia Southern University

38

Persevering Amy

Victory belongs to the most persevering.
~Napoleon

The year was 1980 and I had just been appointed head women's basketball coach at Indiana University. I was tremendously excited to be a part of the great basketball tradition both at Indiana University and in the state of Indiana. Professionally, I had reached one of the high points of my career, having coached a national championship team at the University of Dayton. In successful times like these, we tend to think we know so much, when in reality it is then that we are reminded of how little we truly do know.

Graduating from high school, Amy had won the Indiana Mental Attitude Award, placed second in the selection of the coveted Miss Basketball in the state and was recruited by numerous Division I schools. Amy had decided, however, that her number one choice was the Hoosiers. A new coach was in place and the team had the best chance to become the most prominent intercollegiate women's basketball team in Indiana, her home state. Everything seemed to be falling into place seamlessly... but would it?

Shortly after I arrived at Indiana, Amy came to see me and indicated that she wanted to try out for our team. My comment that she was only 5'4" tall probably did not give her much confidence! The Friday before tryouts, Amy contracted a very serious case of strep throat but on Monday she was ready to show the coach that she deserved a spot on the team. Amy did make it through the first week.

On Friday, however, I told her that she would not be playing for the Hoosiers. Imagine the impact of this news on a young player who had just been named the second best high school player in the state of Indiana!

Amy's response was quite unusual. She inquired if she could assist the team in any other way since she was determined to try out again the following year. It seems that Amy knew even then that she was going to play for the Hoosiers, no matter what and in spite of me. Amy's mental toughness along with her positive reaction to adversity certainly had made an impression on me.

Amy would stay close to the team that first year to make sure that I was always aware of her presence. Her constancy paid off as Amy did start playing for the Hoosiers that next year. Her fortitude had led to the fulfillment of her dream. And what an incredible impact she made both as a team player and team leader! With her on board, the Hoosiers won the Big Ten championship and competed in the second round of the NCAA Tournament. I remember thinking that this young, persistent and hard-working "pint" of an athlete with the engaging smile had taught us all an important lesson: it is not the size of the dreamer but rather the size of the dream that feeds our perseverance.

Having played for the Hoosiers as a "walk on" for one year, Amy was finally offered a scholarship to play out her eligibility. And again, Amy's response was unusual. She had been aspiring to become a medical doctor and was now convinced that she needed to sacrifice her dream of continuing her career in intercollegiate basketball in order to have more time to attain the grades necessary for admission to medical school. It was at this juncture in my association with Amy that I realized how important her faith was to her. Amy's burning desire to be the person God wanted her to be became the main purpose in her life, and she followed the call to serve the sick, the poor, and the needy.

In spite of many skeptical voices, "persevering Amy" would eventually be admitted to medical school and become a pediatrician. But this was only after she was rejected and asked to complete further academic work before re-applying. Most people would have given up at this point. Not Amy. She completed the necessary academic requirements and moving forward slowly, steadily and with admirable determination, fulfilled yet another life dream.

In the three summers that followed and while preparing for the medical profession, Amy spent time as a volunteer in South America, Pakistan, and Honduras. In 1992, she finally was ready to start her medical practice. She had persisted through every obstacle, every setback and every disappointment and had now reached her goal. One year later she was diagnosed with dysautonomia, a disease that affects the autonomic nervous system that would render her unable to practice medicine. Life had dealt her the ultimate blow and once again she was forced to make a critical choice, perhaps her most difficult one yet. Up to that point Amy always had realistic alternatives in her choices but this time there seemed to be only one: giving up her dream. There simply appeared to be no other way.

Instead of surrendering, however, "persevering Amy" would find other ways to fulfill her calling to help the poor and needy. Nothing stops her and today Amy uses her medical expertise, her competitive drive and her joyful personality to help others. She has learned that in spite of losing part of her dream she still won, and that by becoming "poor," she has, in fact become "rich." Perseverance, for Amy, is a lifestyle. She has embraced her step-by-step journey into life's pain, suffering, roadblocks and disappointments without compromising the ability to express her incredible joy of living, gratitude and faith.

Her journey, like all of ours, will take Amy to the next pinnacle and give her perspective. For Amy, there is simply no other way.

~Dr. Maryalyce Jeremiah, Head Women's Basketball Coach,
Cal State, Fullerton

Moon's Shot

Shoot for the moon. You may not hit it,
but you won't come up with a handful of mud, either.
~Leo Burnett

Jamario Moon didn't take the common route to the NBA. One has to wonder how could anybody embark on such a trip, but more importantly where did Moon find the gumption to survive the journey? Only a stubborn belief in his ability earned Moon the long-awaited opportunity of suiting up in an NBA uniform as a twenty-seven-year-old rookie.

And now that he is a member of the Toronto Raptors, the 6'8" Moon has shown the NBA what countless other leagues have viewed—a player with off-the-chart leaping ability and hunger for the game that enabled him to persevere when most others would have packed it in. While Moon can jump through the building, the fact that he stayed grounded while suffering one setback after another, gives a true indication of the fortitude he exhibited in order to finally make it in the NBA.

His career prior to his rookie season in 2007-2008 with the Toronto Raptors consisted of a litany of alphabet soup leagues. There was the CBA, the WBA, the ABA, the USBL, the NBDL, one lower-level league after another, but Moon used each as a stepping stone to the NBA. In addition to playing in the U.S. minor leagues, he also spent time competing in Mexico along with a stint with the Harlem

Globetrotters. Finally, Moon not only won a roster spot, but eventually earned a place in the Raptors starting lineup as a rookie.

Actually it was a certain fear that kept Moon from quitting when the odds weren't exactly stacked in his favor. "I'm scared of failure and I just didn't want to fail and I didn't want to give up," Moon said. "God had a plan for me and if I stopped, I would have failed Him. I didn't want to do that so I wanted to keep going."

After just one season of competing at Meridian Community College in Mississippi, Moon applied for the NBA draft in 2001. Following that decision, he encountered the first of many road bumps when he wasn't selected in the draft. "I thought I would get drafted, go to camp and wind up making somebody's team," Moon said. "I wound up having to go a different route." A much more complex route.

In addition to his minor league experience, Moon played for NBA summer league teams of the Milwaukee Bucks, Los Angeles Lakers and Utah Jazz. He also participated in a Philadelphia 76ers mini-camp in 2002.

And of course there were the minor leagues. He said the toughest of all the lower-level basketball leagues was the American Basketball Association, where he played for the Kentucky Colonels in 2004. Sometimes the checks wouldn't arrive exactly on time. "I still wanted to play, but it's hard to play when you aren't getting paid," he said. "A couple of times I toughed it out and they finally came around with a paycheck but it was hard." Yet not impossible, especially with a mental outlook that was a strong as his drives to the basket.

"I always thought I would make it," he said. "I felt if I kept doing what I was doing and worked hard, I'd be there."

A big break came for Moon in the 2006-2007 season while playing for the Albany Patroons of the Continental Basketball Association. That season he was named the league's defensive player of the year and helped the Patroons advance to the CBA finals before losing to Yakima. A Toronto Raptors scout attended a few of his games and then invited Moon to mini-camp.

Whether it was as a scout, fan, or team executive, it was easy to identify Moon's enthusiasm for the game. "He is just a real fun-loving person who has a smile from coast-to-coast," said Albany vice president and general manager Dave Bestle. "Jamario was doing something he loved and he always believed in himself."

Despite taking an unconventional route to the NBA, Moon quickly earned the respect of his Raptors teammates. "It's not a common thing in the NBA to have somebody that old make it, but so much of it is getting the opportunity and the right chance and circumstance," said Raptors teammate Anthony Parker. "He's definitely gotten the right opportunity in a good situation and he has made the most of it."

Since he had to take the extended route to reach the NBA, Moon now takes nothing for granted. "What I went through makes me appreciate every little thing," he said. "If it wasn't for those different minor leagues I played in, I don't think I would be here because I always had somewhere to keep playing if I wasn't in the NBA." And then showing his gratitude, he added, "I am thankful for those leagues."

Moon has to laugh when he hears NBA players complaining about such things as the travel, the difficult schedule or any other perceived inconvenience related to their job. "I don't want to hear complaining because they should go down and play one month in some of the leagues I played in and they would come back and appreciate where they are a whole lot more," he said. "A lot of people feel they are in tough positions when they are really at the top."

Nobody feels more on top of things than Moon, who understands that his story could provide inspiration for the countless others who are chasing that NBA dream. "Hopefully I am an inspiration," he said. "People have to realize that they should never give up."

~Marc Narducci, *Philadelphia Inquirer* Columnist

Keep Climbing

*You can expect any change, no matter how much for the better,
to be accompanied by drawbacks and discomforts.*
~Arnold Bennett

Imagine waking everyday thinking the only thing you had to accomplish was staying out of harm's way. With the passing of each day you were grateful not for the clothes or the fancy material things our world has become consumed with, but to have had another day.

Then imagine that as the years go by it becomes harder to steer clear of the danger that comes with living in the projects, a Mecca for everything and everyone wrong. There were moments in life I was just happy to be alive. I could look around and know it wasn't the best of places, but it was the best place for me at the time. I think when we least expect it there is a moment in our lives when we will either become a product of the environment, or we experience a divine intervention that changes everything and the outcome is so rewarding.

My moment came at a young age. My savior came in the form of my granny who had raised and taken care of me. She decided one day that I would no longer just exist in this world as a tall awkward child. I would use what I was blessed with—and didn't acknowledge at that time—to get me to a place I couldn't have seen then.

What my granny envisioned wasn't even an option in my mind. To sweat, to be tired, to run up and down a court, and for what—to throw an orange ball into an impossible hole? I'd take my chances if it were up to me, to dodge the odds the world had stacked against me. Yet, the persistence of my granny forced me into basketball practices with other young girls who, like me, were being kept occupied while the negative aspects of life were swept aside by the chance of opportunity.

It took a while but with the help of my coach and my granny's relentlessness, I finally came to the realization that I could not only be good but I had the ability—however raw at the time—to be great! Like most kids it was just something to do, something I was being made to do. Later it became something more. It became that something that burns inside, something that, when you are at your weakest, pushes you past quitting to accomplishment. It became my outlet, my source to milk this world for everything it had to offer even though the chips had seemed to be stacked against me.

Basketball was my ticket to bettering myself physically because it allowed me the chance to play for one of the most well-recognized schools in the country, the University of Florida. I was able to better myself mentally by gaining an education that without that ball wouldn't have been feasible. I left the humble projects and arrived in one of the most beautiful cities in Florida and still, while I was blessed and on my way, I was lost.

I became enveloped in a world secluded from the realities of life. I was a project girl living the life the "rest" of the world was used to. As I had done in the past, I resisted all that was good. While I was in a "better place," I kept close to my heart my urban upbringing. I found myself in a storm of uncertainty, in the doldrums of isolation. I found myself without the one thing I had prided myself on to get me where I was. I found myself kicked off the team—without my teammates and away from everything and everyone who loved me. I reverted to the mentality that not getting in trouble was good enough. When I found myself in the spotlight, I cried.

I was torn between the life I knew so well and a new life. I learned during this transitional period in my life that many things from my past that felt right and comfortable aren't always good. Like

Robert Frost, I chose the path less traveled, and that has made a great difference. While these times of adjustment were admittedly difficult, I needed them to grow as an individual.

A college coach told me, "There is no progress without struggle." I have come to understand the truth of that statement as I have faced many obstacles in my life and in my career. I awakened later in life to the understanding that I was not destined to be a product of my environment, but I was headed for bigger and better things. I was becoming the product of determination. I didn't know it then, but I guess my grandmother did. A 94-foot court is what helped me to persevere and paved the way for me to return to my environment as a success and not as a statistic, as a role model rather than a disappointment. It allowed me to become a professional basketball player who lives a life of tragedy, a life of luxury, a life of pain, and a life of sweet glory.

I made it not knowing what the future promised, but had faith that Someone had a greater plan, and I made a solid choice to let my gifts bloom and grow. I owe everything today to those who pushed me at an early age and made me work in a structured, team-oriented environment until I realized my own promise and became self-motivated. I know now that each day I wake up I have an opportunity to be a better person than I was yesterday. I am thankful and humbled by what life has offered and given to me.

~Vanessa Hayden-Johnson, WNBA player

41

Fight On

Thou wilt show me the path of life: in thy presence is fullness of joy;
at thy right hand there are pleasures for evermore.
~Psalms 16:11

Look through the flying dust and you'll see me, a scrawny eleven-year-old, dribbling a basketball on my way to shoot a winning basket into the rusty hoop hung on a piece of plywood stuck to a fairly straight eucalyptus tree. Floating in the dust are dreams of winning games, the people cheering. Can you see them? Can you hear them? I always could.

What I didn't see was the nightmare that took place many years later on Thanksgiving Day, 1965. Exploratory surgery revealed an octopus-shaped tumor surrounding my heart and lungs.

Relatives, teammates, friends, cards, and flowers began arriving. A friend left a 1962 *Sports Illustrated* cover of me firing a deadly jump shot. This kind gesture was to remind me of better times. The only thing I could see now was the hospital room ceiling — so I stared and remembered.

High school coach Bob McCutcheon told me he thought I could really be a good ball player, but it would require a lot of work. He would put in the time if I would. No one had ever encouraged me like that. Our Santa Maria High team won the California CIF Championship; I set two California scoring records. Then there was the 60-point game, where schoolmates carried me off the floor on their shoulders — those dust-filled dreams were coming true. Junior college all-American honors followed the high school honor. These were better times and there were more.

The University of Southern California was next with its then state-of-the-art sports arena. Our team there won the conference title. I received three MVP Awards along with all-American certificates for my junior and senior years. I was only the second Trojan to be named a two-time all-American in men's basketball, plus an armful of scoring and rebounding records for the time. The University was filled with the Trojan "fight on" spirit. Great teammates and a high national ranking made for an exciting time. It was here that the legendary basketball announcer, Chick Hearn, gave me the nickname "Rudo the Reckless Russian." The USC Hall of Fame and Pac Ten Hall of Honor would come later.

In 1962 I was drafted by the New York Knicks. My pretty-faced high school sweetheart, Carolyn, and I set out to make a mark in the Big Apple on the other side of the country. Not bad for a couple of Russian kids. As a kid I had worked in my dad's strawberry fields trying to find out what my talents were, and Carolyn was the sophisticated product of the Los Angeles area. The way was clear and the future looked bright.

But life, like basketball, is given to bizarre shifts. After two-plus years with the Knicks and a short stint with the Golden State Warriors, I was told just before the beginning of my fourth year in the NBA, "We are sorry but we are going to have to release you."

Without knowing why my energy level and weight were dropping, I was still trying to keep in shape, thinking a team would ask me to join them. One day I worked out, walked into the shower, and passed out. The next thing I felt was water spraying on my face from the shower above and I heard others calling an ambulance.

The 1965 biopsy revealed reticulum cell sarcoma, a rare and virulent cancer. A few days later my temperature began to rise. The surgery had caused an empyema (infection) on my right side. Three tubes had to be inserted into the infection to drain contaminants for a year. I had to fight the cancer and infection. The cancer was treated with radiation, nitrogen mustard and Vincristine, the infection with antibiotics. The Vincristine left me paralyzed for seven months with a resulting slight foot drop. This was cancer treatment in the 1960s. There was no future in sight.

Listen, can you hear soft crying in the deep night? There I am, twenty-five years old, sitting on the edge of the hospital bed with my head on Carolyn's shoulder, her head on mine and we're crying. There are no spoken words, only tears blurring our dreams.

There were some tough come-from-behind ball games, but nothing like this. My weight dropped from 205 to 145. Hair loss, a raspy voice and immobility led to the question—what do you do? "Fight on"—never give up. Obstacles force us to take another path we normally wouldn't choose for ourselves, but give us insights we wouldn't learn any other way.

These are times when support is essential. I was blessed to have a loving wife, a fifteen-month-old son, family, friends, and a growing experience with God. The physicians did all they could do, but there is such healing power in the love, support, and prayers of other people. I was blessed with so much from so many. My mind was freed of any rejection, and I felt the compassionate concern of the people. I didn't get well instantly; it took a couple of years.

Five physicians (one later became the Surgeon General) met to evaluate my condition and said, "Three days is probably as long as John will live." At this time USC coaches announced the John Rudometkin 110% Effort Award. This is presented to a player at the team's award dinner each year.

Forty-plus years later, I run into former Trojan hoopsters who tell me they have received the award. It's a unique feeling to know you are still around to hear how others have received your award.

Physically unable to play hoops again, I entered the real estate profession and also developed a ministry of sharing this message of hope in the U.S. and beyond. Yes, there are detours in life, but God knows the way around the obstacles.

One night the sky was ablaze. The fire chief said we were blessed to wake up and get out. The next morning we went back to see the remains of our home. The family room where my basketball trophies and awards were was the first to burn. There were only a few pieces of metal remaining in the ashes. But fire and smoke cannot burn the "fight on" spirit.

Look again. Here I am sixty-seven years old — it's early spring and the landscape is all green and fresh. With the sound of the creek beside our country home we're enjoying another beautiful sunset.

If you find yourself toeing the free throw line with life's moments ticking away, and dust blocking your view, look up — there's help — keep "fighting on." What God has done for me, He can do for you. He will show you the way, and goodness and love shall follow you all the days of your life.

~John Rudometkin, former University of Southern California and NBA player

42

NT Never Quit

It's always too soon to quit.
~*Norman Vincent Peale*

Krystal Thomas is a champion in anyone's book. By age eighteen the 6'5" center had led her high school basketball team to back-to-back state championships and was named state finals MVP both years. She had played in national tournaments like the McDonald's All American Game, the WBCA All-American Game, the AAU Nationals and Nike Tournament of Champions. She had been named Miss Florida Basketball, the Gatorade State Player of the Year and earned *USA Today*, EA Sports, McDonald's and *Parade* First Team All-American honors for her high school career. She had earned a full scholarship to play for the Lady Blue Devils of Duke University because of her remarkable basketball career as a teenager, and she's just getting started!

This outstanding athlete is on the fast track to the Olympics by leading her USA Under-19 Team to a World Basketball Championship and gold medal. She is already a "regular mention" on the sports pages covering Duke Basketball, where she was named the ACC rookie player of the week after only two games! Krystal towers over her competition and is a powerful force under the rim. Yet the greatest story doesn't relate to her sports accomplishments. It's in challenges she overcame to even make it to the gym.

Krystal was the baby girl that made Natalie Thomas a mommy. Natalie and her husband, Victor, would have five children and a storybook life until a series of crises would come, taking both parents away when Krystal was just a young girl.

Shockingly, her dad was the first to be taken from her. Victor was one of the most respected law enforcement officers in his agency when an FBI sting led to his arrest for drug trafficking and eventual incarceration when Krystal was only eleven.

Tragically, only a few months after her dad was jailed, Krystal's mom was diagnosed with breast cancer. Natalie battled the disease with the most aggressive treatments available, along with the drive of a mother who was dedicated to seeing her five children experience one more practice, one more game, one more birthday, and one more Christmas together as a family. Her faith in God kept her battling strong for years.

Natalie fought the cancer until her last day on Earth. Even though her body was ravaged by the disease, she had the determination of a prize fighter with a never-give-up attitude. Even as her body was failing, she couldn't stop thinking about her children and how to make it to the next special event together. When the doctors indicated there were no more medical options, her last goal was to make it through Christmas with her family. She died in January surrounded by her children and a few friends.

Krystal didn't cry at her mother's funeral. She read from a carefully worded statement, with a personal message to her mom. "You'll never have to miss another sporting event because you'll have the best seat in the house."

A few months after Natalie's death, Krystal and her teammates qualified to play for their first of two state basketball championships and each player had an "NT" monogrammed on their jerseys so the memory of Mrs. Natalie Thomas would live on after her death. Even though cancer had prevented Natalie from attending many games the last few years of her life, her "never quit" attitude lived on in the lives of her daughters and their teammates.

Natalie's last wish was for all five kids to stay together. Thankfully a family whose daughter played on the team with Krystal offered to bring all five kids into their home to raise as their own. Don and

Sheri Deluzio already had four children yet agreed to fill the gap and function as guardians for Krystal and her siblings. It wasn't easy, but it worked and showed there are always people willing to come alongside to help if you have the courage to let them know your needs.

The Deluzios have a heart as big as Texas and loved each of the kids. Sports brings people together as a family for a season with a single purpose—to compete and win. Yet this decision was for a bigger purpose than winning. It was an incredible demonstration of shared faith for five African-American kids to move in with a large, white Italian family to laugh and cry together as they built stability from what mattered most... each other.

Krystal went off to Duke, and her younger siblings still play basketball at the newly named Natalie Thomas Memorial Gymnasium at the First Academy in Orlando, Florida. I suspect there is a corner of heaven where she watches her kids play their best... because she lives on. Not just in a name memorialized on a building, but in the hearts and drive of each of these five remarkable kids who learned from their greatest teacher that "quit" is never an option.

~Dwight Bain, Thomas family friend, Orlando, FL

Find Yourself a Dream

One's dreams are an index to one's greatness.
~Zadok Rabinowitz

"Never let it be said that you can run faster than you can read, or that you can jump higher than your grade point average."

I was the last person in my family to be born on a plantation. We were very poor, and I used to work in the fields picking cotton for $2 to $3 a day. As a young man, I dreamt about becoming a great public speaker, even though I suffered from a severe stuttering disability. Though I could barely put two words together, let alone speak a full sentence, I was able to overcome those handicaps because I had a dream.

I was raised by my grandmother, Ella Mae Hunter. She instilled in me the belief that anything was possible. She gave me so much love and so much confidence, and she always had words of wisdom for me. She taught me that nothing in life was free; that if you wanted anything in life, you had to earn it, and you should want to earn it. She made me do my lessons. She told me I had to go to college. And she let me play sports.

She taught me to never give up, to find myself a dream, to hold on to it, and to never let go. Naturally, I wanted to make my grand-mother proud of me and I wanted to get an education so that I could get a good job. Fortunately, basketball enabled me to realize that dream. Every time the other kids would make fun of me because I couldn't speak, I would practice even harder. In a way, my speaking disability was a blessing in disguise.

I received a scholarship to Southern University, where I averaged thirty-one points and eighteen rebounds a game, I was a two time All-American and even played against the Russian National Team, and I was the first black player to make the All South team. I was drafted by the Cincinnati Royals in 1965 where Oscar Robertson was my mentor. My first year's salary was $8,000 and my signing bonus was $200 cash! (My, how times have changed!)

In those days the NBA was made up of only nine teams, and there was a limit to how many blacks could be on a roster. After a short time with the Royals and the Milwaukee Bucks, I was traded to the Chicago Bulls, where I went on to lead the team in scoring for seven straight seasons with a total of 12,623 points. I was an NBA All-Star in 1971, 1972, and 1973... All-NBA Second Team 1970-71, and 1971-72... NBA All-Defensive Second Team 1971-72, 1973-74, and 1974-75. Many of these team records were only finally surpassed by Michael Jordan. Of course, if they had the three-point line when I played, Michael might still be chasing me! My jersey, #10, was officially retired on January 14, 1994.

Even though I had a stellar career with the Chicago Bulls, I kept my stuttering disability a secret from my fans. Instead, I decided to do my talking on the basketball court. But when my career ended early due to a back injury, I found that none of my records meant anything when it came to getting a job. Because I could not put two words together without stuttering, no one would hire me. In spite of a degree in food and nutrition, in spite of all my athletic achievements and records, I had to start at the bottom, earning $4.45 per hour as a dishwasher and busboy at Nordstrom's in Seattle.

I could have given up then, but I remembered what my grandmother told me. She said, "Robert Earl, everybody has a handicap; everybody has a disability. What you've got to do is have a dream, and hold on to it. It's not how many times you get knocked down. It's whether you can get up or not that matters." So I decided to become the best dishwasher, the best busboy in the world. I wasn't going to let anything keep me from reaching my goals.

After a while, the owners of the company came to me and told me that they had noticed my hard work, and that if I would be willing to go to a speech therapist, they would pay for it. After several years of intensive therapy I was able to move up in the company and I eventually became their corporate spokesman.

Today, as Director of Community Affairs for the Chicago Bulls, I make over three hundred appearances each year, and I speak to over 250,000 young people about the importance of staying in school, getting an education, perseverance over adversity, and achieving one's dreams. I am considered one of the top motivational speakers in the sports field in the country. After forty-five years of being unable to speak, my dream has finally come true.

Today, when people ask me what I do for a living, I tell them, "**I talk**."

~Bob Love, former Chicago Bulls star

The Best Policy

You can only go as high on the leadership ladder
as your character will allow you.
~John Maxwell

It was important for me, as a Christian who happened to play professional basketball, to try to live as Christ-like a life as possible in all situations. I didn't feel I could be a dirty player or a referee-baiter. You don't get a free pass just because they are your opponents. The Bible teaches us to be good to our enemies, and if you do that you heap coals on their heads.

A lot of players would try to "sell" a particular call to the referees, but I never got caught up in that. I felt that was a cheap approach. My philosophy was to be an example of integrity and faith to the refs and my opponents. I wasn't perfect in these efforts, but I really wanted the refs to have a lot of trust in me.

One night at the end of my career with the 76ers, we were playing in San Antonio against the Spurs. There was a play where the ball was heading out of bounds and I was trying to keep it in play. In the process, I cut off the ref's view and he wasn't sure whether it went off of my hand or not. He went over towards the stands to pick up the ball, and, as he was doing this, he whispered out of the corner of his mouth, "Bobby, did you touch it?"

I was stunned at that point. Am I now a player and a referee, too? I told him the truth and said, "No, I didn't touch it."

The ref replied, "Alright, red ball," meaning the 76ers retained possession.

I find it amazing how the Lord works. Two weeks later we had a game in Philadelphia and the exact same situation took place right in front of our bench. The same referee we had in San Antonio was working the game that night, the ball was headed out of bounds and I was racing after it trying to keep it in play. This time, however, the ball did go off of my hand out of bounds. The ref walked over to me and said softly, "Bobby, did you touch it?"

I thought for a second and said, "Yes."

Our coach, Billy Cunningham, was standing right there while all of this was unfolding. He stamped his foot and said, "Bobby, that's his job! Let the ref make the call!"

I didn't say anything to Billy, but I thought, "My integrity is not worth a possession."

~Bobby Jones, former NBA player

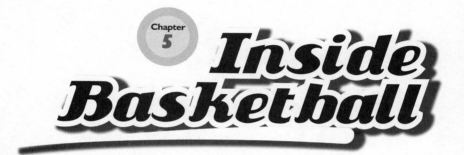

Chapter
5

Inside Basketball

Energy and Effort
Lead to Excellence

Chop your own wood and it will warm you twice.

~Henry Ford's fireplace motto

Swish Your Feet

What pulls people together in an organization is a common purpose.
~Tom Peters

Hall of Fame coach Kay Yow has led the North Carolina State women's basketball team for over three decades. No stranger to beating tough opponents, Yow has notched over 700 career victories. Her perseverance is exemplified by a quote she loves to use: "When you are in a tough place, don't keep. Swish your feet—keep moving, keep working, keep trying—and, eventually, you will overcome and succeed."

Her greatest opponent, though, has attacked her off the court. First diagnosed with breast cancer in 1987, Yow now fights the disease for the third time. "I'm battling an opponent, the greatest foe that I've battled. The home court of an archrival is nothing in comparison to this."

With her chemo treatments taking a toll, Coach Yow was forced to take a leave of absence from her team just four games into the 2006-07 season. Known for her positive attitude and perseverance, not to mention her passion to coach, Yow had no intention of allowing it to keep her away permanently. "I had zero control over getting cancer," she said, "but I have one hundred percent control over how I respond to cancer." After missing sixteen games, she triumphantly returned to the bench, guiding the Wolfpack to a win over long-time rival Virginia.

That marked the beginning of an emotional run of ten wins over the next eleven games, one of the most special coming against cross-town rival and number two-ranked North Carolina. It was Senior Night, all five seniors scored in double figures, and the Reynolds Coliseum floor was named "Kay Yow Court." What a night!

The Pack continued playing inspired basketball, beating undefeated and number one-ranked Duke in the ACC tournament a few weeks later. On its way to the NCAA tournament and eventually to the Sweet 16, the Wolfpack became "America's Team" as fans across the country cheered them on.

Yow's faith and courage made headlines beyond the sports page, inspiring cancer patients everywhere to keep fighting. She admitted having bad days, but told herself "Kay, don't wallow in self pity. You know you will drown. It's okay to have some pity, but swish your feet and get out. Just swish and get out." Those moments of self-pity felt like having her feet stuck in mud. Getting out required action, and that "swish" of her feet helped her get free.

In the midst of this fight for her life, Coach Yow continues to "swish her feet" and continuously talk of her many blessings. Her strong faith in God gives her strength every day and the understanding that everything in life—even her cancer—has a purpose. Jim Valvano, the former men's basketball coach at NC State held that same perspective. Though he lost his battle with cancer in 1993, his legacy lives on through the Jimmy V Foundation, which has raised over $70 million to date for cancer research. Now, in partnership with the V Foundation, the Kay Yow/WBCA Cancer Fund has been established. "My hope," Yow says, "is that this funding will help to change the lives of many men and women who face this opponent daily."

At the 2007 ESPY Awards, Yow won the inaugural Jimmy V ESPY for Perseverance. Visibly touched during her acceptance speech, Yow talked of her special working relationship with Valvano and the impact his passion, inspiration and humor made on her life.

Those who know her, and many who don't, speak that same way about Coach Yow. Her passion, positive attitude and determination to fight every day inspire many to meet the challenges of life with that same spirit, remembering that when they get stuck they can always "swish their feet" and get out.

~Stephanie Zonars, Life Coach

Free Throws

If after a week of practice we are not better then the week has been wasted.
~Vince Lombardi

It all started off with five. It was slightly drizzling, and my dad had told me that I had to make five free throws in a row before I could go home. I was ten at the time and in disbelief. I couldn't believe he wanted me to make that incredible amount. I was also mad. I had spent two hours on those outdoor courts. I had to climb over a fence to get there in the first place; it was cold, and it was starting to rain. He was stubborn though. So I stood and shot until I indeed made five free throws in a row. After every practice, no matter how long it took, I made five free throws in a row. I even got up early in the morning at five A.M. just so I could shoot about one hundred free throws before the day started.

I remember the first time I made ten in a row. I was eleven and I ran around the gym yelling and whooping with joy. I thought it was the greatest thing in the world. Of course after that, I had to make twenty in a row after every practice. Pretty soon the number of free throws escalated from twenty to thirty to fifty, until I got to high school and I had to make seventy-five in a row before I could leave the gym.

One memorable afternoon, there was a hole in the ceiling of the gym I was at, and apparently there was a beehive on the roof. The floor was covered with bees and occasionally one would just start flying out of nowhere. I was on number seventy-three and a bee decided to fly into my ear right before the ball left my fingertips. I shrieked and grabbed my ear and completely missed the shot. My dad didn't even flinch. He just looked at me and said I had to start over. When I started to argue, he just looked at me and said "What are you going to do come game time?" I wanted to ask him, "Would there be many beehives in the stands?", but I decided to hold my tongue. I gritted my teeth and fifteen minutes later I finally made seventy-five in a row.

Not only did I have to make seventy-five in a row, but I couldn't stop until I missed. I used to get mad when I reached my required amount and I missed the next one and my dad made me start over saying that I missed it on purpose. So in high school I would usually get to 120 before I stopped. My highest ever was 175. I never expected, as most young people tend to think, this would ever pay off. It was great that every time there was a technical foul the coach would always send me to take the free throw. But I figured if I just shot one hundred free throws that I would be well prepared. I didn't realize at the time that it was the pressure, the fear of missing the next shot, that I was actually training for, not as much as the actual shot. One game really proved my father's point.

My high school team was playing Royal High School in the Nike Tournament of Champions. We had played Royal High School a week earlier and had lost to them by twenty points, so this game was all about revenge. Royal had one girl on their team who was incredible. Her name was Kelly and she could score at will. To add insult to injury, whenever we were at the free throw line she would pull out a tube of Carmex and rub it on her lips. It was part taunt, part indignation towards the free throw shooter; as if she was so good it didn't matter if we made free throws, her team was still going to win.

With two minutes left in the game, my team was up by six and their coach ordered them to foul. Our coach, seeing this, immediately called a time out and drew out a brilliant game plan. Give the ball to me—every time. I was a little shocked. I wasn't a standout player. I was a role player. I did my job, got my ten points and called it a day. She was pretty much putting the game in my hands it seemed. Seeing my slightly shocked face my best friend and fellow teammate pulled me aside and told me I was the best free throw shooter on the team. I could do it. I said, "Okay, I guess."

So, every time we had possession, my teammates gave me the ball and the other team fouled me. And every time I went to the free throw line and knocked down two free throws. I ended going ten-for-ten that game, all in the last two and a half minutes. The final score was 57-50 and we were victorious. And Kelly didn't get to pull out her Carmex.

~Luiza R. Osborne, Humboldt State basketball player

1,000 Makes a Day

Set short-term goals and you'll win games.
Set long-term goals and you'll win championships.
~Joe Paterno

It was 1995 and my sophomore year in high school in Claflin, Kansas. We were in the middle of our third game of the season in Ellsworth, Kansas, when I went up for a routine lay-up and was undercut by an opposing player. I took a hard fall on my right wrist and hand. Unfortunately, that just happened to be my shooting hand. After being taken out of the game, I could hardly stay still as the pain was as severe as I had ever felt in my life, and soon my wrist was swollen like a balloon.

My coach, Clint Kinnamon, immediately checked on me. Despite my pleas to simply tape me up and send me back into the game, Coach Kinnamon immediately motioned to my mom in the gymnasium stands, and then instructed her to take me to an emergency room as soon as possible.

My mom is a nurse, and thankfully she had some Tylenol with her to help relieve the pain during the trip to the hospital. Unfortunately, the attending physician spoke with broken English, and neither of us fully understood his diagnosis. However, it was clear from him that X-rays revealed I had not broken my wrist, but instead suffered a severe sprain. Despite the pain, I was relieved to hear him report that I should be back on the floor in two weeks.

We quickly returned to the Ellsworth gym in time for me to ride the bus home with my teammates. I was telling everyone that my wrist was fine and not broken, even waving it around throughout the ride home for all to see. Unfortunately, it was after I got home and the pain medication wore off that I began experiencing the most excruciating pain of my life. I spent the night screaming in pain... a night that is forever etched in my mind.

The next morning, my parents took me to a specialist, who quickly revealed through an X-ray that I had indeed a major break in my radius, as well as a chip in my ulna. Although devastating news, I was somewhat relieved to learn that the bone had stayed in place, and it appeared as though I would not need surgery. Only time would heal this wound. The physician informed me that I would be required to wear a hard cast on my right wrist for four weeks, followed by a soft cast for another four weeks.

It was at this time that I realized I could turn this devastating event into something positive, and I dedicated myself to doing just that. Almost immediately, due to the limitations with my shooting hand, I dedicated myself to learning to shoot left-handed. It was a daily struggle, but I was committed to using this time to improve and come back even stronger than before. Yes, I was limited in many ways, but the opportunity was before me. As the old saying goes, "It's not what you do; it's what you do next that really counts."

After four weeks, I was cleared to play with a soft cast on my right wrist, and I was forced to shoot left-handed for the next four weeks. Despite the fact I was happy to be back in uniform, it was not until our team had reached the regional tournament that my soft cast was removed. It was obvious from the start of the playoffs that my right hand and wrist had become very weak from the eight weeks of inactivity and that my muscles had atrophied. My previous shooting accuracy suffered greatly.

Like many high school athletes, I had committed myself to one simple dream... to win a state championship. My dream was close to reality as we were playing in the semi-finals of the state tournament... just one more win and the Claflin Wildcats would play the next day for the state championship.

The most anticipated game in my young career soon turned into one of the most disappointing events in my life. To put it mildly, my shooting performance was awful. I still remember the statistics: four for twenty-one from the field, and we ultimately lost the game by just a few points. I knew I had let down my team, my school and my entire community. I was devastated and completely humiliated by the defeat. If only I had made a couple of those baskets, we would have likely won the state championship.

I had worked so hard throughout my childhood, and when I was needed the most, I couldn't perform to the level I wanted and my team needed. I had worked so hard and overcome the adversity of a serious injury. I was at such a low point during that time that I could have easily and totally given up the game of basketball and never looked back. I was simply that low.

Throughout life, the choices you make as you experience challenges and adversity will shape you and ultimately be the determining factor in your ability to reach your goals and succeed. I had two choices. I could quit, or I could dedicate myself to being the best I could be. Of course, I chose the latter.

I committed myself to a simple and clear goal: to make 1,000 shots a day. I wanted to not just return to my pre-injury ability, but I was committed to returning that next season as an even better shooter.

A thousand shots a day is a major commitment, but I am proud to say I kept that commitment and made 1,000 shots a day until my freshman year in college.

I ultimately achieved some major goals in high school. No, we never won that coveted state championship (something that still haunts me today), but I was fortunate to break several Kansas high school records, including the career scoring leader for girls' basketball. I was selected as an all-state player and eventually named to the *USA Today* Top five team and was named to the Kodak All-American high school team, being named as the Most Valuable Player in that game. I was honored to be selected as a member of the junior world championship team, as well.

I was highly recruited and eventually selected South West Missouri State over Kansas State and national powerhouse Connecticut. It was perhaps the best decision I've ever made in my life, as I was able to play on a great team with some terrific talent, and we literally changed the face of Springfield, Missouri, in the process.

My college coach (Cheryl Burnett) challenged my 1,000 shots a day routine, suggesting it would hamper my ability to have the "legs left" to survive the rigorous college schedule. I developed another practice regimen that focused on quality shooting practice versus quantity of shots made.

My college career was truly a dream come true for me. Not only did our team reach the Final Four, but I was showered with individual honors and trophies beyond my wildest dreams. I was a two-time all-American, recipient of the Wade Trophy and Broderick Cup, and ultimately broke the individual career scoring record for women's college basketball—a record that still stands today.

Eventually, I was drafted by the Portland Fire of the WNBA and named WNBA Rookie of the Year in 2001. After more than a dozen injuries and follow-up surgeries, my pro career was cut short.

While I never sought individual fame or glory, I was both honored and humbled by the recognition. As I look back, I know that all of the success I have enjoyed throughout my life was a result of many things: great teammates, great coaches, a supportive and encouraging family, and yes, those 1,000 shots a day.

Basketball literally opened up a world for me that I never dreamed possible. In retrospect, being injured early in my career played a huge role in my development as a player. I made a choice to overcome the adversity and my life and career were forever changed.

Adversity presents opportunities. Never ever stop believing in yourself and pursue your goals. Yes, dreams do come true—even for a girl from a small town in rural Kansas—and I'm living proof of that. It all started with 1,000 shots a day.

~Jackie Stiles, former high school, collegiate, and WNBA star

Mom's Magic Advice

All who have achieved great things have been dreamers.
~Orison Swett Marden

Mom always had two pieces of advice for my sister and me. "Follow your passion" was one of them.

Growing up as a young man in Orlando in the '80s and '90s, it was impossible not to be passionate about basketball. After all, Orlando—whose most recognized celebrities had been to this point a mouse and a whale—was finally going to get its first national sports franchise. First, there was the campaign to get the whole thing started.

From the very beginning, visionaries got the whole community—including kids—involved in their passion to establish a franchise in Orlando. Then, there were media events and publicity tours to get folks involved in naming the team and choosing the mascot. There were T-shirts, caps, and season tickets for sale even before the franchise was awarded. How could I not become passionate about basketball?

After the franchise was established, the early '90s in Orlando brought all the enticement a young man needed to remain passionate about basketball. There was the all-important first round draft pick of Shaquille O'Neal in 1992 that our family watched with the intensity that must have surrounded families watching the first moon walk. The year after was just as dramatic with the trade for "Penny" Hardaway.

With Shaq and Penny, there were new reasons to remain passionate. There were starting lineup figures to be collected. All over town there were storefront marquees displaying "Go Magic!" Even the delivery of the daily newspaper brought placards you could take to the games or hang on your wall. Of course, not only were my walls decorated with Magic memorabilia, but my bedspread, curtains, and even my wastebasket bore the Magic logo. I went to Magic basketball camps and attended as many games as I possibly could.

I realized early on that no matter how deep my passion for basketball was, I was not destined to become the next Shaq. No matter how hard I tried, I didn't have the speed or accuracy—much less the height. But my passion for basketball remained fervent throughout my high school and college days. I was resigned to the notion that being a devout basketball fan would have to be the extent of my passion.

Life passed on and I graduated from college with a B.A. in psychology. Meanwhile, Mom had developed a neurological disease, which was complicated further by her flat-lining during a hip operation. Her health declined over those years. Despite her diminished mental state, Mom remained steadfast about some things. One of those was her own devotion to the Orlando Magic. The other was her constant encouragement for me to follow my passion. After graduation, I sat down with Mom and asked her what she thought I should do for a career. When she once again encouraged me to follow my passion, I scoffed. "You know my real passion is basketball, mom, and I'll never be a pro basketball player."

Mom's reply was, "Maybe, so. But are there other careers related to basketball you might be interested in?"

She had a point. After all, it takes a huge organization to support the efforts of an NBA franchise. I'd never thought about it before. Maybe she was right. But, where would I have to go to find a career I was qualified for in basketball? Mom's answer to that was quite simple. "The Magic."

All of a sudden, I knew she was right. Here was my passion — my dream — sitting right under my nose! I worked hard and eventually became an intern for the Magic in the marketing department. The person who hired me confided to me later he was very impressed with my passion for the Magic but had wondered whether that intensity would interfere with my doing a good job. His fear was put to rest after I began my internship. After successfully completing my internship, I was offered two different positions as part of the Magic "team." I had made it to pro-basketball after all! Mom's response? "I knew you could do it!"

Mom passed on recently, and I've had some time to reflect on how thankful I am for her wisdom and guidance. And I realize now that I inherited her passion, too.

You may be wondering what Mom's other piece of advice was. It was, "Work hard. Be yourself. And always do the right thing." Basketball has certainly allowed me to follow that advice, as well.

~Matthew Keller, Special Events/Marketing Coordinator,
Orlando Magic

Kim with the Vim and the Will to Win

If you've made up your mind you can do something, you're absolutely right.
~Woodrow Wilson

In 1997, when the WNBA first started, I left my position as the head women's basketball coach at the University of Mississippi to become the head coach of the Houston Comets. As we started putting together our team to play that summer, it was obvious we had an enormous problem—no point guard.

You can't win in basketball without somebody directing your team. Our strategy was to schedule an open tryout. We brought in sixty-seven players, and sixty-two of them were guards. I will never forget one of the guards, Kim Perot.

Kim was small, aggressive and feisty. Frankly, I didn't think she was that good and I never seriously considered her for the team. Some of my assistants urged me not to judge her too quickly, and, sure enough, she survived all of the cuts and made our team.

Our first game that season was against the New York Liberty, and Kim was buried on the bench. We lost that game, and our guards didn't play well. I made a decision that day to go with Kim and told her so.

She replied, "Well, it's nice to know that you've finally realized that you're a good coach and are going to play me. I'll help you win a championship." And that's exactly what happened in 1997. Even with stars like Cynthia Cooper, Sheryl Swoopes, and Tina Thompson, we never would have won without Kim.

In all of my years of coaching women's basketball, I have never had another player like Kim Perot. Whenever I would take her out of a practice scrimmage, she would go over to the sidelines and do push-ups. I once beat her ten straight times in dominoes and she insisted that we play until she beat me four in a row.

We went into the 1998 season trying to repeat as champions, and were down to the elimination game in the playoffs against Phoenix. We were in deep trouble when Kim started yelling at her teammates, "We need to buckle down. Listen to Coach; he'll tell us what to do. We can't lose on our home court!" That was just the lift we needed to nail down that second championship.

Kim had a strong faith in God. We spoke at churches together, and in the off-season we would go do clinics for kids. She was always teasing me. At one clinic she said, "See Coach over here? He didn't believe in me at first. It took a whole year for me to convince him that I was his point guard."

Kim was a great leader; she'd be banged up but would insist on practicing anyway. She told the stars on our team what she expected and they never argued with her. I've never met anybody like her.

Before the next season, I got the shock of my life. Our trainer called and said, "Coach, sit down. I've got some bad news. Kim Perot has been diagnosed with cancer." I was absolutely floored. I loved her and she loved me, and I've never had a relationship with a player like that before or since.

Kim couldn't participate in training camp, but she still came around to see us. She had wasted away to about eighty-nine pounds, but was always such an inspiration. During a game that season, she came to the huddle during a time out and whispered in my ear, "Coach, I know this team is driving you crazy, but I love you." She would phone me from time to time and tell me that she loved me. All of this was going on about one month before she died.

Kim's cancer started in her lungs and spread to her brain. She'd always been in perfect health and took great care of herself. Kim was only thirty-two when she died on August 19, 1999. My wife and I celebrated our wedding anniversary that same day, and it was surely a bittersweet one. The Houston Comets went on to win our third straight WNBA title that summer, inspired by the memory and spirit of Kim Perot.

~Van Chancellor, Head Coach LSU Women's Basketball

That Little Orange Ball

In labors of love, every day is payday.
~Gaines Brewster

Basketball is my passion. That may sound like a cliché, but basketball is truly my passion. A very close friend of mine told me once that I don't have blood running through my veins, I have tiny basketballs. I guess she's right. I will sacrifice food, sleep, going to the movies, going on vacation, just about anything for the game.

When I was about twelve years old my father was killed. The street became the place where I spent most of my time after my father died. I came from a family of seven children and my mother was a deaf mute. The state decided to take the children and move them in with relatives who they felt could better care for us than she could. My brother, sister, and I would be moved to live with my aunt and uncle in the south suburbs of Chicago, in a town called Phoenix.

Our life began in the boring suburbs, and our memories of our city life seemed further and further away. My brother, sister, and I were enrolled in school, and we were the "poor little kids from the city" who had come to live with relatives. Somehow I became friendly with a boy who lived across the alley. Butch, as he was called by everyone, made a basketball hoop from a vegetable basket and nailed it to the telephone pole in the alley. There at that garage, Butch, my brother Boyd, and I played all day and all night.

As time went on, I got pretty good. Then basketball tryouts started in the school I attended. I was fairly tall for twelve years old and I was still the new kid. All that practicing got me selected as the fifth starting player for the Coolidge Elementary School's basketball team in Phoenix, Illinois. I vowed that I would never allow myself to be the last pick again. There's nothing in any history books to make Phoenix famous but to me it's the place where I truly found my heart.

After elementary school I began life at Thornton Township High School in Harvey, Illinois, and played basketball all four years. I was a starter on the freshman, sophomore and varsity teams. I practiced until I became the MVP on all four teams and was even named the *Chicago Sun Times* Player of the Year. I learned more about the game of basketball at Thornton than I did English, math, social studies or anything else.

Now instead of practicing in the alley behind that tiny Phoenix house, I was able to play in this giant gym — and practice I did! I accepted a full scholarship to the University of Cincinnati where Oscar Robertson had become famous. My passion grew stronger and I was named an all-American at the university. I left college in my senior year to pursue life in the American Basketball Association (ABA) and after two years there traveled to Europe where I played in Italy, Belgium, and France, all because of that little orange ball.

After eight years of playing in the European Basketball League, I decided to return home to Chicago, my true home. Since my return, that little orange ball has never left my side. I returned to coach in the high school league, in the junior college level, and then on to Division I college ball. Now my fifteen-year-old son is following in my footsteps, playing on his high school team.

Of course I still play now in a fifty-and-over league and probably will never stop. When I die I will die with that little orange ball at my side.

~Lloyd Batts, former collegiate All-American and
European Basketball League star

51

First Draft

Instead of waiting for your ship to come in, grab two oars and row out to it.
~Vance Havner

In 1978 our women's basketball team at UCLA won the NCAA title and I was on top of the world. Two years earlier I had played in the 1976 Olympics on the first women's basketball team, and I was getting ready for the 1980 Olympics.

In 1978-79, the WBL (a women's professional basketball league) was launched. I was the first draft choice of the Houston Angels but elected not to go pro. I wanted to remain an amateur for the 1980 Olympics; I also wanted to finish my last two classes at UCLA and earn my degree. As I prepared for the Olympics, I received a phone call that changed my life.

Sam Nassi, who lived in Beverly Hills, had just bought the NBA's Indiana Pacers. One day my phone rang and I heard Mr. Nassi say, "Ann, how would you like to try out for the Pacers?" I looked at the phone in amazement. This surely wasn't Sam Nassi. It must be some sort of prank. But it was Sam, and he was serious. He thought it was a great idea that would promote his team as well as me.

Sam's offer piqued my interest. I grew up playing basketball against men — including Wilt Chamberlain in scrimmages at UCLA — and I had confidence that I could compete at the professional level. I also knew there would be people against me if I accepted Sam's offer. I would be accused of making a mockery of the game.

Sam offered me a $50,000 one-year contract to sign as a free agent, and I accepted the deal. The furor began immediately. Bob Leonard, the head coach of the Pacers, flew out to Los Angeles to try and talk me out of it and convince Sam Nassi it was a bad idea.

I was determined to go forward, however. When I was in high school, I wanted to go out for the boys' varsity team but I let people talk me out of it. That wasn't going to happen this time. I've never worked harder in my life and I've never been more focused. I reported to the Pacers three-day free agent camp at the start of the training period and went about my business like any other pro player. Assistant coach Jack McCloskey complimented me when he said that I was fundamentally better than half the guys out there.

Even though I sensed the other players were not happy I was there, I was not intimidated and felt great going through the two-a-day workouts. The media was everywhere and covered me like a blanket. There were two questions asked most frequently: 1) where will you shower? "Back at the hotel," I said; and 2) how will you take a charge from big Bob Lanier? My answer was, "Who else does that, anyway?"

I really wanted to make the team because I knew my attempt would help open the door for other women in the sports world. However, it was not to be. Coach Leonard pulled me aside after the early camp and said that it was great to have me there but he did not have a spot on the roster for me. I stayed on with the Pacers for about two and a half months working in the community and I became the first female broadcaster in NBA history. Later that year I signed with the New Jersey team in the WBL and was named the league MVP.

As I reflect on my brief career with the Indiana Pacers, my experience offers two important life lessons: 1) Don't ever look back and say, "What if?" Having the courage to try is your success. If you don't try, you'll never know what can happen; and 2) Don't let people discourage you and talk you out of your dreams. We all have a gift, so go out and use it. You've got to believe in yourself.

~Ann Meyers Drysdale, General Manager, Phoenix Mercury

52

Makin' Hay and Makin' Buckets

Real success is finding your lifework in the work that you love.
~David McCullough

When I was in elementary school I worked on my family's eighty-acre cattle farm in Harvest, Alabama. I would wake up before school and feed the cows, and then I would spend the weekends cutting and bailing hay, chopping wood and mending fences.

That farm setting allowed my mind to drift, and it often drifted to the game of basketball and playing for a major Division I program. I averaged 16.5 points per game as a senior at Sparkman High, but I wasn't being recruited by what you would call the prestigious schools. I always stayed true to my goals, however.

When I was in school, my dad was an assistant principal at Sparkman High. I would ride to school with him and shoot baskets before class. After school, I went to basketball practice before working at the farm until nightfall. Then I would go inside and study the college basketball games I had recorded. I didn't really date in high school. When other kids were going bowling, I was practicing or doing farm chores.

During my senior season in 2004, we had a 26-6 record but it seems that few college basketball coaches noticed. I received scholarship offers from Missouri State, Troy, Samford and Birmingham-Southern. I wanted to go to Georgetown University.

Georgetown's coach, John Thompson III, recruited me, but he made no promises. I was not invited to Georgetown for an official visit, but when I went to Washington for a high school debate competition I toured the campus. A few weeks later, Coach Thompson invited me to walk on. I walked on as a freshman, made the team and have been a starter for four years. I've learned that if you take the right approach, anything is possible.

I would like to play in the pros after I graduate, but I've also been accepted to Georgetown's law school. Whether it's basketball, law school or whatever, I know where I'll be in the summertime. That's hay-cutting season at the farm.

From sun up to sun down, you've got to work.

~Jonathan Wallace, former Georgetown University Point Guard

Chapter 6

Inside Basketball

Teamwork: Working for a Common Goal

Veni, vidi, vici — I came, I saw, I conquered.

~Julius Caesar

53

"You Don't Want This, Do You?"

If your mind can conceive it, and your heart can believe it,
then you can achieve it.
~Rev. Jesse Jackson

"Believe. Believe in our stuff. Believe in your teammates. Believe in yourself. Believe." The man's not always much for words, but those words Coach Al Skinner chose to scribble on the blackboard of the Minneapolis Metrodome resonated with me for the forty-five minute "eternity" of the NCAA Regional Semifinal. And when it was over, no matter how badly I believed we were going to win, I could do nothing but sit at end of the team bench and stare blankly ahead. I experienced a stillness and serenity completely immune to the fight song of a rival school or the orchestrated shouts of enemy cheerleaders. In that state, time slowed to a crawl bringing me back to the realization that the season was, in fact, over.

People were in motion all around me, but still I sat, head in hands, reflecting on the rollercoaster that was the overtime classic, Boston College versus Villanova. I lingered longer than I should have, ignoring my post-game responsibilities, ignoring the entrance of Georgetown's players and coaches vying for my spot on the bench with their game set to begin. Two minutes of stillness turned into four or five as I replayed the game's momentous turns in my head.

Five minutes turned into ten as I fought back tears. My quiet was disturbed by random basketball jargon. "Why didn't we zone up the out of bounds? Double screen rollback... I've seen it a dozen times on film. Beat on a last second end line out of bounds play!" The final minutes of the contest had been a seesaw battle, but in the end, we lost. Only this time, it really was the end.

For quite a while, no one dared speak to me. The tears welling in my eyes said it all. Georgetown University's coaches and players might have been curious about the stranger at the end of their bench with only moments to go before their game tipped off, but they said nothing.

Finally, as one of their trainers tidied up the area around the bench (one of the responsibilities I had neglected), I saw him pick up a maroon headband. Just before he aimed to throw the used headband into the garbage, out of the corner of his eye, he spotted me and said, "You don't want this, do you?" I reached out my hand, taking the sweat-soiled item, angry that he was about to discard it. It was only a headband, but it infuriated me that he would toss it aside. It is an item never re-used and often left behind, but it belonged to us, to our team. In the moment, it represented our hard work to get where we were. It was our sweat, our tears, our time and devotion to the program. I didn't want someone else to touch that, let alone throw it away.

He didn't know how hard we'd worked, how hard I had worked. How every moment of my involvement with Boston College had been leading up to establishing a career in college basketball. He didn't know how much it all meant to me. Not many people did. To onlookers or my peers, people often thought I was living some type of fantasy camp experience, following college basketball players around, getting free Reebok gear, and traveling on Boston College's bill. But they didn't know. They didn't know how I lost sleep after games, reflecting and strategizing—dreaming of the day I may lead a college program of my own.

To many, they acted as though I was a tagalong to the team, a kid who "probably knew some higher-up." They acted as though they know just as much about the team and the game of basketball because they sat in the stands for all sixteen home games. But they didn't know. They didn't know Coach Coen drinks his coffee black, or that Coach Skinner chews Juicy Fruit before games, let alone our play calls and offensive philosophies. They didn't know what it looks like to see Craig Smith near tears before a game with an injury, or know what Jared Dudley and I talk about the night before the biggest games of our lives. I felt like saying, "You can be a fan, but you're not on the inside. You have no idea." But I didn't; I remained quiet.

And in the quiet of sitting on that bench, the initial shock of the loss began to wear off and my rising anger obviously seemed to be getting the best of me. I needed a change of scenery, so I finally (after nearly fifteen minutes) left our team bench. The battle with my tears had not really subsided; they still threatened to destroy my composure. As I made my way back to our locker room, somehow a headband that was literally sweating through my suit pocket helped me hold on a little longer to the season, and salvage all the hard work we put forth.

Just outside the locker room door was Bill Coen, associate head coach, but also my mentor, a surrogate father, and future employer—someone I had confided in many times about my coaching ambitions. In his eyes, I could see he too was losing the battle with his tears. When our eyes locked, they spoke to each other. "No more games, no Final Four run," something we believed we'd achieve this season ever since the end of the last. From off-season turmoil, to ACC growing pains, we believed we were a Final Four team when others were skeptical. We believed in our stuff. We believed in each other, and we believed in ourselves. Fighting back emotion, Coach Coen said, in reference to the grind and emotional rollercoaster of college basketball, "You don't want **this**, do you?"

For the first time since the final buzzer I spoke, "You have no idea."

~Steve Scalzi, Director of Basketball Operations,
Northeastern University

54

Attitudes Are Contagious: Are You a Carrier?

Ability is what you are capable of doing. Motivation determines what you do.
Attitude determines how well you do it.
~Lou Holtz

I attended a high school boys basketball game a few years back. That in itself is not that big a deal. I see more high school basketball games during the course of a year than I like to count. This one, however, was different. As I watched the action on the floor nothing special stood out. Two teams of very average talent and athletic ability were playing before a gym half full of family, friends and school boosters. However, one player did catch my attention.

The first quarter ended and he had yet to see any playing time. I had noticed him throughout that first quarter as he continually stood to encourage his teammates on the floor while the rest of his teammates sat idly by as if they really didn't care whether they were there or not. After the quarter ended, he alone walked to the end of the bench to pour cups of water and take them to the players who had just come off the floor.

I noted that this young man was a senior and that he was serving water to several underclassmen. I sat there wondering what must be going through his mind as he humbled himself to perform this act of selflessness. I knew that sitting must have really hurt him but he continued, as the second quarter began, to support his teammates without a trace of disgust, pouting, or negative attitude.

As the game progressed he did finally get to play some. He hit a couple of free throws, made a basket, and grabbed a rebound or two. He played hard but every time a buzzer would sound he would look over to see if he was coming out. He knew, as I did, that his playing time was rather limited.

After the game I talked with this young man. As a coach, I am always impressed and humbled by players who seem to be able to put the needs of their team before their own personal agendas and I wanted to get his feelings about the situation. I told him how impressed I had been with his attitude. He told me that it was very hard and frustrating at times to not get to play, especially when he felt like there were times that he could really help his team. He said, however, that he had come to the realization that he was the "Rudy" of his team. He knew that he could either help or hurt his team by his attitude and actions and he had decided to have a positive impact.

I drove home that night having mixed emotions. I really wanted this young man to get the chance to play. I knew how much he wanted to contribute to his team on the floor but the coach in me also knew that not everyone on a team can be in that position. I also felt great pride in his unselfishness, maturity, and the type of person I saw him becoming right before my eyes.

I said a prayer that night thanking God for the example that he had shown me about what it means to be a true team player. I especially thanked Him that this fine young man whom I respect so much is my son, Kyle.

~Kip Drown, Head Women's Basketball Coach,
Colorado State University-Pueblo

Sideline MVP

The first step in problem-solving is to tell someone about it.
~Anonymous

I was the coach at East Carolina University during the 1999-2000 season. Misty Horne, a senior on my basketball team, wanted to come into my office and talk. She had recently torn her ACL for maybe the third time, and I knew what she wanted to talk about. Misty informed me how devastated she was to be injured yet again and how she felt about possibly missing her senior season. She started to cry and wanted to know what I thought about her possibly making the decision to maybe not have the surgery and to retire from playing basketball. Even though Misty was one tough kid, she just did not want to undergo another surgery and rehab.

I felt her pain, and it took all I had inside of me not to cry with and for her. I told her that only she could make that decision. I knew she had prayed and talked with her parents about it, and I wanted her to feel good when she left my office, knowing that I was one hundred percent behind her no matter what her decision. I distinctly remember telling her that even if she did not suit up that season she was still very much a part of our team and I still wanted her to be a team leader, even if from the sidelines. I told her we loved and admired her, and thanked her for what she had already given the team. We embraced and went on to tell the team and staff that Misty would not be playing her senior season. It was a very emotional time for her and her teammates.

We went on that year to have another winning season—the second in a row—and accomplished things that had not been accomplished in a few years. When the Colonial Athletic Association was ready to receive nominations for the Dean Ehlers Leadership Award, I immediately thought of Misty Horne.

The Ehlers award is given annually to the women's basketball student athlete who "embodies the highest standards of leadership, integrity and sportsmanship, in conjunction with her academic athletic achievement." I knew Misty embodied all these things and I had to nominate her for this prestigious award. I did and SHE WON!

We wanted to hide the fact that she won so it would be a BIG surprise at the tournament banquet. The CAA sent cameras to our campus and interviewed me and Misty's roommate and teammate, Danielle Melvin. It was hard to keep it a secret, but we pulled it off.

Off to Richmond we went for the banquet, and when it was time for the Ehlers award, we all got nervous inside. They showed the video and Misty looked at me with great surprise! She looked at me and said "you knew, but did not tell me...." In the video I stated that if I had a daughter, I would want her to be just like Misty. I truly believe that to this day. I also stated in the video that she deserved to win the award and that, even on the sidelines, she had shown great leadership throughout the entire season. We were so proud of Misty and the entire team celebrated this great accomplishment with her.

~Dee Stokes, Head Women's Basketball Coach,
Winston-Salem State University

The Double Win

It's not your wallet or your purpose that makes you rich or poor:
it's your character.
~Woodrow Wilson

Every year we host an eight-team boys' basketball invitational tournament. This particular year we decided to have a double-elimination tournament. Several months before the tournament, we invited seven teams from Illinois and Missouri. Coming into the tournament we were really starting to gel as a team. After starting the season with two losses, we had gone on a streak of twelve wins and only two losses. We were looking forward to an exciting tournament and thought our chances of winning were very good.

One week before the tournament, one of the seven teams cancelled. We frantically worked to fill the vacant spot. As a last resort, we contacted a Christian school in Indiana that had expressed an interest in playing in our tournament. We knew very little about the team from Indiana. The Indiana team accepted our invitation two days before the tournament was to start.

Being the small school that we are—a high school enrollment of forty students—we had only eight varsity players. The starters for my varsity team this particular year consisted of one senior, two juniors and two sophomores. Our tallest player was a 6'2" junior. Everyone else was six-foot or less.

When the roster from the Indiana school was faxed to us, we

immediately knew we were in for a battle if we were to face them. Their roster included seven seniors, four of whom were listed at over six feet tall. The Indiana team was the number one seed in the upper bracket in place of the team that had cancelled. Our team was the two seed in the lower bracket.

The tournament began with Indiana playing the first game. Not only was Indiana bigger, they were also physically stronger. Some of their players looked like they could be in college. The attitude and conduct of the Indiana players and coaches was very poor. They argued or complained about almost every call. They showed no mercy to the team they faced in game one. They crushed their opponent by more than sixty points while still pressing at the end of the game. The losing team was shell shocked as well as everyone else that was in attendance.

In our first game of the day, we beat our opponent by twenty points. Indiana went on to win their second game of the day by a mere thirty-two points, placing them in the final game of the winners' bracket. In our second game of the day, we battled our opponent the entire game and won by ten points. This placed us in the final game of the winners' bracket against Indiana.

The next morning we prepared to face Indiana. I could see that my players were intimidated by the Indiana team and it took everything I had to convince them that we could beat them. We played Indiana very tough the first half and we were only down by two points at half time. In the second half, we were on fire and our defense was never better. We went on to beat Indiana by twelve points.

If this had not been a double-elimination tournament, my story would end here with our team being the champions. Unfortunately, it was a double-elimination tournament and I knew that we would be seeing Indiana again.

Indiana won the losers' bracket and they were now hungry to meet us again in the championship game. We came out flat as Indiana played us very physically and beat us by sixteen points. Now we both had one loss and had to play a second game to decide who would be the champion.

After a short break, the final game began. We went into the locker room at half time down by six points. My players were worn out. I pleaded with them to give everything they had left. The second half was more physical than the first. Both teams battled and the score was tied many times. Indiana went up by two points with thirteen seconds to go. The noise in the gymnasium was deafening. As my senior point guard brought the ball up the court, my assistant and I were frantically trying to call a time out to set up a final play. No one could see or hear us. My point guard, not seeing or hearing us either, proceeded to try to score.

When the referee finally saw us and blew the whistle for the time out, my point guard had just scored to tie the game with 2.8 seconds left. Unfortunately, the referee granted the time out and said the shot did not count. The crowd went from being ecstatic to being stunned. I hurriedly drew up a quick inbounds play for my senior point guard to take the last shot. My team executed the play perfectly and the ball fell through the net as the buzzer sounded. The Indiana coaches became very angry and started complaining about the clock. As they complained, we prepared for overtime.

Overtime did not get any easier. My team battled as the score went back and forth. We finally persevered and beat Indiana by four points to win the championship. Everyone was so excited and I was so proud of my team.

What happened next is something I hope I never witness again. As the trophies were handed out, the Indiana coach accepted the second place trophy then turned around and sat it back on the table and walked away. I was stunned and confused by his actions.

After we received the championship trophy, the MVP trophy was awarded to our senior point guard. As he was being presented the trophy, the Indiana players, coaches and fans proceeded to leave and walked right through the middle of the trophy presentation. As they left, some Indiana fans ran towards the scorer's table and called the scorekeeper and clock operator cheaters. Other Indiana fans were cursing at our fans and calling them various names as they left.

As I stood in the middle of the court after witnessing some of the events that had just happened, I went from being so happy that we had won to wishing that we had lost. I thought that if we had lost, none of this ugliness would have happened. But then, something amazing started to happen. As I stood there in shock, many of the students and my players were going over to other students, workers and fans that had been hurt by the awful words or actions. They were hugging and consoling each other. There was a love for one another that I had never witnessed before. On top of that, no one attempted to retaliate against the Indiana team or the Indiana fans.

That night, we truly persevered as a team and as a school. We overcame adversity on and off the court in a very mature manner.

~Shawn Allen, Basketball Coach,
Mississippi Valley Christian School, Alton, IL

Sitting and Winning

Life is simply a stewardship and not an ownership, a trust and not a gift.
With a gift you may do as you please, but with a trust
you must give an account. Whether it is my talents, my time, my treasure,
or the temple of my body, in all of these I am only a steward.
~D. L. Moody

During the 2005-06 season, the Hope College women's basketball team achieved a 33-1 record and a National Championship. I made a decision in October to carry sixteen players on my team. All the players chosen brought a unique set of gifts and talents. The furthest thing from my mind was the fifteen-player rule the NCAA enforces for the national tournament. However, when March rolled around and the tournament was upon us, the decision on whom to sit was troubling me. What was I to do? Everyone deserved to play due to their roles during the season!

Becky Bosserd, who played off the bench for our team, showed up in my office on Tuesday morning before our Friday NCAA game. She simply stated, "I want to sit." I told her she wouldn't have been my choice. We might need her. She insisted by saying, "I'm good with it, my parents support my decision, and it'll allow you to focus on the next game instead of this decision." Wow! I was blown away by her maturity, focus on a team-first attitude, and willingness to give up her uniform for the good of the team.

The story unfolded like a dream with the Hope women winning six consecutive road games by beating the #10, #4, #3, #2, and #1 ranked teams in the nation. When it was time to accept the championship trophy, it was a unanimous decision: we wanted Becky Bosserd to accept the trophy instead of the captains or coaches. Becky was the first person who we sent out because we felt what she had done was really what our team was all about.

Since the national championship, a local man, Rob Zaagman, has come forth to sponsor a scholarship that will live forever. A Hope student will receive the Rebecca Bosserd Scholarship in recognition of unselfish service to others every year.

In establishing the award, Zaagman noted, "I really feel what she did was very significant, but it goes much deeper than that. It's more a recognition of character than of one event. This is just one way of saying, 'Thank you, Becky, for doing something tremendous for other people.' What she did is never going to be forgotten."

~Brian Morehouse, Head Women's Basketball Coach,
Hope College

Helping Hands

If you need a helping hand, look toward the end of your arm.
~Charles Kettering

As a resident of The Emerald City, my heart swelled with civic and human pride when I read accounts of the Seattle Sonics' visit to New Orleans in January 2008. Professional athletes are often thought of as egocentric, self-serving individuals, but the actions of the Sonics' coaches and players threaten to destroy such characterizations.

When the Seattle Sonics team came to the city of New Orleans to play the Hornets that January, the team was blown away by the devastation that was left from Hurricane Katrina. As the darkness descended on the corner of Canal and Claiborne, they witnessed the homeless who occupied the dozens of tents that littered the underpass of Interstate 10. They had just concluded another day of despair and some coaches were moved to tears. They were staying at the posh Ritz-Carlton, and the harsh contrast when considering the plight of Katrina victims made them feel uncomfortable and guilty.

The day before their game with the Hornets, the team bus was directed to head to the tent area. Players and coaches spent forty-five minutes handing out food to the homeless who had congregated under New Orleans' busiest freeway since Hurricane Katrina. An entire homeless community was there, and it was an amazing scene when the Sonics' team bus pulled over on Canal Street and a group of tall, muscular young men pulled food, water and supplies from the bottom of the bus.

As the homeless people lined up, a frail-looking woman walked over and asked where the line started. There was no line; this was no scheduled stop. After the team had served those in a substance-abuse rehabilitation center near downtown New Orleans, they wanted to do more. The NBA suggests that teams run basketball clinics for those Katrina victims, but the team really didn't think the New Orleans homeless needed to work on their ball-handling skills. They wanted to help directly and reach out to those in Tent City.

One coach remarked, "Our players are just good guys, but a lot of times you do something like this and it's almost like you have to make the players come. With our players, it was the complete opposite; it's a great thing. New Orleans still has major bleeding and exposed wounds from Katrina, and Tent City is one of them. The state has set aside $6 million for the New Orleans Hornets practice facility, but is uncertain what to do with the homelessness issue."

That day they served the homeless, players and coaches lined up outside the bus, each with a food item. Assistant coach Ralph Lewis had sandwiches. Player Delonte West had dinners in a Styrofoam container. Rookie Kevin Durant had rolls.

The homeless ranged from a woman with a broken left arm who gathered all her food with her right arm, to a teenager who pulled out a cell phone during his meal. When the heavy traffic died down, the players scooped up all the supplies and personally delivered them to those sitting in the tents. They were intent on handing out every bit of food and water the Sonics purchased.

Their objective was to try and lift those guys up through a tough time; they wanted to encourage them and urge them to keep fighting. The people in Tent City are pretty much beaten down, and when the players and coaches paid attention to them—treated them as human beings—it meant a whole lot to them. The majority of them were sports fans and appreciated the concern from the team. It seemed to encourage them.

With their mission accomplished, a coach said, "It's a good thing and at the same time it's nothing." But it was a little something that demonstrated that NBA stars can respond with compassion, and the people appreciated it. These Emerald City shining gems, in the person of the Seattle Sonics, had indeed brightened the lives and hopes of Katrina's Tent City victims, personifying the association's motto: "The NBA Cares."

~David Nichols, Seattle, WA

Number Twenty-Five in Your Program and in Our Hearts

A friend is one who makes your grief less painful,
your adversity more bearable.
~William Arthur Ward

I'll never forget that July day in 1984. It was the first time I met Ben Wilson. We were on a Chicago playground in front of a jam-packed summer crowd getting ready to play a pickup game at Cole Park—an outdoor, concrete basketball court on the south side of Chicago. I was sixteen and Ben was seventeen.

Ben was already a Chicago legend. He was a 6'9" point guard who had Magic Johnson written all over him. Ben was going to be a junior at Chicago's Simeon High and was being recruited by every major school. He hadn't picked his school yet, but the University of Illinois seemed to be the frontrunner.

We were opponents that first meeting, but teammates for the rest of our lives. I enrolled at Simeon that year as a sophomore, and our team was really good. We won the state championship that season at the University of Illinois' arena in Champaign. Ben was named the

Illinois state player of the year. In fact, he was the first in Chicago history to ever be named top high school player in the nation.

At the beginning of the next basketball season, the hype surrounding the team was ridiculous. Not only were we the defending state champions but we also returned the nation's best player. I couldn't wait to get back on the court with #25, Benji Wilson.

It was the eve of the next basketball season, and Ben was standing outside the school with his girlfriend. Ben was confronted by two young men who both had guns. They tried to rob him and in the process shot him twice in the stomach with a .22. Ben hung on through the night, but the next morning, at five o'clock, he died in the hospital.

The entire school—the entire community—was devastated. Ben was an amazing person and player. He was an honor student and a young man of strong character. At 6'9", I'm convinced he really was going to be the next Magic Johnson with a jump shot. The funeral was an unbelievable experience. The church was overflowing and the viewing was even more amazing. The line waiting to pass by Ben's body must have been five miles long.

I dedicated my whole career to Ben. I went to the University of Illinois because I knew Ben was going there. I started wearing number twenty-five while at Illinois, and everyone knew the reason why. When I put on my jersey, I told them it's a part of me; it's a part of Ben. My basketball career was dedicated to the memory of Ben Wilson.

Now, all of Simeon High's best players wear Ben's number. All the basketball players from Simeon that went to a big-name college wear twenty-five. It's just a legacy. It's our tribute to Ben Wilson.

~Nick Anderson, former Orlando Magic player

Band of Brothers

Sticks in a bundle are unbreakable.
~Kenyan Proverb

Many of us have received a call that has thrown us for a loop. I got such a call in December 2007, right before Christmas, and it hurt.

The call came from one of my good friends, Eric McMahon, who works for the Memphis Grizzlies. In fact, I aided Eric in every way I could to help him land his position with the team. He had only been working for the Grizzlies for about a year and a half when the call came, but even with that short tenure, he was very significant to the team and its fans. He was Grizz, the Grizzlies mascot.

I had not heard from Eric in what seemed like ages. We typically share stories and compare our teams on a regular basis, but it is not uncommon for one of us to get extremely bogged down in the midst of the NBA season. I had made a few calls to Eric, leaving disparaging messages for him about his deflating Memphis Grizzlies, while the Magic were clearly on their newfound upswing. I also sent him numerous texts, goading him to do a better job at getting the Memphis fans excited, because it was always his fault, in my mind, when the team could not make a basket.

After several unanswered attempts at playfully deriding his efforts, the game I was trying to play was no longer fun. Without his comebacks and verbal counter-jabs, it was pointless. I reasoned that he was probably mocking me by not answering, and thus the joke had been turned on me. However, it was completely uncharacteristic of him to ignore me for so long, even during a busy part of the season. And that is when the call came.

When I finally saw Eric's name pop up on my phone, he had to pay the price. I quickly answered the phone with one of my normal lashings and scolded him for not responding sooner. But something didn't feel right. The air was heavy and Eric was not displaying his normal light-hearted attitude. He still wasn't playing "the game." I cut through the small talk and got to the point. I asked, "Is everything okay?" It wasn't. Eric had just found out he had cancer.

Needless to say, my jaw was on the floor. I wanted to know everything. Are you sure? What kind is it? Is it curable? Did you get a second opinion? How about a third? Can they cut it out? Can you still work? Are you staying in Memphis? Oh my goodness, are you positive?!?

Eric was diagnosed with Hodgkin's lymphoma, stage 3B, which is very serious, considering it is only out of four stages. Little did I know he had been misdiagnosed for the previous three months. He had not felt like his normal self since returning from an overseas appearance, but shrugged it aside as jet lag. Once he noticed some large nodes protruding from areas on his body, he went in to get them checked out. For the next three months, his doctor was uncertain about Eric's situation, but later sent him to the oncologist. It took the cancer specialist only moments to order a biopsy, and three days later I got the call. He would start chemotherapy immediately.

As Eric told me the story, he remained upbeat, but I could hear the fear in his voice. He informed me that Hodgkin's lymphoma is "one of the most curable forms of cancer," and that his doctors were quite optimistic, as was he. Luckily, Eric was in peak physical condition, and he told me he would undergo the chemo and hoped to resume his duties as Grizz within a few weeks. He also did not see himself missing any appearances. Regardless, I reasoned to myself, we were dealing with cancer and I had just lost a grandmother from it weeks before.

The Memphis Grizzlies organization did something for Eric that

I found remarkable. It made me uneasy at first, but then I realized the genius in what they did. They went to the media: Eric McMahon is our mascot and he has cancer. We need your support. And until Eric is better, there will be no Grizz!

There are a couple things here that impress me about the actions of the Grizzlies:

Being a mascot, there is an unwritten code that no one knows who is inside the suit. The mystique helps create a special power for the performer that allows him to rule a crowd with ease. If no one knows who is behind the mask, the performer feels less inhibited to try certain ridiculous things, such as dancing like a fool in front of 17,000 people. The audience respects that, and thus a bond is created. But in this case, the Grizzlies humanized their character, with Eric's permission, in an effort to gather community support for their fallen hero.

Similarly, they refused to find a replacement for their mascot. In my eyes, it was quite profound and very bold of them. They could have easily put an intern inside the suit, hired a local performer, or even fired Eric altogether and held a new audition. I am sure most teams would have chosen one of those options. But the Grizzles did not do that. They acknowledged the hard work that Eric had given, and more importantly, recognized that without him, there was no Grizz. Eric WAS Grizz—not just some guy in a suit! He had honed his craft so solidly that people would have figured it out anyway. The Grizzlies understood all of that.

Finally, the Grizzlies started a program called the "Friends of Grizz," inviting patients of St. Jude's Children Research Hospital to attend games on behalf of Grizz. Eric was planning on attending the games with the children while he was unable to perform, thus unifying their similar battles with crippling diseases even further. They also created and sold bracelets to benefit this new program.

With all that the Grizzlies were doing to support my friend, I felt compelled to do something as well. Working within the mascot community for the last thirteen years, I knew all the guys in the NBA and I knew they would unite to support their brother. I promptly sent out the word to all the NBA mascots and, as I knew they would, they responded.

First, since Eric was going to lose all his hair during the chemotherapy process, we chose a date and those who were willing shaved their heads. About half of the NBA mascot community was bald underneath their fuzzy, oversized heads!

Second, we designed an armband for all the mascots to wear until Eric got better. It was a very conspicuous, white armband, emblazoned with a violet ribbon, which is the universal symbol for Hodgkin's lymphoma support. In the middle of the ribbon was an image of Eric's alter-ego, Grizz. It was quite literally the "band of brothers." Each NBA mascot, as well as a few from other leagues, donned the armband on his biceps for the remainder of the 2008 season. It not only garnered a lot of exposure for Eric's cause, but it certainly showed solidarity between this unique collection of friends.

Finally, and most importantly, I realized the hole that Eric's absence was going to cause the Grizzlies. The mascot for any NBA team is widely recognized as the highest rated entertainment element at the game. I can only imagine what our games would be like without our mascot, STUFF, and therefore I devised a plan I hoped would work. For each remaining home game that Memphis would play, a mascot from a different team would perform in Grizz's place, in Grizz's arena, wearing Grizz's jersey, but performing as their own team's character.

A project such as this had never been attempted before. No team had probably even imagined sending its mascot to support another team. It had never been necessary. Nonetheless, after speaking with Eric's boss and gaining his enthusiastic support, we made it happen. In fact, each team paid their mascot's expenses and supported the cause wholeheartedly.

The Memphis fans rallied around the idea as well. Many could not wait for the next game, going just to see which mascot was performing at the Grizzlies game on that night. It was a wonderful sight to see how each organization supported the cause. It was especially exciting to see an "opposing" mascot performing at another team's venue and cheer on the Grizzlies. The band of brothers came through.

And what became of Eric, you may ask?

The season finished and every date was filled, but much to Eric's dismay, he was unfortunately unable to make a comeback within that season. In fact, there were two incredibly scary periods when we almost lost him altogether from complications involving bacterial infections. His lungs collapsed, his kidneys failed, and his liver began to fail. They were pumping three liters of fluid from his lungs every day. But the story doesn't end there....

As I write this story, Eric has finished with chemo and just went in for his final scan. I literally just hung up the phone with my good buddy, and for the record, there was just as much verbal sparring as there was in the past. Eric underwent his final scan this week and I am elated to report that the doctors have deemed him completely cancer-free!

Furthermore, he is finally getting in shape again, and although he will have to work hard to get back into his original condition, I am sure he will do it. The worst part is behind him. His goal is to make his comeback within the costume for opening night of the upcoming season. He has the entire city of Memphis supporting him, not to mention his tremendous brotherhood.

I can guarantee the loudest cheers that night will not be for the new recruits of the Memphis Grizzlies, or even their superstar players. The loudest ovation of the night will undoubtedly be for Eric McMahon, a.k.a. Grizz. My brother.

~Scott Hesington, Orlando Magic Mascot Coordinator

Chapter 7

Inside Basketball

Beating the Odds: Overcoming Difficulties

Storms make oaks take deeper root.

~George Herbert

61

Down, But Not Out

Undertake something that is difficult; it will do you good. Unless you try to do something beyond what you have already mastered, you will never grow.
~Robert Osborn

Beware. Brad Hennefer is a carrier. His contagious and courageous positive spirit has more than earned the love and support of his family, friends, teammates, and even the opposition. When he prepares to throw off his warm-ups to enter a game for Cherry Hill East High School, the fans are already enthusiastically and rhythmically chanting, "B-Rad, B-Rad, B-Rad."

Something happens when Brad steps on the court that perhaps is not seen in any other high school game in the United States. With the clock counting down, Brad excitedly enters the game and dribbles to the three point line to attempt a three point shot. The crowd goes wild with approval.

Brad has Down syndrome, a genetic condition that causes learning difficulties. His parents, Bob and Nancy Hennefer, knew the day he was born that he would have challenges. They were determined, however, not to treat him any differently than his older brother. The Hennefers advocated to have Brad included in regular education classes in the Cherry Hill School District. The parents acknowledged that they were Brad's first and most important teachers, and they worked daily to amplify Brad's classroom experiences in their home. Brad was the first child with Down syndrome to be included in a regular kindergarten class in his neighborhood school and progress all the way through his graduation in June 2008.

Sports have been an excellent social outlet for Brad, who has bowled, played tennis, golfed, swam, skated, and skied. He got his first chance to play for the Cougars as a freshman. His framed freshman jersey still hangs on his bedroom wall.

I have coached the Cougars since 1976. When I first met Brad, I thought I could include him in the basketball program by giving him some sideline chores, but the thought of him actually seeing game time intrigued me. Four years later, Hennefer has played in over twenty varsity games and has scored approximately thirty points at the varsity level, including numerous three-pointers.

Much like his parents, I did not think it was fair to treat him any differently. He never received a free pass at practice. He went through the same drills on offense and defense as his teammates did. Drew Berlinsky, a friend and teammate of Brad's since their freshman year believes that, "Brad is probably the most popular kid in school. He carries himself in such a respectful and mature way."

It is clear that the Hennefers, Brad's administrators, teachers, classmates and teammates at Cherry Hill East, not only know the meaning of the word teamwork, they are helping to define it.

~John Valore, Head Basketball Coach,
Cherry Hill East High School, Cherry Hill, NJ

62

Chicken Soup for the Soul

Then and Now

Confidence is hard to teach; confidence is only born of one thing: demonstrated ability. It is not born of anything else. You cannot dream up confidence. You cannot fabricate it. You cannot wish it. You have to accomplish it. I think that genuine confidence is what you really seek. That only comes from demonstrated ability.
~Bill Parcells

At the age of ten, I began to suffer from an autoimmune skin condition called alopecia areata. I had no idea what it was. It started out with a small patch of hair loss on the back of my head. I literally woke up one morning and a patch of my hair was gone. The patch was about the size of a quarter. I told my mom right away. She was clueless as to the reason for the hair loss, but more worried about the harm it might cause.

When we went to visit my local doctor, I felt like I was improperly diagnosed. I was told the condition was related to stress and in a short period of time the hair would grow back after I took some prescribed antibiotics. I continued to see many different doctors, tried all sorts of different remedies, but still had no answers or clue as to the cause.

At the age of twelve, during the summer, absolutely everything fell off. The skin disease spread throughout my body and I was officially diagnosed with alopecia universalis, which results in rapid loss of all hair, including eyebrows, eyelashes, and everywhere else on my body. The only good information I was told about the condition was that it is not life threatening, harmful or contagious.

I found out that this skin disease also affects over five million Americans. It is currently believed to be an autoimmune disorder, and there is no standard treatment for alopecia universalis. It was heartbreaking for me, at that age, to receive such news. At the time, I didn't even know how to begin to face the facts. I was scared, embarrassed, confused, upset, and disappointed.

At that point in my life, it was bad enough dealing with the poor living conditions of the ghetto, but now I had a skin condition to add to everything else. There were some tough times. The biggest thing I feared was not what the world would think of me, but what my fellow students would say. The New York City public school system can be pretty hostile and I was afraid to face my peers.

I remember that first day of school back in September so clearly. I tried to do everything I could to hide my new look, but it turned out to be in vain. The other kids noticed my alopecia right away. For the majority of the school year, I constantly wore hooded sweaters, fitted sport caps, just about anything I could find to cover my head and eyebrows, which stood out the most when you would look at me. It was difficult to gain peer acceptance.

I got in trouble many times because in public school they would make you take your hat off in class — no exceptions. I would always put up a fight about taking my hat off and would be sent to the principal's office on a weekly basis. It was awful. The faculty in my school wouldn't give me a break. My mom would have to come to school about every other month just to talk to my teachers about being a bit more compassionate with me.

The worst part about the whole ordeal was the reaction of other kids. Teens can be so hurtful to one another. Even my own friends would tease me. I heard it all from "egg head" to "bald eagle" to "cone head." I also used to get compared to that albino boy from the hit 1995 movie *Powder*. The whole ordeal was rather shameful. Just imagine a daily occurrence of jokes and teasing all throughout my school years and in my own neighborhood, just because I lost my hair.

I was the same Charlie, yet I was treated differently because of hair loss. It actually came to the point where I didn't even want to step out of my house. I would pretend to be sick to avoid going to school. It not only affected my education, but my self-esteem was destroyed.

As hard of a challenge as it was for me as an adolescent, my solution came to me via a recreational outlet—the game of basketball. All of the hardness that I'd developed over time was still bundled up inside me. As a kid, basketball allowed me to express myself in a way that created value and purpose for me. It became my exercise of the body and mind, the development of my character and leadership on and off the court.

What I appreciated most was that we were equals on the basketball court and the only way to distinguish one from another was through our performance, not our looks. The game helped me understand what fairness and equality were all about. I was treated just like one of the guys on the court. I was accepted for who I was, not what I looked like. The fact that I was a gifted basketball player gave me the opportunity to build my confidence more than anything else.

Self-confidence is at the root of self-fulfilling prophecies. If you want to become a great basketball player or just be great at anything, believing in your abilities is a must. You need to believe and be determined to achieve your goals. The things that separate you from the rest of the pack are your mental approach, fearlessness, and self-belief. It doesn't really matter who you are or what you've gone through in life. For me, when it comes to basketball, an aggressive, attacking attitude puts fear in the opposition and creates openings to score. I have this saying I stick by: "I have alopecia; alopecia doesn't have me." I'm the one in control of myself.

I never lost hope for a better living, a better way. My childhood experiences have now led me to provide other youths with motivation and to assist them in making positive changes in their lives, communities, and emphasizing belief in their goals. I have grown to have a great compassion for children all across America who lose hope due to the destruction caused by bullying.

Through my foundation, programs are implemented to address the ongoing problem of bullying in our society in hope that unhealthy, social interactions move towards more positive interactions that will build better relationships. I created the Charlie Villanueva Foundation with a mission to support, through education, motivation, and recreational guidance, projects that enhance awareness about bullying, and to provide assessment and intervention tools. I firmly believe that a childhood should have a foundation of hope and belief. Being able to bring a smile to a child's face and show them that those who are different, for whatever reason, can succeed and overcome brings joy to my life. I'm living proof of it.

When life gets to the point where you no longer look forward to tomorrow, there is a lack of belief. Basketball was my escape and it has given me a sense of belonging. Now the taunts of my early childhood drama have turned into admiring cheers as I have found success in becoming an NBA player.

~Charlie Villanueva, Milwaukee Bucks Power Forward

Keep on Trucking and Instructing

Don't call it education unless it has taught you life's true values.
~Bertrand Russell

A friend told me about the time he was standing around the ESPN booth at a cable television trade show in Los Angeles. Among the athletes on hand that day was local WNBA star Lisa Leslie. As he watched Lisa meet and greet cable executives, he noticed an extremely tall middle-aged African-American woman standing just outside the ring of admirers and autograph-seekers. He soon realized that she had been standing by herself for what must have been nearly two hours. Finally, my friend went up and asked if the woman was a fan of Lisa's. The woman explained that, in a way, she was; she was her mother.

In the course of making small talk he found out that the woman had once worked as an over-the-road trucker. "How many children did you have then?" he asked.

"I had three girls," Ms. Leslie replied.

"That must have been hard raising three girls being on the road as much as you were."

"It wasn't easy," said the woman, rolling her eyes with a chuckle.

"Did their father stay with them while you were on the road?

"No, I brought them with me."

"You brought them with you? What about school?"

"I taught them while I was driving."

My friend did a double take. "Wait, you mean to tell me you home-schooled your daughters in the cab of a semi while you were driving cross-country?"

The woman simply nodded her head and said, "For a while anyway."

My friend turned away from her for a moment and looked over the crowd at Lisa. He watched her quiet dignity. He watched the grace with which she interacted with people. It was at that moment that he realized what those of us who have watched Lisa have known for quite some time: that she is one of the most remarkable women we've ever met and a young lady that any school in the country would be proud to call its own.

He then looked back, stuck out his hand, looked Lisa's mother in the eye and said smiling, "It is truly an honor to meet you, Ms. Leslie."

~Sheila Johnson, President and Managing Partner, Washington Mystics; Partner, Lincoln Holdings, LLC

Blind Ambition

Definiteness of purpose is the starting point of all worthwhile achievement.
This means knowing what you want, having a plan to get it,
taking daily action and not settling for anything else.
~Napoleon Hill

I was the play-by-play voice for Wake Forest University from 1990 to 1996. In 1995, I met a young man who was enrolled in Wake's law school. Doug Armstrong was from Arkansas and had been blind since birth. An Olympics for the Blind runner and gold medal champion, Doug loved all sports, especially basketball. I met him walking into a party. He heard me speak and he turned to one of his friends and said, "The voice of the Demon Deacons is here. I would know that voice anywhere."

After I met him he proceeded to tell me how closely he listens to the games. Even though he had never seen a basketball, a court, or an arena, he told me he could picture the game by listening to me. As it turned out, his father would draw positions, lines, defenses, zone traps, everything associated with the game, on his leg. Doug remembered all the Xs and Os—from where the point guard played to how a team ran the flex offense. Doug was remarkable.

We became friends to the point that I asked him if he would like to go for a jog one day since he still was a runner. When I asked him what time of day he likes to run he responded, "It really doesn't make a difference to me, it's always night."

I discovered his sense of humor when during an early morning run in which he held my elbow and asked me to say "curb up" or "curb down" I tripped and fell. It was dark. He stopped in his tracks and said, "Boy, this is like the blind leading the blind."

That season I introduced Doug to Wake's head coach at the time, Dave Odom. Odom was as blown away as I was and made sure that Doug had a seat behind the Deacons bench for the remaining home games. Doug would place a Walkman headset in one ear so he could experience the sound of the crowd with the other. He listened to Dave's time outs. He knew when Wake scored. He could see the game—maybe better than most fans.

I tell this story to people who ever question what they do in life. Don't stop thinking that what you do serves a purpose. There is probably someone who depends on you and you don't even realize it.

Ten years later it happened again. Now at Virginia, I met a young Cavalier fan named Tyler Gumm, age thirteen, who, like Doug, he has been blind since birth. He hangs on my every word. He has sat next to me in the booth at football games and at courtside during basketball games. Tyler told me he wants to become a play-by-play guy one day. Even though he will never have sight, by listening, he thinks he will always be able to see the game.

~Mac McDonald, Voice of the Cavaliers (University of Virginia),
Director of Broadcasting

Performing Under Pressure

*The Chinese word for crisis consists of two characters...
one meaning danger and the other meaning opportunity.*
~John Kennedy

Anticipation was overflowing in an Indiana high school gymnasium. The teams and fans were packed into the bleachers, hours in advance. Number one and number two in the state were on a collision course, and finally meeting in the regional tournament.

That alone made it special, but as a veteran local TV news sports reporter this, too, was a day I had marked on the calendar. The terms of a non-compete clause with my former station expired, and I was back on the airwaves with a new station. The timing was perfect to re-introduce myself to a familiar audience.

The game was unfolding as everyone expected. There were many lead changes, and the marquee players were living up to their billing. By the third quarter, one player was the clear standout, scoring all of his team's points and sending fans into a frenzy with a thunderous slam dunk.

Suddenly and dramatically the atmosphere changed. This energetic, dominant player appeared dazed, called a time out, and took himself out of the game. Moments later, he was slumped over near his team's bench as the game resumed. In a short time span, this transcended from one of the evening's top sports stories, to the top news event of the day and one of national interest.

This player stood seven feet tall and was one of the most highly sought after basketball players by colleges around the country. He had committed to attend the University of Kentucky, where basketball national championships are expected if not demanded.

When this giant of a young man was wheeled away on a stretcher, the cheering had subsided, the game's outcome was no longer important. Family, classmates and fans on both sides watched helplessly as paramedics worked frantically to restore his breathing and heartbeat.

For those in attendance it was a horrific scene, but in the news business this had all the juicy elements: action, reaction, drama, and pure emotion. Instead of points and rebounds, this was now life and death. This is exactly the type of story I did not want to cover, the type of story that isn't found during a career covering sports. This was hard news.

I wanted to disappear and turn this situation over to some hardened "journalist." However, we had to respond instantly and deal with this unfortunate and difficult scene. The photographer with me and the production staff back at the station all understood the significance, but at the same time recognized a need to show restraint, respect and sensitivity to all involved.

This huge, public sporting event now seemed private. Word was spreading rapidly about what had happened. A prominent radio station was reporting that the player was dead on arrival at the hospital. From a professional standpoint, this was a tremendous opportunity to make a big splash back on the air. However, as a Christian, there was an even greater call to minister to others in a time of crisis in a non-intrusive way. How would I respond—or not respond—in this delicate situation?

I learned during and after the fact that God was at work in many ways and through many individuals. This event wasn't about me.

The confusion in the gym nearly turned ugly as TV and newspaper photographers attempted to move in to get the headline shots and reaction. Fans were already spent emotionally after screaming for help from doctors and paramedics. Officials were unsure whether to resume or cancel the game. It was a no-win situation. Yet in the midst of all the chaos, one of the young men dressed as a team mascot, removed the head of his costume and was leading groups of fans of both teams in prayer. It was an unforgettable, calm, serene moment. For a few moments, we forgot about news gathering or who was the best basketball team. We put down our cameras and notepads, bowed our heads, or got down on our knees as one family.

I found out later, as I was going on the air to report the sad news, a member from my church congregation was actually praying for me, that I would maintain my composure in carrying out my role. It turns out those prayers were answered. My first live report was one of the most trying experiences of my career.

Our station provided news for an independent channel at 10 P.M. I was not hearing that station in my earpiece when it was time to deliver my report. Instead, I was hearing the audio from a program airing over the network from our own TV station. Rather than hearing the news anchors introduce me, I was hearing a circus broadcast. This was a major hardship as we stood outside in the cold near the hospital, fifty miles from the station.

In addition, the station helicopter was hovering overhead, bouncing our signal back to the city. The only way I could receive my cue from the producer was to listen to the wrong station. Having already gone through the wringer emotionally that night, I was close to a "melt-down," trying to remain fluent and composed, while being serenaded by Barnum & Bailey music and a helicopter buzzing overhead.

Clearly there was another force guiding me through all the hysteria. It gave me pause from shoving a microphone in the faces of devastated teammates who left the hospital in tears after receiving the news. It also would have been easy to ambush the coach with premature reports of his player's death outside the locker room, or even "losing it" myself on the air.

Somehow, I had the presence of mind to offer words of comfort and put my arm around the player's mother at the hospital later that night. Much to our amazement, she agreed to stand in front of the cameras and speak publicly about her devastating loss. We received numerous compliments about our treatment and coverage of this event. People at home watching never knew how close to the edge we really were.

It has taken me years to comprehend why it all happened: how a young man with so much promise had been whisked away on such a grand stage and how I was able to handle this overwhelming assignment with some degree of grace and humility.

I know God has a way of changing our environment in the "twinkling of an eye." There was a greater plan for young John Stewart than playing college basketball. Sports medicine now provides more thorough physicals for Indiana high school athletes and more life-saving devices are accessible at sports venues. Thousands of kids and parents learned valuable life lessons as they heard the news of this gentle giant, and his strong, courageous mother facing an unspeakable tragedy.

People in the news media still have to make tough decisions and technical glitches will continue to challenge them, but as we all struggle to find our purpose in the things we do on a daily basis, the extraordinary opportunities come when we least expect them.

~Dick Rea, TV News Sports Reporter

Journey from Fantasy Island

Obstacles are often opportunities in disguise.
~Nelson Lauver

I was born on the tiny Caribbean island of Canouan, population: 500. As a kid I was very skinny and poorly coordinated, so it's easy to see why I was a lousy athlete. I tried all of the sports, but I was just terrible. From the ages of ten to twelve I was growing so fast that I couldn't get my body to do what I wanted it to.

At the age of fourteen, I moved to Union Island and started high school. At this point I was 6'7" and starting to fill out. Being that tall, I was urged to play basketball. I was reluctant to play based on my past sports experiences, but I decided to give it a try. I showed up to play and the basic premise of the game of basketball was explained to me. Immediately I was rebounding, blocking shots and running the whole floor... but forgot to dribble. They failed to explain that part of the game to me. Even though I made a few mistakes in the beginning, I continued to play basketball.

A year later our school went to a basketball tournament on Dominica Island, and it was there that I met two professors—Jay and Joan Mandle—from Colgate University. They were involved with the tournament in a missionary sense. Jay was the head referee and was there training other refs while Joan was working at the scorer's table. Our team was really ragged, but we were having a terrific time. I was still rebounding, blocking shots and running the floor, and I must've made a good impression.

The Mandles discovered that I was only fifteen years old. They suggested that I move to the United States to develop as a basketball player. I liked the idea, so I went to my mother and said I must go! I persisted in my pleading until she finally okayed the move.

In July 1990, I left my island home and flew to New York. I remember getting off at JFK airport and thinking I would be lost forever. I had never been on a plane that big; I'd never even ridden on an elevator. I enrolled as a sophomore at Cardinal O'Hara High School in Philadelphia and lived at the home of one of the assistant coaches. I was a terrible student at that point and also struggled to learn the finer points of the game of basketball.

After my sophomore year I spent the summer with the Mandles in Hamilton, NY. When the summer was over, it just seemed the natural thing to stay there with them. So I moved in with them and started going to high school there. They really helped tutor me at night and all day on Saturdays and Sundays.

I really started developing as a basketball player, and by the time I was a senior every college was recruiting me intensely. I didn't want to cut corners academically, so I decided to go to Colgate University, right in the town that I was living. In the spring of 1997, after my junior year at Colgate, the Golden State Warriors selected me with the eighth pick of the first round. As of 2008, I have played ten years in the NBA. From where I started, that is a miracle.

I left behind everything I knew as a teenager, moved to a strange country and trusted two people who I'd only known a week, all because I wanted to do something with my life. I have had many obstacles which have forced me to navigate them. If there is one word that should be attached to my name, it is "perseverance."

~Adonal Foyle, Center, Orlando Magic

Be a Victor, Not a Victim

Your attitude determines your altitude.
~Zig Ziglar

I was very fortunate to have been raised by parents who put Christ first in their lives and who provided their two boys with a home that was envied by others. They were always interested in giving their boys more than they had as children, as evidenced by their sacrifices to provide us with a private school education.

As I was growing up, sports and competition played a major role in my life. I can remember playing many one-on-one games with my older brother, and recall how much I hated to lose. Along with my passion for sports, I developed a tremendous love for the outdoors, and I will never forget an afternoon in the woods that changed my life.

I was twelve years old and had gone to my grandparents to go deer hunting on their property. As I was positioning myself to get down from the tree stand, my 20-gauge shotgun rolled off my legs. Instinctively, I reached for my gun to stop its fall, not realizing that as I was grabbing for the barrel the gun would fire as the hammer jammed into a wooden step. I can remember that when the gun fired I looked above to see where the slug had hit, and I was thinking how lucky I was to still be alive.

While smelling the aroma of discharged gun powder, it was at that split-second that I felt a heavy weight at the end of my right arm and I realized that I was the victim of a terrible accident. The flesh on my hand was mutilated and burned, not from the slug but from the muzzle blast which destroyed its unintended target. Blood gushed from my hand, so I controlled the bleeding by clamping my wrist with my left hand.

Doing my best to control the bleeding, I jumped from the ten-foot-tall stand and began walking briskly along the half-mile logging road to my grandparents' house. When I arrived there I remember my grandfather saying that he had seen similar accidents in the military.

There followed a thirty-minute drive to the nearest hospital. The doctor told me it was a miracle that I had not bled to death or, at the very least, gone into shock. Eight hours of reconstructive surgery followed and the surgeon was able to save my thumb and little finger, which exceeded my expectations from the time I first looked at my shattered hand.

Two weeks later, I was released from the hospital and began the painful rehabilitation with doctors and therapists. The worst part was the removal of the dead skin, and the best therapy was getting to resume the normal activities of a twelve-year-old boy.

My first day home, I remember getting out a basketball and, with my right arm in a sling, dribbling full speed up and down the road in front of our country home. My determination, fueled by an encouraging family, led me to start on the junior high basketball and baseball teams the next season—shooting basketballs and throwing baseballs with my thumb and pinky.

As I continued my high school sports career, I threw a baseball with my right hand impairment (I never considered my limitation a handicap) and I shot the basketball with my right hand until my junior year. I had limited motion in my wrist, so I taught myself to shoot left-handed because I was not satisfied with my shot.

I played on regional and state championship teams in high school basketball and baseball, and was honored by being selected to all-state football and baseball squads and to all-star and all-tournament teams in basketball. However, the award that I treasure most is a plaque from Forrest Falls Christian School. It is inscribed, "Special recognition to Tony Duckworth: You have turned a misfortune into a shining example of courage and determination."

Four surgeries later, I reflect on the impact that hunting accident had on my life. I realize that next to receiving Christ as my Savior, this has been the most important event of my life. My accident has enabled me to touch lives through athletics and given me ministry opportunities. I challenge you, the reader, to ask yourself, "What would my attitude be if I suffered a physical or material loss?"

The world is full of individuals who have decided to give up because of a problem or tragedy. Conversely, there are overachievers who rebound from extreme difficulties with a "never quit" attitude. Pastor Chuck Swindoll summarizes the overcomer's drive to succeed, saying,

> *The longer I live, the more I realize the impact of attitude on life. Attitude to me is more important than facts. It is more important than the past, than education, than money, than circumstance, than failure, than successes, than what people think, say, or do. It is more important than appearance, giftedness, or skill. It will make or break a company, a church, a home.*

> *The remarkable thing is we have a choice every day regarding the attitude we will embrace for that day. We cannot change our past. We cannot change the inevitable. The only thing we can do is play on the string we have and that is our attitude. I am convinced that life is ten percent what happens to me and ninety percent how I react to it. And so it is with you. We are in charge of our attitudes.*

Tragedies serve a purpose in our personal growth, yet many individuals allow circumstances to block them from reaching their potential. It has been said that we control few things in this life. Our reactions, attitudes, and perspectives, however, are within our power to control. How will you respond to the trial and tragedies of your life?

~Tony Duckworth, Athletic Director, Maryville University

He Got Me In, I Got Him Out

The trouble with a college education is that it
gives you more things to worry about.
~Anonymous

I grew up in Kentucky, where basketball is king. I had an older brother, Byron, who was an all-state player and highly recruited out of high school by all the major programs—Kentucky, Indiana, Louisville and many others. He finally picked Furman University in Greenville, South Carolina, because of early playing time and an excellent math department. He headed off to Greenville with a lot of fanfare.

I was a year behind Byron and played basketball as well. I sat the bench my senior year, and I was always Byron's Little Brother Bobby. I was an average student but my SAT scores were not high enough to get me into a lot of schools. I had a difficult time gaining admission into any college and at the last minute I applied to Furman. Because my brother was already a rising star at Furman, the school accepted me—without a basketball scholarship.

Byron and the coach, Lyles Alley, never got along. Byron was struggling with starting, then being benched and then back starting again. His scoring average dipped to around twelve points per game his third year.

The next year was Byron's senior year. As a red-shirt sophomore,

I was good enough to walk on the team. We had a number of players get hurt or leave school, and, before the second game against Georgia Tech, Coach told me I would be starting that night. That was the first time I had ever played a basketball game with my brother. The next day *The Atlanta Journal-Constitution* published an article with the headline, "Bobby Pinson Scores 15, Brother Byron gets 12."

We didn't have a very good year that season and Byron's relationship with Coach Alley never healed. In April, after the season was over, he and a bunch of buddies went into downtown Greenville and got a little bit out of control. They were partying too hard and causing a ruckus. These players were disgruntled with Coach Alley and elected to hang him in effigy from a lamp post. Some Greenville police officers spotted the players, apprehended them and the whole thing was reported back to the university. Needless to say, it was a tense moment all the way around.

The real question was if Furman would allow my brother to graduate after this display of disrespect and disregard for the school had transpired. After much debate, the school allowed Byron to get his diploma and graduate with his class. As it turned out, the main reason they let him graduate was because I still had eligibility and they didn't want me to be upset or leave the team.

So in the end, it seems the only reason I got into Furman was because of my brother. The only reason my brother got out was because of me.

~Bobby Pinson, former Furman University basketball player

Losing Rufus

Life is like a grindstone, and whether it
grinds you down or polishes you up depends on the stuff you're made of.
~Knute Rockne

The most rewarding aspect of being a coach is the relationships with athletes during a formative time of their lives. Kids can offer you many views of life, and often have as much influence on a coach as the coach has on the kids. I consider it an honor to be entrusted with the life of a young man who many times is going away from his home for the first time.

All the kids that we come in contact with are special in their own way, and learning that "way" is an exciting challenge for coaches. Occasionally there are kids who come along who have more influence on your life as a coach than you could have ever dreamed possible. Such was the case for me with a young man from Maxton, North Carolina, named Rufus Leach.

While I worked as an assistant to Buzz Peterson at Appalachian State, I was recruiting the junior colleges in Florida to find a couple of impact players to bring into our program. I, along with many other coaches, had discovered a tremendous shooting guard with the strength of an ox, yet the deft touch of a surgeon, playing for Santa Fe Community College. Rufus was the unquestioned leader. He was the best defender and the best shooter on a very talented team. We wanted Rufus at Appalachian State University.

Upon further investigation, it became apparent that Rufus was not going to qualify academically to play Division I basketball. This was a major disappointment to Rufus and to me. I had many engaging conversations with him leading up to the time when I learned of his academic shortcomings. Many other coaches backed off, but I continued to stay in contact with Rufus. He insisted that he would do whatever he could to be a Mountaineer. He was on a mission.

While sitting in my office one afternoon, I was taken by surprise when I looked up to see Rufus standing in the doorway with a million-dollar smile. He had driven 600 miles from Gainesville, Florida, just to get in our faces and find out what he had to do to be part of the university and our basketball program. He was not to be denied.

Coach Peterson and I explained all that would be necessary for him to become a basketball player here. He would have to have the grades and he would have to pay all his own expenses for his first year as a student. This would be difficult for a young man from a single-parent household with limited resources. Rufus was not discouraged. He said, "I'll take it and I'll make it! I'm on a mission!" He returned to his junior college and began preparing to attend Appalachian State University.

Rufus took a job making biscuits at Bojangles in the mornings before classes and had a second part-time job in the evenings. In between jobs, he was constantly in the library, and was clearly the most celebrated intramural basketball player on campus. He would visit practice from time to time just to remind himself what all his hard work was for. A chance to be on the floor with the varsity was his burning desire.

Rufus passed all of the classes that he needed in order to become academically eligible to play for Appalachian State. He had worked so hard that he was now on track to obtain his degree in communications. In 1999-2000 he would, in fact, become a Mountaineer.

It did not take Rufus long to have an impact on our program. In his first game, he scored twenty-eight points at Oklahoma State. He wound up having a spectacular season, leading Appalachian to the Southern Conference Tournament championship and a spot in the NCAA Tournament. When we walked on the floor to play Ohio State in the first round, the satisfied look on Rufus' face was absolutely priceless. He knew how much he had gone through to reach this point, and Rufus was justifiably proud.

He was the team's leading scorer and our best defensive player, although he never started a game. He never questioned why the team's leading scorer did not start; instead, he chose to focus on what else he could do for his team. Rufus made 103 three-pointers, establishing a new school record. He made his presence felt.

The next summer while working his summer job, he and a teammate had a day off and they chose to visit Watauga Lake. While swimming, Rufus inexplicably cramped up and, due to his muscular composition, he was quickly lost underwater. Repeated attempts to find him were fruitless, and on June 9, 2000, we lost Rufus. We were completely devastated.

During the celebrations of Rufus' life that followed, it became abundantly evident as to the large number of lives that Rufus had impacted. His influence on the many people he encountered was both genuine and powerful.

A monument honoring Rufus outside the Appalachian State University arena sums up his effort: "He was a man on a mission… mission accomplished!"

~Houston Fancher, Head Coach, Appalachian State University

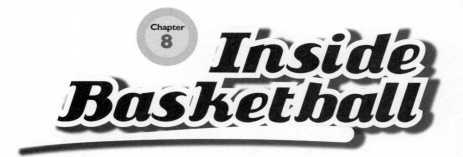

Chapter 8

Inside Basketball

Achieving Greatness

Lord, grant that I may always desire more than I can accomplish.

~Michelangelo

Missing to Make a Point

Give a little love to a child and you get a great deal back.
~John Ruskin

I learned early on in life that sharing meant sacrificing. My granddad, Nathaniel Jones, taught me about the virtues of sacrifice and dedication. As a boy, I worked at his service station in Winston-Salem, North Carolina. I rotated tires, changed oil—all that stuff—and I loved it.

I was given responsibility, and if I didn't fulfill my granddad's obligations I quickly learned the consequences. Some people would say it was a rough childhood, but it brought out the best in me. We were raised to give back and never take things for granted.

In 2002, when I was a senior in high school, my granddad was tied up in his home and murdered by three teenage boys. He was sixty-one. Ironically, the murder occurred the day after I signed a letter of intent to play basketball at Wake Forest University. He was with me when I signed the LOI, he gave me the Wake Forest hat to put on after I signed, and that was the last time we were together.

My granddad was my best friend. I talked to him every day. I don't think anybody was as proud of me and my accomplishments as he was. He was always bragging on me about how good I was. He just made me feel special.

After my granddad's senseless death, I figured there was no better way to honor him than with my play on the court. The hardest thing was to get back on the court and play, but my family helped me to be strong. My granddad would want me to play.

Before my next game after his death, I decided to honor his memory with my best performance on the basketball court. My aunt mentioned scoring sixty-one points for my granddad, and I thought that would be just lovely. But I thought to myself that there was no way I could do that. Before tip-off, my heart was racing because I knew I wanted to do something special for him.

Without almost anyone knowing what I had planned, including my parents, I scored twenty-four points in the second quarter alone. This was one of the times when I felt that there was no way—I don't care what kind of defense they played or who they put in front of me—there was no way they were going to stop me from getting to that goal. They whole game I just kept thinking about my grand-dad—thinking he was in heaven, watching that game.

With two minutes left in the fourth quarter, I had fifty-nine points. I took the ball to the hole, made the lay-up and got fouled. I lay there for a second and was just overwhelmed because I knew that moment in time was something that I would never forget. It felt like I could've just died and gone to heaven right there; it felt like my purpose for being here was almost over.

I was six points away from the state record for most points in a game; but that number didn't matter, sixty-one did. I walked to the free throw line, the referee gave me the ball and I shot an air ball right out of bounds. I walked over to the sideline and my coach took me out. I just looked at my dad and started crying.

Scoring those sixty-one points for my granddad made me stron-ger, but it was still hard to go on. My granddad did so, so much for our family. I'm thankful for my granddad, and I'll never forget him. Ever.

~Chris Paul, Point Guard, New Orleans Hornets

Accentuate the Positive

Treat people as if they were what they ought to be,
and you help them become what they are capable of being.
~Goethe

Imagine my surprise when my then thirteen-year-old daughter asked me to coach her basketball team that competed with other non-varsity teams in Worcester, Massachusetts. Having never coached before—but having familiarity with basketball from a fan's perspective—I was honored that, as a teen, my daughter even wanted to associate with me.

Since I was working with teenagers, I vowed never to speak a bad word to my team. Several of the players had never played organized basketball and some had never dribbled a basketball. At our first practice I instructed them that if one of their teammates made a bad play and a teammate made a negative remark, the offender would be removed from the game. We stressed being positive all the time.

Our first game was against the preseason favorite. They hammered us. During the game, two players asked to be taken out because they were frightened and didn't know what to do on offense or defense. We lost four of our first seven games.

We limped into the second half of the season; however, we started to emphasize positive imagery during practice—like visualizing that the free throw would go through the hoop before actually taking the shot. The players evolved from non-believers into believers with amazing results. We won the next seven games, beating two teams that had beaten us in the first half of the season.

Our next challenge was the playoffs. In the semi-finals, we had to beat a team that had clobbered us twice. Our team played the game of the season, topping our rivals by fifteen points! We actually held them to fewer points in the entire game than they scored in the first period of our previous meeting. Next on the tournament schedule was the championship game against a team that had beaten us twice — the one that crushed us in the season opener.

Two of my players related to me that prior to the game the girls on the other team felt that there was no way they could beat us. Talk about a reversal of fortune! Before tip-off, I told my players not to worry about any aspect of the game since we knew we could win. I instructed them to focus on the thought of receiving the first-place trophy and to reflect on the progress they had made since the season opener.

Seconds before game time I called them to the foul line and said, "Forty-five minutes from now there will be a minute left in the game and you will be leading by twelve points. I will then call a time out, we will return to this foul line, and we will give thanks for our effort."

The game began. The other team scored first but then our kids went nuts, leading 16-4 after one period, 23-9 at halftime, and up by twenty at the end of the third quarter. Players who had not scored all season were throwing up twenty-footers and hitting nothing but net. The kids were playing harder and better than ever, and the result was truly a dream come true.

With 1:22 remaining, I called a time out. We gathered at the foul line and I pointed to the clock and scoreboard. We were not up by the twelve points I had forecasted — we led by twenty-five! One of the kids tapped me on the shoulder and said, "Hey, Mr. DiPietro, that visualization thing really works!"

Being positive prevented me from yelling at a player for blowing a lay-up, missing a pass, or making a turnover. I could have destroyed the confidence of thirteen- and fourteen-year-olds with negative criticism. Being positive positively pays!

~John DiPietro, Worcester, Massachusetts Radio Executive

Willing to Win

Encouragement is oxygen to the soul. Good work can never be expected from a worker without encouragement. No one ever lived without it.
~Abraham Lincoln

In 1976, I was a reserve senior guard on the basketball team at Mississippi State University. The first Monday of January that year we began our preparation to host the University of Kentucky Wildcats that Saturday night in our new arena, Humphrey Coliseum. At the time, Kentucky was coming off an impressive win over Notre Dame and was ranked number two in the country.

Before our Monday practice, I asked our head coach, Kermit Davis, if I could address the team. He said yes. At center court before practice, I told my teammates that I was a senior and this was my last home game against Kentucky, a team we had never beaten in my four years at State. Then I raised my voice and bellowed these words, "We are going to beat the Kentucky Wildcats on Saturday night." With that, practice began, and I noticed a new enthusiasm in that practice and more intensity than I had seen from our team in previous practices.

On Tuesday, as Coach Davis called the team to center court for the start of practice, I again asked if I could say a few words. He reluctantly agreed. I told my teammates that if we listened to our coaches, practiced as hard as we could, and prepared like never before, we could shock the college basketball world on Saturday night. I again ended my talk with the bold statement, "We are going to beat the

Kentucky Wildcats on Saturday night." Practice that day was again intense and had a couple of flare ups, but it was evident that our players were getting ready for a monumental challenge.

On Wednesday, as we approached center court, one of my teammates grabbed me and said, "Hey, Weiner (that was my nickname on the team), don't say anything today."

I said, "OK."

After Coach Davis finished his pre-practice comments, I said, "Coach, can I say something?" I could tell my teammates were irritated with me, and one said under his breath, "Come on, Weiner, cut it out." Coach Davis again agreed to let me speak, and with a voice as loud as I could muster I hollered, "Fellows, we are going to beat the Kentucky Wildcats on Saturday night."

Before Thursday and Friday's practices I did the same thing before practice, and my teammates and coaches started to look forward to hearing my bold prediction.

The week of the Kentucky game was the first week of my student teaching assignment at Starkville Middle School. I was an education major at State and the spring semester meant practical teaching experience in a school setting. The boys in my physical education classes were in the seventh and eighth grades and loved the Mississippi State Bulldogs. On Friday of Kentucky game week, I gave my students the same proclamation I had given my teammates during the week, "We are going to beat the Kentucky Wildcats tomorrow night."

The boys were skeptical, but excited about coming to the game. I then asked them if they wanted to help me get our team ready. They quizzically asked, "How?" I explained that on football Saturdays on our campus, the cheerleaders and sororities came to the athletic dorm, where the student-athletes were housed, and decorated the lobby of the dorm in maroon and white crepe paper, balloons, and signs urging the football Bulldogs on to victory. I told my middle school posse that we were going to do the same thing on Friday night for the basketball team.

With the permission of their parents, I picked up about five of the boys, and drove them to a local general store where we bought all kinds of decorations, balloons, and poster boards to decorate the athletic dorm for the players. The Mississippi State athletic dorm never looked more spirited with maroon and white crepe paper, balloons, and signs everywhere, one which boldly read, "The Dawgs are going to beat the Kentucky Wildcats tonight!" When my teammates came downstairs on Saturday morning for breakfast, they were all amazed at the lobby decorations and the outpouring of support for this big game. We were ready.

Before a sell-out crowd in Humphrey Coliseum that night, the Mississippi State Bulldogs and the second-ranked Kentucky Wildcats battled for thirty-nine minutes, nose-to-nose, and toe- to-toe. With just thirty-nine seconds to play, and my courageous team up by one point, the Wildcats fouled our point guard Al Perry, who stepped to the line for a one-and-one opportunity.

What happened next was a play that will live with me forever. As Al Perry's free throw bounced off the back of the rim, our freshman guard, Ray White, a 6'5" jumping jack from Gulfport, left the fourth spot on the lane, leaped high into the air, and in one motion, rebounded the miss and shot it back toward the basket. Time seemed to slow down for that one instant, as Ray's rebound shot hit nothing but the bottom of the net.

The Dawgs were now up by three points (no three-point line in those days), with time running down. The Hump went crazy. I went crazy. I was on the bench, as usual, cheering for my teammates. When Kentucky missed on their next possession, the Mississippi State Bulldogs rebounded, made meaningless foul shots at the end, and came away with a hard fought 77-73 victory. We had beaten the Kentucky Wildcats on Saturday night!

The crowd was ecstatic and our players were jubilant. But the best moment for me was just before we entered the hallway to go to our locker room. I found my coach, Kermit Davis, who gave me an opportunity to play basketball in the SEC, and gave him a big bear hug. It is a moment that I cherish to this day.

My fiancée at the time, Ellen Anger—now my wife of thirty-one years—was with me as we drove away from Humphrey Coliseum to go celebrate with my teammates. On Coach Davis' post-game radio show, I was surprised to hear him say to the long-time voice of the Bulldogs, Jack Crystal, the following: "Jack, tonight was a special night for Mississippi State and a lot of people deserve a lot of credit for this victory. But one young man, a senior on our team, who didn't even play in the game tonight, deserves as much credit for this victory as anyone in our program. Joe Dean, Jr. told our team all week that we were going to win this game and beat Kentucky, and his will was part of the courage and determination that you saw on the court here tonight."

The thing that makes me the most proud about Coach Davis' words and the lesson that I learned from that experience, is that you don't have to be the star of the team to make a contribution. I made a contribution to my team in my own special way.

As my father preached to me growing up, one of the greatest privileges in life is being part of a team. Thank God I have been a part of a team since I was in the fifth grade. And I am still just trying to make a contribution.

~Joe Dean, Jr., Athletics Director, Birmingham-Southern College

73

From Coal Mines to Gold Mines

I will not give up. I will keep on striving until I climb over, pass through, or tunnel underneath—or simply stay and turn the mountain into a gold mine.
~Rev. Robert Schuller

Mine was a journey that had begun in the mountains and valleys of rural West Virginia and ended on the gold medal podium at the 1968 Olympics. It is a story of how basketball, though not without its own disappointing moments, had given a young man a guiding light through life's challenges. As I stood on the platform to accept my gold medal as a member of the United States Men's Olympic Basketball team, I was flooded by many memories from my journey.

I thought about what I learned from the coal miners back home. I thought about the older guys and my teammates in Richwood. I thought about the days of playing basketball just because I loved to play.

I have always said basketball kind of dragged me along, and it did. When I was in school, learning did not come easily for me and was a source of frustration; however, basketball allowed me to get on the court where I could do things other people couldn't do. I began to find out I actually could excel the way other people did in algebra and chemistry. It became a hook.

As a junior in high school, I thought very seriously about

dropping out of school and going into the service. I told myself, "This isn't working." Had it not been for basketball, dropping out of school might very well have happened. That's what basketball did for me: it became an anchor that allowed me to get over some rough spots. I found some balance because basketball was an outlet for me. You hear all the bad stuff about athletics, about people pushing their kids to play sports but not for the right reasons. There are some really, really good reasons to play. All of us need a platform where we can feel good about ourselves.

As I stood on the Olympic platform in Mexico City I felt good about myself. I was proud to represent my country, my state and my schools. And I was thankful for all that the game of basketball provided me.

~Mike Barrett, 1968 USA Men's Olympic Basketball team member,
as told to Pat Hanna

Editors' Note: Following the 1968 Olympics, Barrett played three seasons in the old American Basketball Association. He gave his gold medal and white Olympic uniform to West Virginia Tech, and his blue uniform to Richwood High School. As much as he represented his country, he also represented the two schools and the people associated with them. He remains a supporter of both schools.

74

Courting Commitment

People never improve unless they look to some standard
or example higher and better than themselves.
~Tyron Edwards

I was unable to attend the ceremony in which they unveiled the naming of Ken and Kathy Shields Court at McKinnon Gym. I read that the players ringed the playing surface to pay respects to the honorees and I am so sorry I could not make it to stand in that line. Work commitments and moving a family 3,000 miles left me no opportunity to be there. I can only imagine the spectacle and the emotions that must have coursed through everyone's hearts. My father-in-law, Bill Snow, sent me the articles and I read every one of them trying to put myself there because it was a milestone for me as well.

The years I spent in McKinnon Gym were not my best years. At the time, I was in a very selfish, confused state. It seems like those were lost years. I was part of the team but, also, not part of it. My priorities had become compromised and I was not as dedicated as I should have been. Looking back, I have some nagging regrets. It was just where I was on life's journey.

The Shields' contributions to who I am and where I am are unquestionable. The pure focus on excellence that they cultivated has been formative for me. I may have not even known it at the time, but I was getting a lesson that would serve me well. For four years, I was a witness to a passion, an intensity, a humanity that was delivered in the context of teamwork. That gym was a classroom. I learned things that I have transferred into my workplace and my home life. They are now serving me very well. After reading the quotes in the paper, it is so clear to me now that the wins were not really the objective (though they were nice). It was to deliver to the players a way of life, a compass for the years ahead.

I remember Ken speaking at an event in Prince Rupert one summer when I was back home. He said something that will stick with me forever. "Everything I have, I owe to basketball." I can now say that I truly understand that statement because it holds true for me, too. Those are words I use all the time now as kids ask how I started out. The first real job I got in radio was the result of being on Paul Carson's TV interview show on CHEK after we won the first championship. It directly led to my job at CJVI, then to CHEK, then to CKVU in Vancouver, then to Orca Bay, and now to Maple Leafs Sports and Entertainment.

You can draw a direct line from being on that gym floor for all of those practices at McKinnon to the dream job I have today. I feel, in large part, it is because of those lessons on that court. The accountability, the demands, the precision of strategy, the leadership were all there. I see it as clearly as day now that I am in the leadership position. I was at business school and didn't know it. As I look back, I realize that the Shields were the first great leaders that I had in my career. Their ability to communicate, to plan, to invest in players, to manage their expectations, to pull the collective together, were all skills that I would need to acquire some day. Man, I was sure not going to get that from a degree in linguistics!

My kids are seventeen, fourteen and eleven now. I hope some day that they meet their own Ken and Kathy Shields. I hope some day I can do the same for some other kid. Coaching is a term that is used a lot in business today. I feel that I have an MBA in that subject because I learned from the best. That is something that did not show up in the stats sheets with the wins and losses, but is undeniably their legacy.

I am welling up with tears. The things that they have done for me are so important to me. There are days that I think of the teams that we had. The faces come back, the intensity of the practices, the crowds, the time outs, the training, the pressure. The guys who made the team. The guys who didn't. It was a proving ground. They made it so. What a gift they gave us all.

That ceremony represented a lifetime of commitment and purpose, of dreams and heartbreak, of men and women who enriched the lives of others. I can still smell that gym right now. The sounds of the court are so imbedded in my brain. Their voices still echo across the years. They got us to believe in the quest. They got us to places we didn't think we could get. They taught us the lessons of life. I will never forget them.

~Chris Hebb, Senior Vice President, Broadcast and Content,
Leafs TV/Raptors NBA TV, Maple Leaf Sports & Entertainment Ltd.

75

A Thirsty Kid

*Desire is the key to motivation, but it is determination and commitment to an
unending pursuit of your goal — a commitment to excellence —
that will enable you to attain the success you seek.*
~Mario Andretti

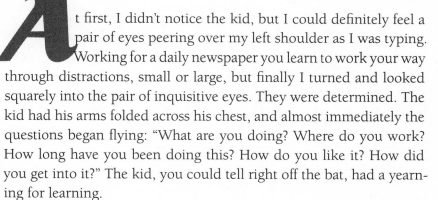

At first, I didn't notice the kid, but I could definitely feel a
pair of eyes peering over my left shoulder as I was typing.
Working for a daily newspaper you learn to work your way
through distractions, small or large, but finally I turned and looked
squarely into the pair of inquisitive eyes. They were determined. The
kid had his arms folded across his chest, and almost immediately the
questions began flying: "What are you doing? Where do you work?
How long have you been doing this? How do you like it? How did
you get into it?" The kid, you could tell right off the bat, had a yearn-
ing for learning.

On and on the questions came at the press table at the NAIA
tournament in Kansas City, Missouri, some three decades ago. After a
short conversation, I assumed that would be that, and the kid would
move on. That wasn't the case. There was more to come from the
kid. It was the beginning of a very brief but interesting and not-so-
personal relationship which continued for several years — in periodic
flurry-like style — almost exclusively through the mail.

As time passed, the kid got my address and then came more
questions. He asked if he could send me some of his basketball copy
to read and give him my take on it. He sent it to me, and I did that. At

a later date the kid wanted to know what I thought of the University of Kansas. Was it a good journalism school? How did it rate with others from around the country? How good was Missouri's J-School? How did KU compare to MU? The kid, obviously, was determined.

Slowly but surely I learned that this was not just another inquisitive youngster looking for some fast answers to quench his thirst for knowledge. The kid was serious about basketball and made it known in his unique way that he was in the game to stay. He had made it clear that somehow, someway, he would find his niche in the game, and was in it to stay. It was, he pronounced without saying a word, how he was going to make his living some day. Several years would pass from one contact to another but each time, in his own little way, I could sense that air of determination from the kid. Sure enough, some years later he started a national basketball magazine. He was no longer a kid. Holy hoops!

The kid now had his own national magazine, for heaven's sake! It was abundantly clear — he didn't need to say anything, his actions spoke volumes — that he wasn't going to stop there. As he got older, I began to ask questions about the kid. Each and every time the answer from reliable and knowledgeable sources was basically the same: the kid — make that the young man — was determined. Very determined. Over time, I lost track of the kid but I began finding out how he was doing with his career, usually in *USA Today*.

The text was generally the smallest possible, but the words came out loud and clear: the kid was on the move and there was no stopping him. Every several years he seemed to move from one position to another. And he wasn't just making subtle little moves. He was now in the NBA! He was with the Knicks, the Clippers, the Nuggets, and the Trail Blazers. Each time I read the news I was in awe, still feeling his unspoken determination. Later he became the director of player personnel for the Miami Heat and then the general manager of the Boston Celtics.

I only talked to the kid a couple of times over the years, but I'll never forget all the good things he had engrained in his personality when he didn't stand much higher than three or four basketballs.

In his very early years, I saw displayed an unusual depth, integrity, maturity, perseverance and courage. The kid from Buckhannon, West Virginia, did precisely what he had set out to do.

He had gone on to make his living in basketball—from founding the award-winning *Blue Ribbon College Basketball Yearbook* to his position today as vice president/general manager of basketball operations for the Memphis Grizzlies. The kid didn't talk long and hard about living his dream. At least I never heard it. He simply lived it. That kid, Chris Wallace, was something else.

~Tony Jimenez, *Basketball Times* Columnist

76

This Kite Flew Higher

Some men dream of worthy accomplishments
while others stay awake and do them.
~Edward Simmons

My love of the game of basketball was sparked by my Dad's love for his sons. Growing up in Houston, Texas, I was the last of four children, five years younger than my only brother, Chris. My father, Robert Kite, was a very nice and kind man who was always concerned about others. He was very intelligent and loved to read and to learn. Sports were also something he enjoyed. He had high jumped and wrestled in high school, but was never a star athlete.

One way that my dad spent quality time with his sons was to attend sporting events with us. The Houston Astrodome was about ten minutes from our house, and an Astros game or college football game was a fun way to spend time with my dad. In the late 1960s, the University of Houston Cougars basketball team, led by All-American Elvin Hayes, excited fans as they pursued an NCAA Championship.

Back then, the Cougars played at off-campus Delmar Field House with a seating capacity of about 5,000. A ticket to see U of H and the "Big E" play was tough to come by. My brother, my dad and I stood in line for an hour or more several times for general admission seating. While waiting in line one rainy Saturday morning, my dad wrote "Little E" on the back of my yellow rain jacket. I was a very tall six-year-old and Elvin was my favorite player. Seated in the bleachers, with the Cougars running and the pep band playing, it was exciting to watch Elvin pour in the points as the crowd chanted "E, E, E, E...."

Chris and I also participated in sports, playing baseball, football, basketball and competing in track and field. Dad would occasionally play catch or rebound for us. He put up a basketball goal in our driveway which became a neighborhood gathering spot. Dad and Mom were big supporters—hauling us to and from practices, attending games and volunteering as scorekeepers, umpires or concession stand helpers.

With our age difference, I never played on the same teams or leagues as my brother, Chris. Even in the neighborhood pick-up basketball games, I was usually relegated to "scorekeeper" or "referee" when friends his age were around to play. But I wanted to be like Chris. I dreamed of playing basketball and football like he did for Pershing Junior High and Madison High School. At age fourteen, he played on a highly successful church league basketball team, Maplewood 2nd, which qualified for a prestigious national tournament in Salt Lake City.

By then I was a fan of Kareem Abdul-Jabbar of the NBA's Milwaukee Bucks. Chris' Maplewood jersey became my "Maplewood Bucks" jersey, as I would often wear it under my shirt to elementary school, dreaming of playing like both Chris and Kareem.

In 1971, the San Diego Rockets relocated to Houston and struggled to stay out of the cellar and to draw fans. But for my dad and his boys, any Rockets game was a good game. Sharpshooting forward, Rudy Tomjanovich was one of the Rockets we admired the most.

In 1971, I played on my first organized basketball team at the YMCA. The next year I made the Pershing Junior High roster. In the summer, I had the chance to attend two basketball camps. A special instructor at the first camp was our local favorite, Rudy Tomjanovich. He looked at me, a gangly eleven-year-old, well over six feet tall, and saw a young player who could one day reach 6'11". Rudy spent extra time working with me during the camp. A few weeks later, the host instructor at an overnight camp I attended in College Station, Texas, was "Big E", Elvin Hayes. Elvin shot jumpers with us, taught us to throw outlet passes and, coolest of all, shot the breeze with campers at the dorms as we munched on fruit and cookies after the evening session.

From age ten, my long term goal was to play professional basketball in the NBA. I knew that there would be many intermediate goals and lots of hard work for a YMCA basketball beginner to become an NBA player, but I loved the game and was determined. Basketball heroes like my dad, Chris, Rudy T. and the Big E created living models for my dream.

In 1983, I realized my dream as the first-round draft pick of the Boston Celtics. I was a rookie back-up center on a team with future Hall of Famers Larry Bird, Kevin McHale and Robert Parish. We are playing the Houston Rockets in the Boston Garden. Coach KC Jones told me to check in the game to give Parish a breather. Houston made a substitution and Elvin Hayes, now a Rocket in the final year of his career, checked in. My defensive assignment was Elvin and he guarded me at the other end of the court! "Little E" vs. "Big E" in the Boston Garden for a few minutes—the dream was a reality.

After the game, I shook Elvin's hand and thanked him for being a basketball hero to me. I later called my dad and Chris, my other heroes, and told them about my epic match-up with the Big E. Heroes can help us paint the picture of what our dreams can be.

~Greg Kite, former NBA player

77

If You Want to Play Indoors, You'll Have to Leave Town

He lives so far out in the country, he has to walk toward town to hunt.
~Jim Crotty

This was the first night basketball game I ever saw. It was played in cold weather on a dirt court in North Carolina. Denton High School had no indoor facility, but that hadn't deterred the coach, who also ran the telephone company in town. Vernon Cashatt had gone to the local hardware store and bought several metal wash pans, punched holes in them and inserted light sockets with bulbs. He then strung them up over the bare court. Presto! Let there be light.

Electricity was new to the town and this was an exciting occasion. Denton was playing Southmont, and this was a match of neighboring rivals. When they played, one basket was uphill and the other downhill, and oft times the wind drift had to be dealt with. There was little wind the night the lights came on, only the piercing cold. The spectators gathered beside bonfires to keep warm. The players had only their coursing blood to fuel their bodies.

At halftime they, too, gathered around their own bonfire.

Denton won the game and great was the joy to behold. This was only the start of something this town had never seen before. These five players went on to win the county championship, and the excitement was only building. They would move on to Raleigh to play in the state tournament.

At Raleigh, the tournament was played in the gym at North Carolina State University. As fortune would have it, Denton came into the finals against another team from their county, Welcome, long most bitter rivals. The trip to Raleigh in those times wasn't an easy one—perhaps two and a half hours today—and only a handful of locals were in the stands.

The game came down to the last few minutes when Spike, the biggest player on the team, sank the basket that gave Denton the lead. In the end our boys won, 13-8. The teammates that played indoors only when the game was out-of-town, who had played their first night game at home under light shining beneath wash pans from the local hardware store, were champions!

One of the most vivid memories of all is that when the news of the score arrived touting Denton as champions, my older sister was so excited she fell off the porch into a rose bush. Clay, the star of the team, was her boyfriend. They were later wed and stayed married for sixty years. Oh well, that was country life back then.

~Furman Bisher, *The Atlanta Journal-Constitution*
Sports Columnist

Shining a Light

*Those who bring sunshine to the lives of others
cannot keep it from themselves.*
~James Matthew Barrie

he girl in the wheelchair at the edge of the court wore a red T-shirt that read "#11's Sister." For all the words unspoken, all the sights unseen on this night, for the sister sitting on the baseline, and the sister cutting down the victory net, the shirt said enough. Because Lizzie was there to wear it.

Elena DelleDonne won four Delaware state girls' high school basketball titles in five varsity seasons at Ursuline Academy, was named the nation's number one girls' basketball player and top recruit as a senior in 2008, and was chased by both Tennessee and Connecticut before choosing to play her college ball with the Huskies—just a four and a half hour drive from Lizzie.

Elizabeth "Lizzie" DelleDonne, five years older than Elena, walked on her own. That was one of her victories. She cuddles on the couch with her father, rides in a golf cart with her sister, pulls her mother tight and smells her hair. Lizzie is blind and deaf, with autism and cerebral palsy, her world consisting of smells and tastes and hugs and simple hand strokes of communication. And presence. There are the days she won't stop crying, when the kicking and hair-pulling and thrashing show off her surprising strength. But on the good days, and even the bad, she is there, shaping her sister and her family.

Wearing that T-shirt in 2005, Lizzie was part of Elena's second state title. It was the first basketball game Lizzie ever attended, the roars from the crowd that cheered for Elena sending a message from one sister to the other. Lizzie couldn't hear them, but she felt the gym shake. The cheers never seemed to end. Elena emerged as a star in her home state, scoring 2,818 points, the most in Delaware high school basketball history—girls or boys. That included a state-record fifty points in one state championship. Her string of eighty consecutive free throws set a national high school record. Her state player of the year awards matched the one her brother, Gene, earned for high school football.

Elena is 6'4", a player with the size of a center and the ball skills and shooting stroke of a guard. Brother Gene is a 6'7" football player at Middle Tennessee State. Their father Ernie is 6'6" and mother Joanie 6'2". But it's Lizzie at 5'8"—the sister many fans knew nothing of—who remained the center of attention at home.

"It's like we're a team at home," Elena said, "and Lizzie's the all-star player and everyone has to worry about keeping her well. We all have our roles in the family. She's the one who keeps us humble in the family. OK, I won a state title, but she wasn't supposed to walk, and look at her now. So, she really overshadows everything I've done in my entire career."

Rather than casting shadows, Lizzie shines rays of light on Elena's world, ensuring the game she played so well remained a game. For two months in the summer before her senior year of high school, during a crucial period in the recruiting calendar, Elena told college coaches not to contact her, turned down a tryout for an Under-19 USA Basketball team and focused on her other passion.

She volunteered with special education children at the Meadowood Program at Forest Oak Elementary School in Newark, Delaware, which Lizzie had been a part of when she was younger. Where others may be unsure or intimidated, Elena found comfort and relief in the walks and crafts with children who repeatedly had to ask the name of the girl known to every basketball fan in the state.

"Elena identified with them, and really tuned in to them," Ernie DelleDonne said.

Her interaction with basketball was limited to rebounding for some of the students. While facing the tension of a recruiting decision, the player who had been a star since playing varsity ball in eighth grade found that the joys of basketball had evolved into a job. Maybe it was burnout. Maybe it was her reaction to her understanding of the world beyond the game, to the awareness developed by the Thanksgiving turkey left in the oven when a seizure sent Lizzie to the hospital; by the more than thirty surgeries Lizzie has faced; by the daily routine of watching your parents care for your sister, knowing it will never get easier.

So often as she grew up, the two hours of basketball practice provided a break for Elena from the chaos that could inhabit Lizzie's world. But when Elena needed a break from basketball, it was to Lizzie's world that Elena turned. Basketball has been a passion and a joy, a palette for her talent, an entry into opportunity. The game has taken Elena down so many roads, to so many places Lizzie will never know.

But on a quiet couch or in a rocking arena, with the game or without it, she'll always be Elena's sister.

~Doug Lesmerises, Columnist, *The Plain Dealer*,
Cleveland, OH

Editors' Note: Elena has since transferred to the University of Delaware where she is playing volleyball.

79

A (Blue) Devilish Dream

Every good thing in the world was once only a dream.
Dream your own great dreams.
~Dr. Phil McGraw

In the spring of 1963, I was a high school basketball coach in Punxsutawney, Pennsylvania. The NCAA Final Four was held in Louisville that year. Since I had never been to a Final Four, I was thrilled when I received a call from an attorney friend, Jesse Long, inviting me on his private plane to Louisville. He said, "I can get you to the Final Four, but I cannot help you with tickets or a hotel room."

I took Jesse up on his offer, somehow found a place to stay, and bought a scalped ticket for the championship game in Freedom Hall. That was the year Loyola of Chicago upset Cincinnati in a classic Final Four contest. I saw it all from the last row behind the basket up in the nosebleed section—the worst seat in the house. I took the whole game in, had the time of my life and flew back home on Jesse's plane.

I had been writing letters to various college coaches for years hoping to move up in the coaching ranks from high school to college. After the Final Four that spring, Fred Shabel, an assistant to Vic Bubas at Duke University, left to become the head coach at the University of Connecticut. I wrote a letter to Coach Bubas and applied for the assistant's job. I had never met Vic, and I knew it was the longest of long shots.

At the end of May, Vic invited me down for an interview. We met for four hours talking basketball, and later he took me to a social event. I'm sure it was to get a read on how I would handle myself.

I went back home not knowing what sort of impression I had made on Coach Bubas. One day at school they came and got me out of class for a phone call in the principal's office. I had never had a phone call at school before. I picked up the phone and it was Vic Bubas who said, "Chuck, how would you like to be a Duke Blue Devil?" I was ecstatic and accepted the job right away.

I loved my new job at Duke. I was on the road a lot scouting and recruiting. I coached the freshmen and helped Vic with the varsity. We had a terrific season ripping through the NCAA tournament and ended up in the Final Four, played in Kansas City. We got to the final game and lost to UCLA, which was the first of Coach John Wooden's ten NCAA titles.

In March 1963, I bought a scalper's ticket and sat in the last row of the upper deck of the Final Four. One year later, I was sitting next to Vic Bubas helping coach the Final Four championship game. I went from the worst seat in the house to the best! If it can happen to me, it can happen to anyone. There's always hope. Never fear moving up the ladder.

~Chuck Daly, Hall of Fame NBA Coach

Inside Basketball

Leadership:
The Coaches' Corner

The first great gift we can bestow on others is a good example.

~Thomas Morell

80

The Coach from Iona

There would be more I love yous, more I'm sorrys, more I'm listenings;
but mostly, given another shot at life, I would seize every minute of it —
look at it and really see it — try it on — live it — exhaust it —
and never give that minute back until there was nothing left of it.
~Erma Bombeck

A s we go through life, we meet people who touch our lives unexpectedly, wonderfully, and magically forever. It could be the briefest of encounters, but it can leave a magnificent impact, an eternal fossil that crystallizes over the years telling a perpetual story of love, inspiration and courage. This is my story of just such an encounter many years ago, in a basketball gym, with a basketball coach from Iona.

When I was a kid, I played basketball endlessly. Life was basketball and basketball was my life. It was the summer of 1976 in Philadelphia and I was heading to the Father Judge High School basketball camp. I was fourteen.

Every camp has "guest speakers," and you just hoped that you got somebody good. This week we did. He was Rollie Massimino, the head coach of Villanova, one of Philadelphia's Big 5 schools, who would later lead his Wildcats to an amazing upset victory over Georgetown in the 1985 NCAA National Championship. The other guest speaker was some coach from some school called Iona College...

wherever that was. Coach Massimino was great; I learned how to dribble a basketball with my head up. But it was the coach from Iona, who taught me how to live with my head up and how to never give up.

So, this skinny Italian coach who looked like Al Pacino walked into the gym and my eyes never left him. He was electrifying, excitable, animated, his eyes nearly popping out of his head as he spoke, his voice a raspy roar. I had never seen anyone as passionate about anything as he was about teaching kids how to play basketball.

He spent an energetic, fundamental-filled hour with us and I was sad to see him go, but thrilled that I enjoyed his talk so much. As he sat us all down at half-court, he started to talk about basketball and life and how they were very much alike. I guess he saw some blank stares, so he said, "Let me show you guys." Then he looked right at me. Me! I was not even in the front row; I was in the middle of the group and we were all wearing white camp shirts, yet there he was pointing at me, asking me to get up and come over to him... in front of everyone! I was a shy kid growing up, but I had to go, my buddies were watching me, the high school coaches were looking at me, but most of all he wanted me to do something special with him. So, I hustled nervously over to this stranger, who in the next five minutes would have an impact on my life that would carry on forever.

He asked my name, then said, "Marc, let's play around the world." I thought, "That's it? Just a little game of around the world. What's that got to do with life?" Well, he must have read my thoughts, as he had this sly smile. He said, "You shoot, I'll rebound." "Around the world" is one rebounder and one shooter; the shooter shoots; then moves to the next spot; usually once around the perimeter. He rebounded my first made basket, said "Good shot," and snapped a hard chest pass back to me. I shot again, made another one, shot again, again... my confidence was high and then something didn't happen.

He didn't tell me to stop, we kept playing... then something did happen. I got tired and I started to miss and miss again... but I refused to quit. Not here, not in front of everyone... not in front of the coach from Iona. So, I dug deep and finished out the drill... he kept track of my makes and misses, nine for twenty-fix, ouch! I was dead tired and disappointed in my performance. I walked dejectedly back to the group, still trying to catch my breath. Coach came up to me before I sat down and in front of everyone, put his arm around my shoulders, put his hand on my heaving chest and said loudly, "Gentlemen, THIS is hard work!"

I can still feel his arm around me; I can still hear his voice, as his touch and his words and his inspiration, captured in time, have carried me through a lifetime of ups and downs, highs and lows, happiness and sadness. Not a day goes by that I do not hear the echo of his words, "...this is hard work."

He went back to Iona (later to NC State and a national championship) and I went to Father Judge, played basketball; went to St. Joseph's University, but did not play (too slow, too small). But I worked hard in everything I tried; I wanted to be the best; I wanted to learn everything; I wanted to be as passionate as him. That simple drill taught me to work hard, to work through adversity, to work through "tired"... and it was not about the shooting percentage; it was about the "working hard." That's what mattered. And in life, working hard matters.

When I tried out for a team, I heard his voice, "Gentlemen, this is hard work." When I went to college and finals were brutally tough, I heard his voice. When I started my first job and I had to give my first presentation in front of a thousand people, I heard his voice. When I was out of work for the first time in my life, with a mortgage, kids in school and bills that needed to be paid, his voice boomed, "Gentlemen, THIS is hard work." That basketball camp so long ago, that drill, his words, are immortal for me in every way.

Yet the coach himself proved to be mortal. Years later, I heard he was diagnosed with cancer, but I heard his words again whispering in my ears. He would work hard, harder than ever before. In the end, it was simply a matter of God wanting him more and God worked hard to welcome the coach from Iona home with His arm around his shoulders.

Shortly before he died, the coach from Iona won the Arthur

Ashe Courage Award and he gave his now famous acceptance speech at the ESPY awards, speaking to millions of people all over the world. "Don't give up, don't ever give up," he said and I was fourteen years old again. I cried because this coach, this man would soon be gone from a world that needs people like him. I need people like him.

When he finally died, a part of my childhood died with him... but only for a moment. Although I only knew him for a short time, his spirit, his passion, his inspiration lives on in me still.... I will share this gift with my kids. I will share this gift with the kids I coach. I will carry the memory of this brief encounter with Jim Valvano forever in my mind, in my heart and in my soul.

~Marc Balara, Fifth-Grade Coach Boys' Basketball Team, Marlton, NJ

What's In a Name?

*Remember that a person's name is to that person
the sweetest and most important sound in any language.*
~Dale Carnegie

I grew up in the Philadelphia area and attended Malvern Prep School. I was a good basketball player in high school, which led me to LaSalle University where I played four years of college ball from 1966-70. I then went into the Army for eighteen months where I played and coached basketball.

When I got out of the Army, I was trying to find myself, so I went to Villanova University to get my master's degree before going back to Malvern to coach at my alma mater for four years. I then jumped into the college ranks and have had a long career as the head coach at the University of Pennsylvania and now Temple University.

The most important lesson I've learned in coaching took place during the 1986-87 season when I was an assistant coach at LaSalle under head coach Speedy Morris. The highlight of the season took place when the highly-ranked Tar Heels of North Carolina arrived in Philadelphia to play LaSalle at the famous Palestra on the campus of the University of Pennsylvania. The historic gymnasium was packed to the rafters with energy, fervor and excitement that is difficult to describe, even to this day.

Just as the game was getting ready to start, both coaching staffs came out of the locker rooms. I was the third assistant on our staff, an absolute nobody. As the LaSalle coaches arrived at our bench, I looked up and saw North Carolina's legendary coach Dean Smith walking towards me. He shook all of our coaches' hands and said to me, "Have a good game, Fran."

I was absolutely dumbfounded. How in the world did Dean Smith know my name? He must have read our media guide, seen our pictures and remembered all of the names. That fleeting moment with Dean Smith — the Dean of College Basketball — has never been forgotten by this coach. We lost the game that night, but I learned a life lesson that I've applied throughout my coaching career.

To this day, I read our opponent's media guide before the game, learn the names and faces of the young assistants and then say to them what Dean said to me. My doing that won't mean as much to them as Dean's thoughtfulness did to me, but I still think it's important.

I guess the lesson from all of this is that you never know what a thoughtful gesture, a kind word or a gracious act will mean in the life of some person you may never see again. Dean Smith proved that to me.

~Fran Dunphy, Head Coach, Temple University

A Clear Conscience Gets a "W"

The world's shortest sermon found on a road sign is: Keep Right.
~Dr. Tony Evans

I am now beginning my eighth year at Columbus State University, the first six spent as an assistant coach for men's basketball. I was named the interim head coach on April 17, 2006. We had a great recruiting year and signed a junior college all-American to add to our returning guards. We also signed a big, physical 6'8" player, giving us size to go with our speed and quickness.

On January 17, 2007, we suffered a home loss to the number six team in the nation, Clayton State. At eight A.M. the next morning, I received a phone call that three of our players had been found smoking marijuana in their dorm room. Two of those players were starters, our leading scorer and our biggest post player. I immediately met with our coaching staff to discuss our options. The assistant coaches suggested various suspensions, running punishments, and community service work. The assistant coaches knew we were on an interim basis and that our future at Columbus State depended on how well the team performed, so they did not want the players to be dismissed from the team.

After deliberating with the assistant coaches, I needed to spend some time alone. I was fighting an internal battle, "Do I keep these young men on the team and gray the line between right and wrong, therefore bolstering my chances of shedding the interim tag, or do I dismiss the players and face the remainder of the season with no players over 6'4"?" My stomach was in knots and this was literally making me sick. I finally came to the decision that I had to do what was right—I had to dismiss these guys from the team. I knew that I had to be able to face my children and teach them right from wrong. I cannot tell my children one thing and then have them see me do something else.

The choices these young men made were wrong and I could not allow them to represent our program, our university, or me any longer. I knew my job and my future were on the line and I also knew that most people would judge me and my staff on wins and losses. However, I had to be able to live with myself, to sleep, and to teach my children the difference between right and wrong with a clear conscience. Looking at it from a wins and losses standpoint, it was a tough decision. On the other hand, in my heart I knew what had to be done. I called the players in and dismissed them from the team. Immediately the knot in my stomach went away and I felt like a load had been lifted from my shoulders.

After losing those players, our tallest guy was 6'4". We had to completely change the way we played. We had to scrap a lot of the plays we had run all season and put in some completely new things. We went on the road and beat that same Clayton State team and we also won another double-overtime thriller over a conference opponent. Our team bonded, played together and was a joy to coach. We absolutely overachieved and finished the season with a 17-12 record.

After the season ended, the head coaching position was officially advertised and a search began. I was a candidate and was fortunate to make the top five for final interviews. Two of the other top five candidates were from Southeastern Conference schools and another was an assistant on a team that advanced to the Final Four in 2006. My family and I held strong to the belief that we were the right people in the right place for the job. We also knew that whatever happened, it would be the right thing and would eventually work out.

On April 17, 2007—one year to the day after I was given the interim position—I was named the new head coach. I fully believe that the decision I made impacted the supporters and committee members more than our wins and losses. They knew we were in this for the right reasons and wanted to win and have success in the right way. They knew we were here to help student-athletes become better people by being held accountable for their actions. They knew we would not sacrifice integrity for wins.

In the end, we were rewarded and blessed for doing the right thing.

~Doug Branson, Head Men's Basketball Coach,
Columbus State University

Don't Be Afraid to Coach

You gain strength, courage, and confidence by every experience in which you stop to look fear in the face. You must do the things you think you cannot do.
~General George Patton

When my playing days in the NBA ended, I was really kind of at a loss. I didn't know what career path to follow and spent a lot of time trying to figure out what to do with my life. I got a break when the Lakers added me to their broadcast team in 1980. I enjoyed the broadcast world and thought that was where my future lay, but then some strange things began to happen. The Lakers, with Magic and Kareem, won the NBA championship in 1980 over the Philadelphia 76ers, when Magic, a twenty-year-old rookie, scored forty-two points in Game Six of the NBA Finals.

The next year, in 1981, the Lakers were knocked out in the first round by Houston — an indication that things were not well in Laker-land. Early the next season the team made a coaching change and, amazingly enough, I was named the new head coach. I had never coached anything in my life and was the most unlikely candidate. The Lakers were loaded with great players — Kareem, Magic, James Worthy and company — and my coaching career actually got off to a great start. I thought this profession is not all that tough... nothing to it!

After about two weeks, however, the tide turned and I began to run into some real difficulties. It was at that point that the Lakers owner, Dr. Jerry Buss, came to visit me. He sat me down to give me a word of encouragement and a good pep talk. The statement he made that I still remember was, "Pat, don't be afraid to coach the team." He meant that I was the boss and I was responsible; don't be looking over your shoulder all of the time; don't look back later and say, "Why was I afraid to step up and lead?"

That meeting with Dr. Buss took place more than twenty-five years ago, and I still consider that the best piece of leadership advice I have ever received. I often tell young coaches that coaching is over-rated, but leadership is not.

~Pat Riley, President, Miami Heat

84

Cotton Matters

All great people spend time alone preparing and practicing their art.
~Wynton Marsalis

"Y**ou know what we're here for!"** Those words echoed through my head every time our team bus arrived at a game this past season as I was coaching for the Kansas City Knights. The only problem was I couldn't bring myself to say them, because only Cotton Fitzsimmons, my coach with the Kansas City Kings, could say them the way they were meant to be said. The intensity with which he said them never varied. It didn't matter how many times you heard them in a season, it was a welcome cadence, a sound piercing the quiet nervousness of a pre-game bus ride from the hotel to the arena. In the raucous atmosphere of an intense game, it would bring things back into focus and remind us all of the task at hand.

To Cotton, every game mattered, every minute, every second. Whether it was the first game of the season or the seventh game of a hard fought play-off series, they were all the same. Arriving at the arena was not unlike going to church. You knew you were about to set foot on the hallowed grounds of the arena, where in a few hours you would be putting everything on the line—your dreams, your hopes, your livelihood, your place in this mysterious world.

The memory of that blond, confident little man getting off the team bus with no other place in the world he would rather be than in this moment, leading his favorite team—made up of his favorite players (and I was his favorite player)—off to battle, brings a smile of joy. How did this diminutive man—5'7"—inspire a basketball team to go beyond itself, to overachieve game-after-game? I believe it was the "voice," and that "voice" was backed by an unshakeable, compassionate, joyful spirit. When you heard the "You know what we're here for," you never heard fear in the "voice," you never sensed nervousness.

What you did hear was the pure delight and joy we should all feel in getting to do something most people only dream about.

You heard in that "voice" that we were all just a bunch of big kids having fun and our coach is nothing more than a kid at heart, too! You heard in that "voice" that we have been working our butts off and now we are going to show the world "we can flat-out play!" You heard in that voice the only thing your coach wanted—what was best for you. And what was best for you was to play as well as you possibly could so our team would win and we could all walk out of this building proud of ourselves with our heads held high. Pretty simple. Players are sensitive and a player can sense if a coach is more concerned about his own welfare than your own. Cotton was always more concerned about ours.

I loved my relationship with Cotton. It was a special relationship and I believe one of the reasons it was so special was that I was his favorite player! I realize that I was one of many who felt that way. I believe we all felt important to Cotton, because he was so important to us. This was Cotton's gift. He was able to tailor each relationship he had with each player to that player's personality, strengths and weaknesses. If a player needed a father figure, a best friend, a coach to crack the whip—whatever the need—Cotton was there.

When I am coaching, as our team bus arrives at the arena, I will force myself to say those words no matter what, in memory of him, "You know what we're here for!"

And behind it, I will be reminded about Cotton and what really matters!

~Scott Wedman, former Head Coach, Kansas City Knights

85

Friendship and the Fratello Fraternity

A friend is one who joyfully sings when you are on the mountaintop,
and silently walks beside you through the valley.
~William Arthur Ward

Mike Fratello was head coach for the Atlanta Hawks in 1986 when his daughter Kristi had a birthday spend-the-night-party with several of her little girl friends at the Fratello home. The next morning one of the girls, whose parents would not allow her to ride a bike, got up early and was fascinated with Kristi's new ten-speed bike. She wanted to ride it. She took the bike without anyone's permission and down the hill she went. She was unable to stop the bike, hit a neighbor's garage, was thrown from the bike and suffered severe head injuries requiring emergency brain surgery.

Unfortunately, the girl's parents had both been recently laid off and were without any medical coverage. Needless to say, the medical bills began pilling up... and up... and up. When Mike received the news of the girl's accident, he rushed back from training camp to stay with the family in the hospital. As the young girl lay in a coma, Mike felt helpless; surely, there was more that he could do.

Mike decided that something needed to be done to help the family with their medical bills. Mike started calling some of his coaching friends—Willis Reed, Dick Versace, Tommy Lasorda—and asked me to help put on a Friends of Fratello Foundation luncheon that people still talk about today.

The luncheon started as a Mike Fratello roast, but the stories they told about each other were so fascinating that the luncheon lasted past three P.M. We could have used eight microphones because everyone wanted to get in on the act! Businessmen were calling to say they were not coming back to the offices that afternoon.

After everything was said and done, we made enough money to pay almost all the medical bills for the little girl. Today that little girl is thirty-two and is doing extremely well thanks to the efforts of Mike and his friends.

When it came to charity work, Mike Fratello had one of the biggest hearts.

~Rachel Styles, former House Manager,
The Omni Coliseum, Atlanta, GA

86

Called to Lead

Where God guides, He provides.
~Vance Havner

My first job as a head coach was at a Division II school in Texas. While there, I received a message that one of my brothers was killed in an auto accident. I loved being a head coach, but felt strongly that I should be close to my family in Orlando, even if the move would require me to take an assistant coaching position.

Jerry Richardson, at the time the head coach at the University of Central Florida, called to offer me an assistant's job. I gladly accepted the job, packed, put Texas in the rear-view mirror, and headed toward Orlando. During a stop in Mobile, Alabama, I phoned my parents and they informed me that Jerry Richardson had lost his life in an auto accident. I was dazed by this second monumental event. The remainder of the trip to Orlando is a blurred memory.

Upon reporting to the UCF athletic department, I was offered the job of interim head coach. The prospect of becoming a head coach under these circumstances was a daunting task. Even though I felt overwhelmed, I knew that God had directed my journey home to Orlando to be with my family. Being overwhelmed is the inherent feeling that pervades the realm of a leader, particularly in times of crises. The best leaders I know never feel as if they have "arrived." They are continually at work, and when they meet their goals, rather than being self-satisfied, they prepare for the next set of "overwhelming" challenges.

My first year at UCF, we were 13-15, and improved our record to seventeen wins and eleven losses the following season. Through it all I have learned that coaching, particularly during adverse times, reveals character strengths and flaws. I also believe that God calls us to accept life's challenges so that we can confirm our total dependence on Him. My faith in God empowered me to accept a leadership role that was, at that time, well beyond my mortal abilities. God selects us to face challenges whether we want them or not.

~Lynn Bria, Head Women's Coach, Stetson University

87

A Father's Inspiration and Love

Effort is the difference between commonplace and first place.
~Roy Williams

I played college basketball at the University of Alabama-Birmingham from 1985-1989. My biggest fan and number one supporter was my father. During this time my father was working a factory job in Springfield, Ohio. He used to work daily ten- to twelve-hour shifts for over thirty years to support his family of three children.

My father instilled in me that with hard work and education you can be successful at anything you put your mind to. The main reason I have had some success in my life is because of the lessons my father taught me about basketball and education. My father went to night school for ten years to get a business degree from Purdue University. So, whenever I thought about quitting or not giving one hundred percent in school, I was always reminded of how he would work his ten- to twelve hour day and then go to night school to finish his degree in order to provide a better life for his family. He always told me, "No one can ever take away your education. So get as much education you can, because it will pay off in the end." Inspired by his words, I received my bachelor's degree from UAB and a master's degree from Hardin Simmons University.

On the weekends, even though he was tired, he would find

enough energy to take me to the YMCA to work on my individual basketball skills. He taught me how to dribble, how to shoot, how to come off screens, and how to work hard to be the best player I could possibly be. He would send me to the best basketball camps in the nation. I went to the Purdue camp, Hoosier basketball camp, All-American Camp in Ohio hosted by Bob Huggins and Dave Krider (who used to pick the *Street & Smith's* All-Americans).

The number one camp in the USA back then was the Five-Star basketball camp in Pittsburgh, Pennsylvania. I attended that camp, which helped me get great exposure. My father's financial and time investment enabled me to receive a full scholarship to play basketball at UAB.

While I was in college, he would get off work around six P.M. on a Friday and drive through the night to be at my games on Saturday afternoon. The drive took about ten hours. Some days I did not know he was coming. He would just show up knowing I would be totally surprised. One Saturday we were playing in Iowa at 11 A.M. and I looked up and he was sitting in the stands.

My father taught me that I can overcome any adversity or obstacle. In 1988 my father was diagnosed with throat cancer. He probably developed the cancer by working over thirty years in factory air filled with toxins. After going through radiation, he drove to a game because he knew it was a big game for me. I really did not want him on the road driving, but this was a tournament, so he would have a chance to see me play two games over the weekend. It is hard to explain the inspiration he provided when I saw his face before the game. I went on to have the two best games of my career at UAB. I made the all-tournament team. After I received my award I rushed over to my father and hugged him. I cried and told him how much I loved him.

My father beat cancer and lives today. He is still the only man I have ever idolized.

~Dylan Howard, Head Men's Basketball Coach,
Hardin Simmons University

88

Lessons on Basketball and Life from Coach John Wooden

The person who is afraid of asking is afraid of learning.
~Booker T. Washington

Imagine taking a long and extremely difficult college course for no credit. The only reward is what you might learn. That was all that was promised when I was offered a UCLA basketball scholarship.

My future coach, the legendary John Wooden, minced no words. "Swen, if you come to UCLA you will play very little in actual games, maybe not at all because I've got someone coming in who is extremely talented. However, if you work with us, practice with and against this player, by the time you graduate I feel certain you'll get a pro contract. You'll be that good because of the role you'll play on our team."

That "extremely talented" player was Bill Walton. Walton led UCLA to two national titles and was three-time college player of the year. One reason I accepted the challenge was the reputation of Coach Wooden. He was known to be a man of integrity and honesty with a strong emphasis on the development of his players—not only as athletes but as human beings. When I came to UCLA, Coach Wooden had already won six national titles and set records that still stand.

Believing Coach Wooden was the easy part. The hard part came during days of challenging practices. I knew before enrolling at UCLA I would be a backup, but that didn't change the reality I faced during my three years on the team. Like all young athletes, I wanted to play in games, but that was not to be. For the most part, the only playing time I enjoyed was at the end of games when the outcome was no longer in doubt. At times, I became frustrated and discouraged, which put my motivation to practice and learn at risk.

But I never gave up. I understood my role. I was 7-foot-plus, strong and muscular. My role on these successful and talented UCLA teams was to challenge Walton in practices every day. According to Coach Wooden, for three years the team greatly benefited from the role I played, and Bill Walton benefited, too. In fact, Walton has been known to say that going against me every day for three years was the toughest assignment he faced as UCLA's center.

Coach Wooden helped me stick with "the plan" for three years. He engaged and motivated me to focus on what I could learn rather than the immediate rewards most athletes seek. That is an impressive example of successful teaching by any standard.

How did he do it? First, he helped me see the vital contribution I was making to the team. Second, Coach Wooden took time to learn everything he could about me: my background, family, interests, etc. He studied me in practice every day just as he did with each player on the team. Learning all he could about each player, Coach Wooden designed a detailed plan for every practice that not only focused on the team as a whole but on what each player needed to make progress.

Finally, by his actions everyday Coach Wooden taught a definition of success that kept all the players focused on being a learner: "Success is the peace of mind which is a direct result of the self-satisfaction in knowing that you have made the effort to become the best of which you are capable." This personal definition was crafted in the 1930s by Coach Wooden as a very young man. It guided him all his life, and it was a lesson he taught every player—but not by lecturing about it. In fact he seldom mentioned it. But it guided his actions every day. No matter how big the game, Coach Wooden never talked about winning. He spoke constantly about making the effort to become the best of which you are capable.

What about me? After, graduation I was drafted in the first round of the ABA draft, and earned rookie of the year honors. I went on to a long professional career and set records for rebounding, some of which still stand today. My story teaches an important lesson about being a learner. No one, not even Coach Wooden, can be a great teacher without a committed learner. I took advantage of an opportunity which many might have missed, and I focused on learning to be the best basketball player I could be. But I also learned a lesson for life, expressed in my poem, "Success."

Success

Some say success is in fortune and fame,
Or winning the crown in a championship game.
Some say success is in riches and gold,
Or trophies and medals — That's what we've been told.
We worship the winners who shine in the race,
And shame all the trailers who hold second place.
We train our poor children to only be best.
"Success is just when you're ahead of the rest."
We tell them success is an A or a B,
And that something is wrong if they bring home a C.
"What's wrong with the teacher?
Why can't my child pass?
My child's name should be at the top of the class.
My taxes are spent and remain in their pay,
So why is my genius not getting an A?
My child is not average," they say as they're riled.
"That place is reserved for the neighborhood child."
But God in His wisdom, when making this race,
Did not make us equal in talent and grace.
For some of us run, but then others are lame.
But both share success if they try just the same.

If you came up short when you went for the A,
But gave it your all till the very last day,
And effort was made to be all you can be,
You're still a success if you brought home a C.
When you know that you gave it your all, then you'll find,
That self-satisfaction gives sweet peace of mind.
And that peace of mind, that you only possess,
Is your declaration that you're a success.

~Swen Nater, former UCLA and NBA player
as told to Ronald Gallimore, Strength and Conditioning Coach

Let 'er Rip

Remember, a diamond is just a chunk of coal that made good under pressure.
~Dr. Henry Kissinger

My third year as head coach at the University of Evansville, we opened the season playing the University of Louisville. The previous year we had lost (by ten points) to them on the road. Obviously, we were the underdog, and I played that up with our team as much as possible prior to the game. Louisville had a roster of players that were bigger, faster, and stronger than my team, but I knew if we executed well we would have a chance.

At the beginning of the game, we had a loud and boisterous crowd. With seven minutes and thirty seconds to go in the game, we were down eleven and fighting for our lives. Our crowd had grown silent, radio listeners had turned off the game, and for most of the fans, "that was all she wrote."

Thankfully, my team still had a rally left in them. We went on a 12-0 run and by the 3:20 minute mark we had taken the lead. Our kids were excited, but the pressure kept growing. Even though we had Louisville back on their heels, I could tell our players were starting to play tighter. Shortly after we took the lead, Louisville called a time out. Just three minutes and sixteen seconds separated a team whose gear you can find in most stores in the Midwest from a school whose enrollment is around 2,400 students.

Like every coach, my idea for this time out was to passionately motivate my team to victory or make some incredibly strange move that would enable our team to maintain this lead and secure the upset. At the moment I started to kneel down to put my wonderful plan in action, I heard and felt a ripping sensation that I knew was coming from the hind end of my pants. My eyes must have been as big as grapefruits and my face grew white and pale. Now remember, this was supposed to be one of the greatest moments of my coaching career, the time out of my life. Instead, my players were reading my face and asking me what was wrong!

Horrified, I filled them in on my mishap and asked a few of them to check my backside to make sure that I wasn't flashing some poor, innocent soul sitting on the other side of the gym. By this time, my team was laughing. I was laughing, and I was assured the tear must have only been the lining. Sure enough, my shoe had caught the lining of my pants when I knelt down to talk in the huddle. It was now hanging out of the bottom of my pants!

Someone up above must have had a hand in this one because an amazing thing happened in that huddle. My original time out—the passionate, strategic call to action—would have only added pressure to a team that was already tight. My pants ripping and the laughter that erupted took the pressure off. Even though I barely had any time left in the huddle to talk about our pending situation, our team took the court relaxed, focused and confident. We won the game by two points and our local paper ran a large picture on the cover of the sports section to highlight the upset.

I learned a valuable coaching lesson that day. One of my biggest responsibilities as a leader during difficult situations is to take the pressure off my team. It is amazing what people can accomplish when they are focused and relaxed.

Although, I'm going to have to find some new ways to take the pressure off. I can't afford to rip out the back of my pants for every big game.

~Tricia Cullop, Head Women's Basketball Coach,
University of Evansville

Dig Deeper

I can't do it never accomplished anything. I will try has performed wonders.
~George P. Burnham

I grew up in a basketball family, the daughter and sister of two NBA coaches. My brother, Eric Musselman, has been an assistant coach with the Minnesota Timberwolves, Atlanta Hawks, Orlando Magic and Memphis Grizzlies. He has been the head coach for the Golden State Warriors and the Sacramento Kings.

My father, Bill Musselman, was a coach in the NCAA, the ABA, the CBA and the NBA. He was head coach for Ashland College, The University of Minnesota, San Diego Sails, Cleveland Cavaliers and Minnesota Timberwolves. In 2000 my father was an assistant coach with the Portland Trail Blazers when he suffered a stroke and was later diagnosed with bone cancer.

Days before my father died, at age fifty-nine, he could not walk. His eyes had circles underneath them the color of darkened grapes. His voice was raspy and low. His weight had plunged. His kidneys no longer worked. He had cancer.

The last day we saw him we arrived at the hospital early. He asked to be put into his wheelchair and taken to the chapel. He sat in the middle of the center aisle, hands folded, head bowed, praying to God. He then asked me to say a prayer. When I finished, he whispered to me to take him back to his room and grab his dark sunglasses, which he wore like James Bond in Bangkok, day and night throughout his life. When I returned, I put them over his eyes and then in a low voice he said, "Take me outside."

It was a beautiful sunny day and we wheeled him outdoors.

He turned his face to the sun and spoke to my brother Eric. "E, hand me that phone," he commanded, waving his hand. Dad grabbed the phone and then dialed with more energy than we had seen in weeks.

"Biggie," he said to Damon Stoudamire, Portland's 5'9" point guard, "It's Bill Musselman."

And then my father came alive. His voice boomed with an enthusiasm we hadn't heard in weeks, but had heard so many times in locker rooms and on sidelines. My brother and I were mesmerized and captivated by his words and the rhythm and strength of his voice.

We heard him barking at Stoudamire: "What is going on with you? You have got to dig deep. You have more inside you. Don't let anyone keep you down." His voice got louder and gained momentum. "Dig deeper! You have to go deeper! Get in there, fight, be strong, and be tough; we all have more to give then we think! Push yourself! Use every ounce of your potential! I know you have more, I know you can find more inside, we all can."

Dad's arms were waving like a symphony conductor. His jaw was clenched. His words were crisp and clear for a man who had lost all of his speech six months earlier from a stroke. Eric and I stood there a bit shocked but smiling and hanging onto each of my father's words.

On that day in the glorious sunshine, wearing his sunglasses, my father gave us our last life lesson, one last bit of advice that makes you believe that you have something glorious inside you. As Dad spoke to Biggie, he let us know that we have been given a gift from above and must dig deep to find it and then do everything possible to use it wisely and with impact. We must all live up to our potential, and our potential is infinitely greater than we can ever imagine.

My father was a great believer that if you kept your focus and were willing to work harder than you ever thought possible, even when your dreams didn't happen on your timeline, you could still accomplish great things.

My dad was interested in why people prevail and why people surrender. The will to triumph fascinated him. When I look back at his life, his greatest gift wasn't a fantastic basketball mind; his greatest gift was the dedication to follow his dream. Behind his steel blue eyes was a life full of passion. My father once told me, "Two percent of basketball players are born with endless talent, the kind of talent that would take a complete fool to mess up. The other ninety-eight percent are going to succeed because of how much they put into it and how deep they dig into their soul."

I looked back at the road my father traveled and it was filled with great successes, but also some controversies and brutal failures. But he never lost sight of where he wanted to go. Dad's life was cut short but he had something inside him that kept him moving forward, something that gave his life fullness and energy. His love for basketball was so powerful that no matter how much he succeeded or how miserably he failed, he still felt value in his quest. He was a focused warrior.

At Dad's funeral, an older man came up to my brother and introduced himself. He said, "Over thirty-five years ago I was driving down the two-lane highway on the way to Orville, Ohio. I saw a boy about eleven or twelve years old dribbling a basketball on the side of the road. I pulled over and said, 'Son, where are you going?'

"He kept dribbling and replied, 'Orville.'

"Then I asked him, 'Do you know Orville is ten miles away?'

"And the boy nodded, 'Yes.'

Then I asked, 'What are you going to do when you get there?'

"He looked up at me with this strange kind of smile and answered, 'Dribble back home with my left hand.'

"That boy was your father."

Now there is a guy who knew how to dig deep!

~Nicole Musselman Boykin, Dallas, TX

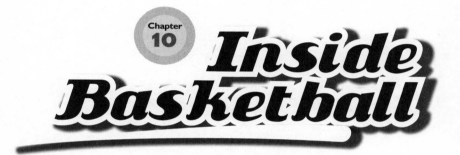

Living Large
On and Off the Court

*Our main business is not to see what lies dimly at a distance,
but to do what lies clearly at hand.*

~Thomas Carlyle

A Big Man
with a Big Heart

We make a living by what we get, but we make a life by what we give.
~Sir Winston Churchill

In the summer of 1992, the biggest basketball player in the sport joined our team. Shaquille O'Neal was the tallest, widest, most popular rookie the NBA had seen since Patrick Ewing almost ten years prior. A star from day one in the league, Shaquille was the major sports story for television, magazines and radio. While he stood seven feet tall, he seemed so much bigger.

Shaq instantly became a spokesperson for the NBA and made his rounds in the basketball circuit. I was fortunate enough to travel with him to a clinic in Brazil that first summer. Along with other coaches, NBA security and plenty of media, we accompanied Shaquille to several schools to help promote the game of basketball. Our final stop was a Brazilian basketball game where Shaq posed for photos, shook hands, kissed babies and was as warm and as personable as you will ever see a professional athlete. It was remarkable how open he was.

After the game, it was late but we were hungry. It was about midnight and Shaq told the driver to stop at a pizza place so we could get something to eat. Outside the pizzeria, a little girl in rags was selling gum. Shaq asked how much, and the little girl—maybe seven or eight—told him twenty-five cents. Shaq bent down to the little girl's level and gave her $1,000 and a big hug! The little girl ran away, heading home. It was quite a day for her and her family; she probably got more money that day than they saw in a year.

The best part about the entire interaction was that there were no cameras, no reporters and no promoters around. Out of the kindness of his heart, Shaq wanted to bring more than just basketball to this girl's life. The biggest player in the NBA also had the biggest heart.

~Tom Sterner, former Assistant Coach, Orlando Magic

A Busload of Love

Sentimentality comes easily. But caring is hard—it involves doing.
~Anonymous

In the mid-1990s, with Shaquille O'Neal as its star, the Orlando Magic was the NBA's hottest show at home and on the road. One night in mid-season, the Magic were playing the New Jersey Nets in New Jersey before a packed house. The Magic won the game handily. After the contest was over, the Magic team bus was backed into the arena tunnel to protect the players from the fans and the inclement weather.

As I gazed out the door of the visiting locker room, I realized the crowd in the hallway was bigger than I had ever seen before. Of course I realized that Shaq had family ties to the New Jersey area, which could explain why the crowd was extra large.

Most of the players had successfully made it onto the team bus except for Shaq. Heavy security surrounded him as he stepped into the hallway and headed to the bus. I had already made my way through the crowd unscathed. I stood on the first step of the bus and watched Shaq and his "escort service."

As I had walked to the bus, I noticed a very small boy being supported by leg braces and permanent walking canes. His mother and father were close by his side to keep the crowd from overwhelming him. He held a piece of paper and a pen. His eyes were glued, like the others, on the locker room door in anticipation of Shaq's appearance.

In my mind, the little boy's presence had now taken priority over everything else. As Shaq and his entourage made their way through the crowd, the thing I feared the most happened. The wave of momentum of the crowd not only blew by the youngster but nearly knocked him over. The little boy was just too small to get Shaq's attention.

I saw this unfolding from my perch on the bus step, and my heart almost stopped beating. I'm sure things like this happen frequently in stadiums and arenas, but I felt in my heart, "Not today."

I knew when Shaq was safely aboard the bus the driver would take off, without me on it, but I had to do what my heart was telling me. I ran desperately, pushing my way through the crowd, to get to the boy. When I got to him, he and his mother were crying because he had missed his moment with Shaq. Time was running out.

I grabbed the boy's mother and father toward me and said, "Listen! I just saw what happened with your son. I'm an executive with the team, and I'm asking you to trust me and follow me if you can." They both gave me a puzzled look but nodded yes. I then reached down with both arms and gently scooped the fragile child up and started running to the bus. I heard the security guard yell, "All clear; move out!"

As I heard the guard yell those words, I ran up the steps onto the bus with the little boy still in my arms. I started down the aisle and all the players—including Shaq—knew exactly what I was doing. Shaq reached out for him and the other players gathered to sign his small sheet of paper. He not only got his autographs, but, for a short while in a crowded bus in New Jersey, he was a part of our team.

When it was time to go, Shaq gave him one last hug and handed him over to me. I walked down the steps of the bus to the two tearful parents. They offered me their sincere thanks, and as I wiped my tearful eyes, I offered mine.

~John Gabriel, former General Manager, Orlando Magic

Making Forgetting Unforgettable

The beauty of memory is that it still sees beauty when beauty has faded.
~Paul Boese

In the NBA, amazing things happen every day. LeBron James gets a triple-double whenever he wants, Dwayne Wade dunks over seven-footers like it's going out of style, and Tim Duncan hits turn-around jumpers with three to four guys guarding him every night. The league truly is filled with gifted athletes who do incredible things seven days a week.

But in the years I've worked in the NBA, I find the greatest memories are built on providing unique experiences for special fans. For some fans, coming to the game isn't just about the amazing performances by the world's most talented athletes. Those are just the bonuses. For some, coming to the game is about exhilaration, elation and the ability to forget about life's daily realities.

For a young father with a ten-year-old son, coming to a Sacramento Kings game meant forgetting about cancer, life, and even death.

I received a call from a colleague telling me about her friend, Kevin, a forty-one-year-old man who was in the final stages of lung cancer. He was a long-time Kings season ticket holder who had been unable to attend games for a while because of his illness. My colleague said that Kevin wished he could attend just one more Kings game with his son Zach before he passed away. So she asked if there was a way to get him tickets in seats that would accommodate his wheelchair, wife, son, father, cousin and hospice caregiver.

These simple requests are things the Kings owners, Joe and Gavin Maloof, always want to accommodate. I immediately contacted the strategic people in our organization who could make this happen. The evening that was provided for this family was an incredibly heartwarming experience for everyone involved. Although many observers may have believed the family members were the benefactors of this special evening, in reality, it was the people providing the experience who felt the greatest blessing.

Kevin's family was met at the VIP entrance, escorted into the building and through the player's tunnel to their special courtside seats. Zach was wide-eyed and beyond excited at the special treatment he and his family received. Little did he know that the courtside seats were just the beginning of his family's memorable evening.

During the first quarter, the family was visited by Big Mike, the Kings emcee, and Slamson, the Kings mascot, who delivered a special Kings prize pack with Kings hats and jerseys. Throughout the game, the family was treated like royalty. The smiles from Kevin, Zach, Kevin's wife, father and cousin were priceless. It was clear to everyone that a special memory was being made for this family.

After the game the family was escorted to the area outside the Kings locker room. Before long, Kings players came out to say hello. Kevin Martin was first, then came Ron Artest and members of the coaching staff. Each time someone came to say hello, Zach's eyes opened wider and wider. Before he knew it, Zach and his dad were being escorted into the locker room to meet the entire team.

Each player spent a few minutes talking to Kevin and Zach and everyone signed Zach's hat. The look of joy on this boy's face and the look of satisfaction on his dad's face was one of the most moving and memorable moments that the people making this experience possible had ever experienced. Kevin's wife, Chris, pulled us aside to express her heartfelt gratitude. She explained that the organization had provided so much more than tickets to a basketball game; it had provided a wonderful, positive lasting memory for her son to share with his father and for her to share with the two of them together. By the time the family left the arena, there was nary a dry eye among the people who helped provide this experience for this special family.

Ten days after this memorable evening, Kevin passed away. As friends and family gathered at the house, Zach made sure everyone saw his Kings autographed hat and listened to him detail the night when he and his dad were special Kings VIP guests.

For one night, a father forgot about his cancer. A son forgot about his future without a dad. And everyone who made it happen realized how blessed we are to provide unforgettable memories based on forgetting, even if only for a while.

~Donna Ruiz, VP Human Resources, Sacramento Kings

Be Careful What You Wish For

The problem with humility is that the moment that you discover
that you have it, you no longer do.
~Truman Capote

I was an advance scout for the Orlando Magic, and I was in New York working my first ever game at Madison Square Garden. I remember getting my schedule weeks earlier and marking that date with great anticipation. After all, this was historically one of basketball's biggest stages and "The Garden" was one of the few classic venues left in the NBA. All of the other arenas had been imploded and rebuilt.

I got there extra early that evening and took my own private tour. I had an all access pass and that night I used it very well. Just before game time, I went to get settled in my seat and began an evening of star gazing. Very quickly I spotted Andre Agassi, then Claudia Schiffer. Spike Lee was a regular and he was in his usual seat. Right among all of these stars in the front row was me! Throughout the game, during each time out or break, the cameras would zoom in on a star and they would show them on the big screen overhead. All night long, I would see everything from the biggest models to the hottest rappers and rock stars, actors and athletes; you name it they were all there.

While watching the screen with each break, the thought occurred to me, "I wonder what level of status it takes to be on that screen?" It really didn't matter, because in my mind I was soon to be a head coach in the NBA and I would be on that screen someday! You see, I really wanted to be on that screen like those other celebrities.

The night went on and I did my job and was working diligently when the New York Knicks ran a play that I had not seen before. This was unusual because I had watched the Knicks enough to know most everything they did. I began charting the action that took place on that particular play, looking down at my play sheet. As luck would have it, one of the players from the Knicks threw a pass that went errant and into the first row hitting a fan in the face. Me!

I can still remember the pain the ball had caused me physically. My nose was bleeding and my eyes filled with tears immediately. My glasses sat cock-eyed on my face and my hair was a mess. The physical pain soon became measurably less as my dream became my greatest fear. As I wiped the blood from my nose and the tears from my eyes, I looked up and saw the big screen. I did it! I was on the big screen! Normally as the stars are shown, the crowd cheers. When I was shown, the crowd (all in one corporate gasp) moaned, "OOOOHHHHH!"

I never made it as a star on the big screen and my fifteen minutes of fame were more like ten seconds of shame. Be careful what you wish for.

~Richie Hughes, former NBA Scout

95

The Long Road to the Final Four

It's not only important where you stand,
but it matters in which direction you are moving.
~Dr. Bill Bright

Bruce Seaton and Arthur Lee II live in different cities in the Los Angeles area. They are regular guys with regular jobs. One is white, one is black. Without basketball, they never would have met. Because of basketball, they spent hundreds of hours in the same car driving to college basketball games.

Both Bruce and Arthur have sons who were exceptional high school basketball players, Mark Seaton at Servite High in Anaheim and Arthur (Art) Lee III at North Hollywood High. Though not highly recruited nationally, each son played well enough to earn a basketball scholarship to Stanford University, both entering in 1995.

Stanford is a world-class academic institution, but as of 1995 Stanford's basketball history had been less than glittering. Stanford had not won a conference championship since 1963 and had made only three NCAA Tournament appearances in fifty-three years, with only one victory.

Parents of Stanford players, many from distant places like Michigan and Virginia, attended games infrequently. Airfare was expensive and it hurt to see the team lose. I currently broadcast

Stanford games on radio and I played at Stanford when wins did not exceed losses. My parents attended only one home game, my last.

So I was surprised, during the first two seasons of Seaton and Lee's college careers, seeing the same two men—one white and one black—seated in the player ticket section of the arena. I had a first conversation with Bruce Seaton, with Arthur Lee II standing nearby.

"Guess you guys spend a lot of time at LAX (airport)," I said as we started to discuss the fathers' travels to the games.

"Oh no," Bruce replied, "Arthur and I drive to every game."

"From Los Angeles?" I exclaimed. Los Angeles is nearly 400 miles south of Stanford's campus. "Do you drive up the day before? Where do you stay? How do you get time off from work?"

Seaton, who worked at the Port of Los Angeles, smiled. "Actually," he said, "we don't do hotels. On game day I do a half-day of work, then I go pick up Arthur and we drive up to Palo Alto for the game. We go Interstate 5 to California 152 to U.S. 101. After the game, we get in the car and drive back all night and go to work the next morning."

The Seaton and Lee car journeys up and down California became local legend. Most Stanford games are on Thursdays and Saturdays. Not only would Seaton and Lee drive Thursday for the Thursday night game and drive back for the Friday workday in L.A., they would repeat the roundtrip for the Saturday game.

And while the dads were spending hundreds of hours driving up and down California highways, the sons were starting down a long road as well—the NCAA "Road to the Final Four."

During the 1996-1997 season, Stanford made it to the NCAA Sweet Sixteen by defeating Oklahoma and Wake Forest in Tucson, Arizona. Against favored Wake Forest, Stanford rotated several players, including Mark Seaton, to defend All-American Tim Duncan. They then used a tip-in by Art Lee in the final seconds to secure an upset victory. Yes, Bruce Seaton's car made the 500-mile trip on Interstate 10 from Los Angeles to Tucson.

Though it did not win another game, that 1996-97 Stanford team became the first to reach the Sweet Sixteen since World War

II. So hopes were high for 1997-1998. Art Lee would be the starting point guard. Mark Seaton would be a key reserve. And Bruce Seaton's gasoline card would get a workout.

In the first weeks of the 1997-1998 season, Stanford had the greatest start in its basketball history. By mid-January Stanford had built an 18-0 record and a number four national ranking. And though losses would later stain Stanford's record, Stanford took a 26-4 record into the 1998 NCAA Tournament. The elder Seaton and Lee had never enjoyed the highways so much.

Stanford was awarded the number three seed in the 1998 NCAA Midwest Regional. Two wins in the opening weekend in Chicago would mean a trip to St. Louis for the regional semifinal and final. Seaton and Lee decided not to drive to Chicago—they would decide what to do if Stanford won the first two games.

Stanford won both opening weekend NCAA games. Meanwhile, the number one seed in the regional, Kansas, lost its second round game. One of four Cinderellas advancing in the Midwest Regional—Purdue, Rhode Island, Valparaiso and Stanford—would win two games in St. Louis and make it to the Final Four in San Antonio.

Back in southern California, Seaton pondered his St. Louis travel options. He could take Highway 15 north, then in Barstow go east on 40 and then in Oklahoma get on 44 northeast which goes straight into St. Louis. But what if it snowed? And driving required extra vacation days. So Seaton reluctantly decided to fly to St. Louis.

Stanford faced number two seed Purdue in the regional semifinal and won by eight. Meanwhile, due to connecting flight problems, Bruce Seaton had to take a bus from Kansas City to St. Louis and missed the game. As he walked into the St. Louis arena two days later for Stanford's regional final game versus Rhode Island, Seaton's vocalized preference for driving over flying to games was never louder.

But would Seaton and Stanford have another week of travel beyond this one? To get to San Antonio and the Final Four, Stanford would have to beat a Rhode Island team whose coach won the NCAA title three years earlier. Stanford had not been to a Final Four since 1942.

With one minute remaining in the 1998 Midwest Regional final, it seemed that the Stanford season—and Bruce Seaton's travels—would end. Rhode Island led by six points. All Stanford could do was quickly foul Rhode Island players and hope they missed free throws.

But then Art Lee made a three-point basket. Then, following a Rhode Island free throw, Lee made a brilliant pass leading to a Stanford lay-up. Stanford suddenly was down by only two. Then, after two Rhode Island free throws, Lee drove the length of the court for a basket and was fouled. He made the free throw. Stanford was now down just one with thirty-two seconds remaining.

On the ensuing Rhode Island backcourt inbound pass, Lee deflected the ball into the hands of teammate Mark Madsen, who dunked the ball and was fouled. Madsen made the free throw and with twenty-six seconds left Stanford was suddenly—incredibly—ahead by two points. Rhode Island could not answer thereafter, suffering a turnover and three missed free throws. Stanford won, with Lee hitting two free throws in the final seconds. The fathers screamed with joy.

Lee scored thirteen points in the final two minutes, the greatest individual Stanford basketball achievement ever. The improbable journeys of fathers and sons—Bruce and Mark Seaton, Arthur and Art Lee—had led to the ultimate destination, the Final Four.

Alas, Stanford lost to Kentucky—the eventual 1998 champion—in overtime in the national semifinal in San Antonio. But Art Lee scored twenty-eight points in the game and would grace the cover of *Sports Illustrated* the following year. And Mark Seaton played in that Kentucky game and was enshrined, briefly but forever, in CBS' *One Shining Moment* video highlight archive.

And one more time, dads Bruce Seaton and Arthur Lee were driving together in San Antonio, with thousands of miles and memories behind them.

~John Platz, Radio Announcer, Stanford Basketball (1988-Present) and Stanford Basketball Point Guard (1982-84)

96

Chillin' with the "Polar Bear"

The world hates change:
yet it is the only thing that has brought it progress.
~Charles F. Kettering

I never really dreamed of a college degree when I was playing basketball in high school. My only dream was to one day be playing in the NBA along with the guys I used to watch as a kid growing up in a predominantly white, affluent Baltimore suburb. Back then the stars of the Washington Bullets, Earl "the Pearl" Monroe, Gus Johnson and Wes Unseld, were my idols. I loved playing basketball and used to dream of competing against the Knicks in Madison Square Garden who were led by "Clyde" Frazier, Willis Reed, Dave DeBusschere and Bill Bradley.

My high school team was one of the top scoring teams in the state and I averaged eighteen points a game. My best friend, Reese Jennings, also played on that team and was a shooting guard who averaged twenty points himself. One of the colleges that recruited him was Morgan State in Baltimore. Morgan State was in the process of winning the NCAA Division II Championship that year with their star center, Marvin "The Human Eraser" Webster. Marvin was seven feet tall and averaged twenty points, twenty-two rebounds and eleven blocked shots. In 1975, he was the third pick of the NBA draft. Morgan State was a historically African-American college, and, although there were a few white football and lacrosse players there, they had never had a white basketball player.

My guidance counselor told Coach Nat Frazier that although I was white my best friend was black, and that if he was interested in both of us that I might be interested in playing basketball at Morgan State. Coach offered both of us tickets to a game at the Civic Center in Baltimore and the rest was history. The game drew a capacity crowd of 12,000 (more than the Bullets were drawing) and The Eraser was dominating a 6'11" center from Maryland Eastern Shore named Joe Pace. Joe later played for the Bullets and Celtics. Marvin was a junior and had one more year to go before turning pro.

Coach Frazier offered both Reese and me a full ride and in the fall of 1974, I enrolled at Morgan. I had no idea what I was in for. *The Baltimore Sun* ran a story, as did the local news channel, that Morgan State had recruited its first white basketball player, a 6'5" all-county player from Severna Park.

I loved every bit of my time at Morgan, living all four years on campus, the only white student to do so. The players were all very supportive and our team was very close. Although I did not play much my freshman year, I started as a sophomore and played quite a bit from then on. I was a co-captain along with Reese my senior year. My most memorable basketball experience was in 1977 when we won the MEAC Championship, defeating Howard University. To this day that is the only Morgan team to have won the league championship. Reese and I were starting at the guard positions the night we won. In three of my four years I was not only the lone "white guy" on the team, I was the only one in the league, which consisted of other historically black colleges.

I had a multitude of nicknames but they were all spoken more affectionately then in a derogatory sense. I was dubbed everything from "Whitey" to "Honkey" to "Hondo" to "Bird" (who was at Indiana State) to "O'Koren" (the star at UNC). But the one that many used was "The Polar Bear," given because the Morgan State mascot was the Golden Bear. The fans from the opposing schools would constantly try to rattle me with insults, but my teammates always showed me how to laugh it off... and it worked.

I received my degree from Morgan in 1979 and the education I received has been a springboard to a life blessed by God. I learned far more from my experiences on the basketball court than the subjects taught in class. I learned about culture, diversity, humility, perseverance and faith. The players and many students were like family to me. While at Morgan, a number of students shared their faith in Christ with me which led me to become a Christian in my junior year and that has had a tremendous impact on my life.

Today I am a vice president of sales for a medical device company and am also a volunteer chairman on the board of directors of Youth for Christ. I attend a few games each year along with my youngest son who loves the game and loves going to Morgan. My experience at Morgan State made me who I am today. I will be forever grateful to all those teachers, coaches, students, and players who helped shape my experience and who once called me "The Polar Bear."

~Jim Gorman, former Morgan State College player
and successful businessman

Life Lessons on Lottery Day

What we make is a living; what we give is a life.
~Winston Churchill

The most important date in the history of the Memphis Grizzlies franchise took place on May 22nd, 2007. The NBA Draft Lottery in "picturesque" Secaucus, New Jersey, was going to re-launch the Grizzlies' fortunes with the acquisition of one of two future NBA superstars—either Greg Oden or Kevin Durant. According to the hoop pundits Oden, the seven-foot man-child from Ohio State, was going to be the next Bill Russell and Durant, the 6'10" phenom from Texas, was destined to wear the mantle of Magic Johnson.

The Grizzlies finished the 2006-07 season with an NBA worst record of 22-60, thereby having the highest percentage chance (25%) of snagging the number one pick and reenergizing their future.

In my seven years in Memphis I never saw such a fanatical level of enthusiasm throughout the community. Fans who had drifted away from the franchise where dusting off their credit cards and check-books ready to re-enter the world of Grizzmania. At Draft Lottery watch parties throughout the community, fans were overflowing bars and restaurants waiting for the great Grizz moment.

I had just left a downtown location, which was rocking with several hundred Grizz fans, to go back to my office and watch this historic moment by myself. When Deputy Commissioner Adam Silver opened the envelope for the sixth position and showed the Milwaukee Bucks logo my heart stopped. This meant that we were not going to get either of the first two picks in the upcoming draft. We were dropping all the way to fourth.

I cursed the fates with a combination of expletives worthy of a drunken sailor and a Marine drill instructor. Then I remembered that my night wasn't finished. I straightened my tie, put on my suit jacket, and walked a few hundred feet down to our practice facility to participate in the second graduation of the senior class of the Grizzlies Academy.

Grizzlies Academy opened in 2003 for students fifteen to seventeen who are two years behind expected grade levels of the Memphis City school system. Small classes, tutors, a reading specialist, extended hours, a social worker, and a rigorous curriculum led by one of the state's top educators, Jane Walters, were put in place for the students to graduate in three years. When I walked up to the stage and saw the beaming smiles of pride on the faces of the fourteen graduates and their families, friends and teachers, I knew that our mission as a basketball team was more important than an errant ping-pong ball.

In the artificial world of pro sports and the funny money that rules our economies, watching these young leaders of tomorrow receive their diplomas exemplified that what we make is a living and what we give makes a life.

~Andy Dolich, former President of Business Operations,
Memphis Grizzlies

Being Useful

If one cannot be used, it only means one is useless.
~Dr. Maya Angelou

I have had a long and diverse career in basketball. I attended Wake Forest University and was the starting center for the Demon Deacons from 1968-71 after being named one of the top fifty high school players in the country in 1966-67. I was drafted out of college by the Cincinnati Royals (now the Sacramento Kings) in the 1971 NBA draft, and I played in forty-two games with the Royals during the 1971-72 season. I concluded my playing career overseas by playing seven seasons professionally in Belgium, France and Italy.

When the Charlotte Hornets started up in 1988, I was an original member of their broadcast team and moved with the club to New Orleans where I continue doing Hornets TV commentary. I have had a wide variety of experiences at every level of basketball, and have learned a lot of lessons along the way. One of these lessons stands out in bold relief.

After my pro days were over, I served as an academic advisor of athletics at Wake Forest. The local March of Dimes chapter was staging a fundraising dinner and asked me to help. The legendary Dr. Maya Angelou was an adjunct professor at Wake (in fact, she still is). The March of Dimes had written her to see if they could auction off a home-cooked dinner by Dr. Angelou at her house. Somehow the request was misdirected and they did not get an immediate response from her.

One of the committee members was aware that Dr. Angelou and I were friends and asked if I would intercede on their behalf. I agreed to do so, and I called Dr. Angelou to explain the situation and see if she would participate. Dr. Angelou agreed immediately.

Obviously I was delighted that I had been able to help, but now I was fumbling around for words of thanks. I said, "Dr. Angelou, I hope you don't feel I'm using our friendship on this request and taking advantage of you."

Dr. Angelou honestly replied, "Mr. McGregor, if one cannot be used, it only means one is useless."

How profound! When I called Dr. Angelou, I was not expecting one of the most valuable pieces of advice I have ever received, but I sure got it. I've never forgotten her words and they still impact me to this day.

~Gil McGregor, New Orleans Hornets TV Color Commentator

Somebody's Watching

Example is not the main thing in influencing others. It is the only thing.
~Dr. Albert Schweitzer

St. James Episcopal Church in Baton Rouge, Louisiana, gave me a big assist that helped launch my basketball career. I was an altar boy there at a time that I had been cut from my high school basketball team. The church gave me a great chance to play for its team in a church league.

To show my gratitude to the church, I always attempted to repay it in a positive way by setting a good example throughout my professional basketball career. It is no secret that young fans idolize professional athletes and imitate their moves. As I look back at my eleven-year pro career, there is one decision I wish could be erased from my "highlight reel."

I was in my second year of pro ball and I had just won the scoring championship. I was approached by an advertising agency that made me an offer to do a cigarette commercial.

"I don't smoke," I explained to them.

Their agent replied, "Athletes endorse products all the time and don't really use them."

I thought about the duplicity of lending my name to their campaign and thought about the young people who would be impacted by me.

"Do you want the money or not?" the agent prodded. "I can always get another star."

The money was attractive, so I reluctantly agreed to shoot the commercial. I dismissed the endorsement from my memory, but was reminded of the commercial when I reported to camp two years later. A rookie from the Midwest had joined the Hawks team. As we sat in the locker room, he reached into his pocket and pulled out a cigarette.

I asked quizzically, "You smoke?"

He explained, "Oh, yeah. I have ever since I saw your commercial on TV. I figured, 'If it's good enough for Bob Pettit, it's good enough for me.' So I started smoking."

The revealing discussion caused me to feel like my 6'9" frame was shrinking to about three inches. I was stunned by the reality of the influence that I had on this young man. Sometimes, you just don't realize your influence on other people.

That cigarette commercial was one ad campaign that I will never forget. I've learned to always be a positive example because, more times than not, somebody's watching.

~Bob Pettit, former St. Louis Hawk,
one of the 50 Greatest Players in NBA history

The Crash that Changed My Life

Therefore if any man be in Christ, he is a new creature:
old things are passed away; behold, all things are become new.
~2 Corinthians 5:17

In 1989, I was the Deputy Commissioner of the Continental Basketball Association, which at the time was the minor league system for the NBA. I had worked for one of the league's teams in various capacities, including marketing director and radio play-by-play announcer. Just three months earlier, my wife Diane and I had moved to Denver, where the CBA office was located.

On the morning of July 19th, I got up early to catch a seven A.M. flight from Denver to Chicago. I was traveling with my boss and great friend, Jay Ramsdell, who was the commissioner of the league. Jay and I were set to fly to Chicago, then make a connection in Chicago and go on to Columbus, Ohio, to attend the CBA's college draft. We never got there.

Jay and I got the last two seats aboard United Airlines Flight 232. It was a jumbo jet with 296 people on board. Completely full. I end up in row 23, Jay in 30. There are thirty-seven rows in a DC-10. We took off for Chicago under perfect weather conditions—sunshine, no wind, eighty-three degrees.

About halfway to Chicago—exactly an hour into the flight—at 37,000 feet and over northwest Iowa, a catastrophic event took place within the aircraft that eventually led to the death of 112 people. The number two engine, which sits in back and on top of the plane, exploded. The sound and the feel ripped through the cabin and the plane immediately began to lose altitude.

My first thought was that a bomb had gone off. Panic seemed to consume the cabin. Dishes flew from tray tables while the sounds of screams followed the sound of the explosion. I figured we were going down, that this was it for everyone on board. I reasoned we would eventually hit the ground and all of us would be dead very soon. I held onto my armrests as tight as I could, fighting both the drop and the oncoming nausea that follows heavy turbulence.

After about thirty seconds, I could feel the plane start to come out of its drop. We were starting to ease back up. And level off.

The panic slowly began to subside and we waited very anxiously for someone to inform us as to what had happened and what sort of predicament we were now in. That came about ten minutes later when our cockpit captain came on the public address system. He informed us that the number two engine had exploded, causing "a lot of damage to the aircraft." He later told us that we had been given a directive to make an emergency landing in Sioux City, Iowa, and that we were to listen to the flight attendants as they would take us through the emergency landing procedures.

The captain made sure we understood very, very clearly, that we were in trouble. Because there was so much collateral damage to the plane as a result of the engine explosion, the cockpit crew had very little control of the plane and knew there was simply no way to land the huge aircraft safely. "I'm not going to kid anybody," said our captain. "This is going to be rough." We knew it would not be an emergency landing. It would be a crash landing.

At 3:59 P.M., Flight 232 made contact with the edge of a runway at the Sioux Gateway Airport at 255 miles per hour. A normal DC-10 landing is about 125 mph at touchdown. We also hit at a nineteen degree angle, which meant the right wing hit first.

The initial impact was nearly indescribable. Bodies were thrown about the cabin in the first couple of seconds. Some were still strapped to their chairs. Others were thrown from their seats. Smoke and fire started to fill the cabin. I remained in the brace position the flight attendants had shown us. I held the seatback in front of me with all the strength I could muster.

The plane then began a long, fast slide. About the time I thought we might actually coast to a stop, the plane began to flip forward into an almost cartwheel type motion.

After we flipped over, the plane, unknown to me, began to break apart. I ended up in a piece that was rows 19 through 28, a fairly small section compared to some of the others. The piece I ended up in flipped over once, then slid upside-down and backwards for another 4,000 feet. We finally came to an abrupt halt in a cornfield next to the airport. We had traveled more than a mile after hitting the ground.

When we stopped, I was hanging upside-down in my chair, my seat and seatbelt still completely intact. Unlike many of the people around me, I never lost consciousness. I felt no pain and saw no blood on my clothes. So, I unbuckled and slipped onto the ceiling.

Eventually, I made my way to the back of plane, away from the heaviest smoke. I passed several passengers who I knew had not survived, who had died on impact. There was no choice but to move on, away from the smoke. I found myself moving toward those who were moving themselves, doing my best to get them away from the smoke and fire.

After a few minutes, I saw an opening, and people moving through it, to the outside. It was where the tail section had broken off and was easy to get through once I got back there and could see it. After assisting several survivors through the opening and into the cornfield, I ducked out myself, only to find myself back in a moment later.

I heard a baby's cry. The next thing I knew I was back inside the wreckage. I didn't weigh any risks. I didn't think it through. In fact, I didn't think about anything. I just reacted. It just happened. I heard a baby crying and before I could figure out exactly what was going on, I was outside the wreckage with a baby in my arms.

Eleven-month-old Sabrina Michaelson survived the crash along with her parents and two older brothers. They were reunited some forty-five minutes later when her parents found her in the arms of a woman I handed her to.

But 112 other people were not as fortunate. One of those fatalities was my boss and great friend, Jay Ramsdell.

Besides the questions, "How did you ever get back on a plane again?" or "How do you still fly after surviving a plane crash?" I think the most often asked question of me is: "How has the event changed you?" I can easily give a one word reply: "Completely!"

I am simply not the same man I was before the plane crash. I never, ever thought I would say this but I am, in many ways, a better person because of Flight 232. I battled survivor's guilt, tried to fight off anger and went to war with depression. Then, about a year after the crash and because of the crash, I became a Christian, which is the greatest thing that has ever happened to me, the greatest decision I have ever made.

Jesus Christ has completely changed me and the priorities in my life. And all for the better.

With the inner strength that can only be gained through a relationship with Christ, I got back into broadcasting, which I had dabbled in for years before the crash, and eventually was fortunate enough to make it to the NBA. I believe He has allowed me to move from tragedy to triumph.

Jesus means it when he says in the Bible—"Behold, I make all things new."

~Jerry Schemmel, Broadcaster, Denver Nuggets

You Leave the Biggest Footprints Walking the Second Mile

Nothing will more effectively inspire you to change
than having a beautiful example to follow.
~Anonymous

In March of 2002, I was coaching at Bishop Ready High in Columbus, Ohio. It would be my last year of high school coaching before going to Denison College. We had a good year and played for the state championship. We lost in the finals by the score of 54-51 before 15,000 fans at the Ohio State University arena.

We were disappointed about the loss, but still realized we had a memorable season. About a month after the tough loss, I was attending a dinner with my wife when a woman, who appeared to be in her forties, walked over and said to me, "Aren't you the coach at Ready High?"

I replied, "Yes."

She then said, "My father, who was in his eighties, loved your team. He'd been sick for several years, but he went to one of your games and fell in love with your team. He was very impressed with the way they played—so hard as a unit and they were always encouraging each other. My dad had cancer, but insisted on seeing all of your games. Two weeks after the state tournament ended he died, but he passed away happy."

I now have a whole new outlook on the impact that basketball can have in our country. What is done out on the court is exactly what human beings are capable of doing in life—sacrificing, sharing, contributing and showing individual effort for a collective good.

I never met that man, but that experience really impacted me deeply. You don't ever know who's watching you; you don't ever know the effect your actions are having on others. In a world where people try to give six hours of work for eight hours of pay, a group of "second-milers" always leaves an imprint.

~Bob Ghiloni, Head Coach, Denison College, OH

Chapter
11

Inside Basketball

Overtime Points

Hoopster-in-Chief

Leadership is the wise use of power.
Power is the capacity to translate intention into reality and sustain it.
~Warren Bennis

In early May 2008, then-Senator Barack Obama came to Chapel Hill, North Carolina, to rally support for his presidential campaign. He spoke that evening to a large crowd at the Dean E. Smith Center. He was scheduled to stay overnight in Chapel Hill, so he asked the athletic department if they could set up a pick-up game for the next morning so he could get some exercise. We obliged and, according to his schedule, set the game up for seven a.m.

We were a little apprehensive regarding the potential turnout from our basketball team. Getting college students to wake up and be anywhere at seven a.m. is nearly impossible, especially since then-Senator Obama's visit coincided with final exams. To my surprise, the entire team showed up and was ready to play.

They hooped it up for an hour and fifteen minutes. For much of the time, then-Senator Obama was guarded by Jack Wooten, a 6'2" walk-on who scored a grand total of five points the previous season. Jack was all over Obama and blocked a couple of his shots and even stole the ball from him. Head coach Roy Williams, who was there watching the scrimmage, yelled to Jack after the second block, "Jack, that's the first guy you've guarded all year...let him score!"

Afterwards, everyone got together for a memorial photo. Obama, tongue-in-cheek, said to Jack, "Secret Service came about this close to taking you out!" Coach Williams added the final touch, "Jack, you've just assured yourself a lifetime of IRS audits!"

Obama looks bigger on TV, but he's about 6'2" and he is very slender. But, as we were all witness to, he has a huge presence and commands the room, whether it's at the podium or on the hardwood.

~Steve Kirschner, Associate Athletic Director
for Athletic Communications, University of North Carolina

The Fist

If you don't think cooperation is necessary,
watch what happens to a wagon when a wheel comes off.
~Will Rogers

I grew up in Reston, Virginia, and accepted a scholarship at Duke University to play basketball for Coach Mike Krzyzewski. "Coach K" is a legendary coach and a terrific teacher. One of his most poignant metaphors is "the fist," an illustration of the importance of teamwork in basketball.

Coach K would hold his hand up with the five fingers outstretched, and he would tell us that these five fingers represent a basketball team. He explained that the five fingers stand for: trust, communication, collective responsibility, caring and pride. Coach would say, "As long as those fingers are out-stretched you don't have much of a punching device, but pull them together into a fist and you have a lethal weapon. Lift up one finger and you lose a lot of power; lift up a second finger and you've lost all the strength. So, just like a fist, a basketball team must merge all five closely together."

When the time out huddles at Duke were concluded and it was time to go back on the court, we would never collectively shout, "Win!" or "Defense!" but rather, "Together!" And, we always lifted our fists together as a reminder of the importance of teamwork.

~Grant Hill, former Duke University star and NBA player

The Wrong Basket

Do not think you are on the right road just because it is a well-beaten path.
~Dr. Billy Graham

Many people will say, "It doesn't matter what you believe or who you believe in, just as long as you are sincere." A person, however, can be sincerely wrong.

A few years ago, our church built a Family Life Center. Immediately the men wanted to start a men's basketball league in which they wanted me—their pastor—to participate.

Due to bad knees I had not played competitive basketball in five years. However, believing it would be good for fellowship, I agreed to play.

The first game was both comical and frustrating. I suppose since I was the pastor, they felt I should be the point guard. My one job was to bring the ball up the court and pass it to another player. That player would then turn to the basket and shoot—no matter where he was on the floor. The player could have eight people hanging on him (three from his own team) and still throw up a shot. After the first half, I had not taken one shot.

In my frustration, I decided I was going to shoot the first time I touched the ball in the second half. After the ball was in-bounded, a shot was taken; one of my teammates hauled down the rebound and immediately passed it to me on the baseline. I was wide open. Catching the ball fifteen feet from the basket, I quickly adjusted my hands on the ball to shoot. As I shot the ball and felt it gracefully come off my fingers, I knew it would go in. Suddenly I heard one of my teammates scream, "No!"

I thought, "How arrogant! He must have shot ten times in the first half without scoring and he is telling me not to shoot?"

A great sense of satisfaction rushed through me as the ball went perfectly through the rim, swishing through the net. Only one problem—I forgot that the teams switched goals at the half. I shot at the wrong basket. I had just scored two points for the other team.

No one was more sincere than I was. But I was sincerely wrong.

~Dr. Dwayne Mercer, Senior Pastor,
First Baptist Church, Oviedo, FL

A Stitch in Time
Didn't Save Speedy

Time is a versatile performer.
It flies, it marches on, heals all wounds, runs out, and will tell.
~Bennett Cerf

I was coaching at LaSalle University and we played at Villanova before a standing room only crowd. I called a time out, and when I bent to address my team, my pants ripped. At halftime, my wife interceded on my behalf and sewed the pants. She was sewing while I was in the locker room in my underwear speaking to the team. My wife ran out of thread so she used a safety pin to close the pants seam.

Early in the second half, I leaped, heard a ripping sound, felt a breeze, and something was jabbing me. The pants had re-split; the safety pin popped, and was sticking me in the posterior. It was a monster rip, clearly evident to the Villanova Wildcats fans who happily chanted, "Speedy ripped his pants."

As one might imagine, I got a ton of exposure on the blooper reels.

~Speedy Morris, Philadelphia area High School Coach and former
Collegiate Coach

A Champion Who Gives Ten Percent

The world is full of two kinds of people, the givers and the takers.
The takers eat well — but the givers sleep well.
~From God's Little Devotional Journal for Women

Ike was a little-used forward during his junior year. When I took over the SMU program his senior year, we needed someone to score and rebound for us. I saw him in individual instruction when I got the job and I felt he could do those things for us. I told people in the fall that Ike could have played for me at UNC. They thought I was "blowing smoke." There was one problem — Ike didn't believe in himself. He didn't have the confidence.

During the first half of the year, you could see it in his eyes. My staff and I kept pushing him and encouraging him to "take over" games, but he seemed reluctant. We designed plays for him and kept going to him and going to him. Finally it clicked! Ike started to dominate games. He had thirty points at Rice! He had twenty-one points against Memphis! Ike finished with ten double-doubles. Over the final seven league games, he averaged twenty points and eleven rebounds and ended up making third-team All-Conference USA!

After the season, it was evident that Ike was going to get paid to play basketball. He and his family never could have imagined that before. It was exciting to think about his basketball future.

One night Ike and I were leaving an SMU function in San Antonio and as we walked toward his car—a beat up compact car with over 100,000 miles on it—I asked him, "Ike, what are you going to do with the money you are going to make?" I assumed he was going to say, "Buy a car, Coach!"

Ike replied, "I am going to tithe to my church!"

Wow! This is why I coach!

~Matt Doherty, Head Basketball Coach,
Southern Methodist University

Got Game

Experience teaches slowly, and at the cost of mistakes.
~James A. Froude

I was a rookie with the Utah Jazz and we were playing the Chicago Bulls at home. Early in the game, there was a long rebound that I scooped up. I headed for the basket thinking I had an easy lay-up. From out of nowhere, Michael Jordan was there and blocked it from behind.

A photographer got a good shot of the play just before the block and, afterwards, gave me a copy. Two years later, I was with Sacramento and the Bulls came to town. At the shoot-around, I asked Michael to sign the photo and he did.

Later that season, we went to Chicago and the same thing happened—a long rebound which I got and then took off for a lay-up. Again, Michael blocked it and knocked me to the floor.

While I was down on the ground yelling at the referee for a call, Michael stood over me and smiled, "I'll sign that one, too!"

~Jim Les, former NBA player and current Head Coach
at Bradley University

The Butler Did It

If you find a path with no obstacles,
it probably doesn't lead anywhere.
~Frank A. Clark

In many old books and movies, when detectives solved crimes, it often turned out that "the butler did it."

Well, to tell the truth, when it came to juvenile crime in my hometown of Racine, Wisconsin, when an accuser claimed, "The Butler did it," chances are they were right. My name is Caron Butler. I am a 6'7" forward for the Washington Wizards today, but "yesterday" I was making more of a name for myself on police rap sheets than I was on scoring sheets.

When I was fourteen, I was caught with drugs and an unloaded gun. I was sentenced to six months in an adult detention center and was then transferred to the Ethan Allen School for Boys in Wales, Wisconsin. I landed in solitary my first week there because of a fight I had with a rival gang member who had challenged me.

It was at Ethan Allen when I began to develop my game; it was also the place where I decided that I needed to turn my life around when I saw my mother cry during one of her visits with me. You never want to make your mother cry.

I spent a total of fifteen months in jails. A lot of criminals "use" their time in jail to become better criminals, figuring out how not to get caught. My goal after I was released from jail was to learn how to become a better person.

I became involved with an at-risk youth center in Racine, and that got me involved in AAU basketball. Then I attended the University of Connecticut for two years before I entered the NBA draft.

I play with intensity because my past drives me to do it. Every time I step onto the court, I have something to prove. I'm "hooping" for everybody in Racine who never made it out of the 'hood.

~Caron Butler, NBA Forward, Washington Wizards

A Polite Spike

Personality can open doors, but only character can keep them open.
~Elmer G. Letterman

Before every Knick game, I would go to Madison Square Garden to prepare the press tables and make sure that all the stats were available for the media. There was this really nice, polite young man who would be there, too. He would ask for the stats and ask if there were any better seats than the ones that he had. I usually knew where there might be some empty seats, and, when I could, I would move him down to a better spot.

Red Holzman, the general manager of the Knicks, once saw me doing this and asked why I would go out of my way to help this no-name kid. I replied that he was a sweet young man who loved basketball, the Knicks in particular. From that point on, when Red had an extra ticket he would give it to me to give to our "friend."

That "no-name" friend went on to become a film director and the most well-known Knicks fan in the world: Spike Lee.

~Gwynne Bloomfield-Pike, former Secretary, New York Knicks

How Dry I Am!

*Get the right perspective. When Goliath came up against the Israelites, the
soldiers all thought: 'He's so big we can never kill him.' David looked up at
the same giant and said, 'He's so big, I can't miss!'*
~SermonIllustrations.com

The Amherst (Massachusetts) College men's basketball team
was 11-1 and ranked number one in the Northeast region.
After a lackluster performance and a loss on a Saturday afternoon, my two sons (Matthew, four, and Michael, two) wanted to visit
me in the locker room. I told my wife to give me five to ten minutes
with the team first.

When my sons came into the room, you could hear a pin drop.
Most of the players, still in uniform, were sitting by their lockers
crushed by this tough defeat. My boys sat alongside me as I sat on a
bench in the middle. The younger one, Michael, swung his feet and
said loudly, "Dad, what's the matter?"

I told him that I was sad.

Michael swung his feet again and said, "Why?"

I told my son that my team had lost a big game and hadn't played
very well.

Michael swung his feet again and said, "Well, you know what?"

Trying to remain patient, I said, "What?"

My son, with all of the players anxiously awaiting an answer,
said proudly, "My pants are dry!"

The players all began to chuckle and what was a dismal mood had been broken and Amherst was right back on track.

It's all about perspective!

~Dave Hixon, Head Men's Basketball Coach, Amherst College

Follow the Bouncing Metaphors

We all experience bad bounces and turnovers along the way,

There are air-balls, and losses, and flagrant fouls that happen every day.
We can't allow these things to defeat us and keep us from our goals,
Rebounding is the key here, with all our hearts and souls.
Get assists from fellow players, cooperate as a team,
Work your plan together to create a winning scheme.
That loose ball has your name on it, out there on the floor,
Dive after it, get those floor burns, and then for an encore...
Take a charge, lead the break, drive right on down the lane,
For you have your game-face on and know "no pain, no gain,"
Jump up, rally and get on the ball,
Face your foes confidently by giving it your all.
Be committed as a team, stay focused, in the zone,
Together we can do it, you are not alone,
Press on and persevere, this is my request,
Execute your game plan and always do your best.
As winners in the game of life, before our final score,
We must live and love and swish our dreams by always giving more.

~Ken Hussar, Speaker and Musician, Lancaster, PA

The Pistol
and the Hawks

Men are equal; it is not birth but virtue that makes the difference.
~Voltaire

I was there when the Atlanta Hawks signed Pistol Pete Maravich to his huge first contract in 1970. It was a big deal, as he was supposed to be the "great white hope" who would fill up the seats even if the team wasn't very good. As you might imagine, the Hawks' primarily black team wasn't exactly thrilled that this untried kid was getting more ink than the likes of Joe Caldwell, Bill Bridges, Walt Bellamy, Walt Hazzard, and Paul Silas put together.

Training camp began and it was a disaster. Pete could shoot and he could pass but his defense was non-existent; he reverted to his college one-on-one philosophy far too often. The racial tension on the team was very high. The Pistol wasn't a very popular fellow with his peers.

Then a funny thing happened: the guys got to know Pete Maravich. They discovered, to their amazement, that this seemingly cocky kid was really scared to death of the situation and that he was a really nice guy. Within a year he still couldn't play much defense, but his teammates saw how hard he tried and their dislike turned from grudging respect to actually liking and then loving him.

Race was forgotten. They saw Pete Maravich as a man and

he did the same with them. Pete was an exceptional kid, but the aforementioned teammates were great players and great people, too.

Both "sides" looked beyond color and liked what they saw. Why can't we all do that?

~Skip Caray, former Atlanta Braves Broadcaster

Tommy Gun Shoots Fifty-Two

The point of living and of being an optimist,
is to be foolish enough to believe the best is yet to come.
~Peter Ustinov

Tom Heinsohn, the former Holy Cross and Boston Celtic great, was considered the best college basketball player in the country his senior year at Holy Cross. That year a strong Holy Cross team hosted a very weak Boston College quintet in the Worcester (Massachusetts) auditorium. It was a grand night for the Cross and Heinsohn. He broke the auditorium scoring record with fifty-two points as Holy Cross trounced the B.C. Eagles. As a sophomore on that B.C. squad I was a very unhappy witness, as I was guarding Heinsohn.

Some fifteen years later while working for *Forbes* magazine in Chicago I happened to bump into Heinsohn as we were waiting to be seated for dinner in a popular Loop restaurant. I mentioned that I had attended the game when he set the auditorium record. He broke into a grin and allowed that he had played well that night. His grin got bigger when I agreed that he did, indeed, play well and that I should know as I was the guy guarding him.

He hesitated a moment and then surprised me by saying, "I have thought of you often since then."

Intrigued, I asked, "Why?"

Still grinning, he said, "I had hopes of you making the pros so you could guard me all the time and I could score fifty-two points every night!"

~Jack Harrington, former Boston College Basketball Team Captain

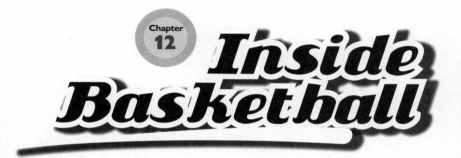

Chapter 12

Inside Basketball

A Final Word from Pat Williams and Family

Great Advice for Athletes and Anyone Pursuing a Goal

As you have read this wide range of stories coming from basketball people at every level of the sport, I am sure you have been as inspired and motivated as I have. I have noticed some common themes running through the different accounts, all of which we can apply to our own lives. Here are the key points to consider:

1. **Dreams** — Walt Disney once said, "If you can dream it, you can do it," and then added, "Somehow, I can't believe there are any heights that can't be scaled by a man who knows the secrets of making dreams come true." All of these people had big dreams in their lives and were not afraid to take action to make them come true.

2. **Preparation** — UCLA coaching legend John Wooden

stated, "Failing to prepare is preparing to fail." He said, "I was seldom once off my seat during the game. I'd tell them, 'Don't look over at me; I prepared you during the week, now do your job.'" How prepared are you every day to do your job?

3. **Focus**—In the special moments discussed in this book, the authors achieve their goals because of an intense focus—a concentration—on their objectives. As Arnold Palmer said, "Concentration comes out of a combination of confidence and hunger." From Chris Paul to Luiza Osborne, their intense focus led to personal successes and memorable moments.

4. **Passion**—Some people call it enthusiasm, others call it energy, but at the end of the day we're all talking about the same thing: finding joy and satisfaction in our pursuit of a goal. Nobody said it better than NFL coaching legend Don Shula, "The thing that drives all real success is passion and enthusiasm for what you do."

5. **Hard Work**—It is essential that in order to be successful you have to work at it. There is no substitute to putting in the effort to be your best. As many of these stories demonstrate, hard work is a crucial component of success.

6. **Taking Responsibility**—Only you can determine your attitude and how you respond to difficult situations. Take responsibility for your actions and your attitudes, and work to improve them every day.

7. **Setting Specific Goals**—One of my favorite stories in the book is from Jackie Stiles about her pursuit

of "1,000 makes a day." She established her goal and stayed committed to it. As she focused on her objective, greatness resulted and she eventually earned a job playing basketball in the WNBA.

8. **Perseverance**—Lance Armstrong stated, "Pain is temporary. Quitting lasts forever." Quitters do not achieve success. In order to be your best, you have to get back up every time you are knocked down.

9. **Deal with Adversity**—Some of the special moments in the book were the results of people overcoming a personal adversity. Whether it was cancer or a mental disability, forgetting the words to a song or remembering a fallen friend, each person found a way to accept the situation and to eventually triumph. As Michael Jordan said, "I can accept failure. Everyone fails at something. But I cannot accept not trying."

10. **Positive Attitude**—Figure skater Scott Hamilton observed, "The only handicap in life is a bad attitude." All of the people in this book took control of their attitudes, had a positive outlook, and were able to reach their dreams.

11. **Pay Attention to the Little Things**—Cal Ripken remembered, "My dad said, 'You take care of all the little things, you'll never have a big thing to worry about.'" As many people in this book explained from their basketball-related experiences, being good at the little things is often the difference between winning and losing.

12. **Confidence**—Confidence can come from many places—hard work, natural talent, teammates—but

it has to be there. Without confidence in yourself, it is very difficult to succeed. Chicago Bulls star Ben Gordon feels the same way, "I never think I'm going to miss. The guy who's not scared to miss should be the one to take the shot."

13. **Strive for Perfection** — Tiger Woods said, "I'm always striving to get better... and in golf, you never get there, you never get to perfection." Perfection may be unattainable, but successes happen in the pursuit of ideals.

14. **Welcome Competition** — Your competition may be an obstacle to your goal, but it's the competition that makes you better. Embrace your competition and use it to your advantage.

15. **Be Self-Motivated** — No one can do it for you. You have to get up, take action and will things to happen. There is no such thing as luck.

16. **Desire/Determination/Drive** — Michael Jordan remembered an experience he had before the 1992 Olympics, "I saw some Dream Teamers dogging it before the Olympics. I looked at them and knew what separates me from them." If you want to be your best and succeed in life, you have to have desire that drives your very existence.

17. **Courage** — Fighter pilot Eddie Rickenbacker said, "Courage is doing what you are afraid to do. There is no courage unless you're scared." So many people in this book faced some frightening situations and came out on top because of their courage.

18. **Team** — Phil Jackson reads Rudyard Kipling's poem *The Law of the Jungle* to his teams before the start of every play-off. The poem ends with the great line, "The strength of the pack is the wolf, and the strength of the wolf is the pack." In each story, no one succeeded without the help of others. It takes a total team effort to win. You must think team-first to achieve your goals.

> ~Pat Williams,
> Senior Vice President,
> Orlando Magic

It's Not the Copa, But...

I write the songs that make the whole world sing...
~Bruce Johnston

Apple bobbing, best costume, and pumpkin-pie-eating contests were all on my Halloween promotions agenda for the Philadelphia 76ers-New York Knicks game in October, 1974. As general manager of the Sixers, I was busy tweaking the details of the fanfare when my phone rang. Barry Abrams, a record promoter who also worked part-time at 76ers games, was on the line.

"I'm working with a terrific young recording artist who has a new song," Barry said. "Could you play it at the game tonight, Pat?" he requested.

"We don't usually do things like that," I responded, "but have him bring me the tape before the game and I'll do what I can." I ended the call and returned to attending to the details of the fan activities.

At six P.M., prior to the game, a long-haired young man approached me and said, "Mr. Williams? Barry Abrams said I should see you. I brought my tape." He handed me a box with a reel-to-reel tape inside.

I then recalled my conversation with Abrams and said, "Do you really want your music played here with our poor acoustics?"

He said, "I have thousands of these tapes and I have been taking them to radio stations, sporting events, dances, birthday parties, any place where people congregate. I want people to hear my music because I know that if they hear it, they'll buy it."

I instructed him to take the tape to Joe up in the sound booth, and I quickly returned to my game-night preparations and the half-time promotions. The arena filled, the Sixers and Knicks took the court, and the game was on.

During a time out, a song was played. It was a nice, easy-listening love ballad. When the song ended, there was light applause, and I thought, "Oh, the guy brought his mom and sisters for support."

About a month later, I heard the song again. The radio deejay announced, "That's "Mandy" by Barry Manilow." That skinny, long-haired young man had a monster hit on his hands and was on his way to stardom.

Push, pursue, and persevere to make your dreams come true.

~Pat Williams, Senior Vice President, Orlando Magic

A Bird's Eye View

It's the willingness to climb mountains that gives one the view.
~Jon Winokur

When the Orlando Magic started their first season as an expansion team in 1989, I was twelve years old. It was a thrill to serve as a Magic ball boy starting that season and for the next six years. There was a ton of excitement in that first season, but it really reached the heights when the Boston Celtics came to town for the first time to play the Magic. Larry Bird was going to play at the Orlando Arena!

I had always heard that Bird would get to the arena hours before his teammates to work alone on his shooting. I got out of school a little bit early so I could be at the arena by three P.M. to see Bird work out. I got dressed and hurried out to the floor. The lights were off, but I could hear the thump-thump-thump of a basketball. Sure enough, there was Larry Bird shooting all by himself.

I crept over to the basket where Larry was practicing and just watched him. He finally missed one and I hustled over to retrieve it and threw it back to him. I continued to rebound the few shots he missed.

Larry said to me, "Hey, kid. Can you shoot?"

As my voice cracked, I bravely replied, "Of course."

He said, "Let's play H-O-R-S-E."

I was numb. It's one thing to rebound for Larry Bird. It's another to play H-O-R-S-E with him.

Larry said, "Are you good for five dollars?"

"Sure," I said.

To no one's surprise, he made his shots and I missed mine. Larry said, "Pay up!"

I grinned and shrugged, "I don't have any money."

Larry gave me a stern look and then just smiled.

That whole game I was sky high. It was enough just having the Celtics in town for the first time, but I couldn't believe that I had just played H-O-R-S-E with "Larry Legend." The next morning, I saw the front page of the *Orlando Sentinel*. There was a big color photo of me firing up a shot with Larry Bird looking on.

That experience was twenty years ago, but it's a memory that will last a lifetime.

~Bobby Williams, former Orlando Magic Ball Boy

I'm Taking You with Me

Nothing will more effectively inspire you to change than having a beautiful
example to follow.
~Dr. Joyce Brothers

Since Dad was working for the Philadelphia 76ers when I came along, it felt like I was born in the Spectrum. I even rode down Broad Street in the victory parade after the Sixers won the NBA Championship in 1983. My life has been surrounded by professional basketball for as long as I can remember.

In the summer of 1986, as Dad led the way in bringing pro basketball to Orlando, I cheered his leap of faith that moved us south. In fact, I helped name the team. Dad recalls that when we first visited Orlando when I was seven years old, in wide-eyed wonder I said, "This place is magic!" Dad ran with that comment and it became the inspiration for the team's name. I remember fighting back tears as I watched the Orlando Magic score their first season victory against the Detroit Pistons in 1989. I was so proud. "This is my dad's doing!"

I have sung the National Anthem in Orlando's Amway Arena more times than I can remember. I've accompanied Dad to several NBA All-Star Weekends where I got to "hang" with the likes of Michael Jordan, Charles Barkley, and Shaq. Yes, it has been an exciting life!

So on a warm July evening in 2007, I fought back tears as I

sat with my dad sharing a bittersweet dinner at a restaurant—the occasion was one I had dreaded for weeks. It was the night I would say farewell to my beloved Dad. My car was packed to the brim. The next morning, I'd be on my way to Nashville, my first big move away from home. For as long as I can remember, I've dreamed of becoming a professional singer. The time had finally come for me to grab that dream by the throat.

As you may have guessed by now, Dad and I are as close as a father/daughter duo can get. I don't do much without seeking his opinion, wisdom, guidance, and counsel. At the age of twenty-eight, I've finally realized an important truth I wish I'd gotten through my head a long time ago—Dad is always right!

When I was a little girl, he was my hero. Now that I'm grown—well, he's still my hero—I have developed an unbelievably deep respect for this man who has taught me everything I know. As I get older and reflect on my childhood, I realize that just about everything I do and say is a result of what he has ingrained in me. Yes, this goodbye dinner was going to be tough.

It only seemed fitting that before leaving home, I tell my Dad how I felt about his influence in my life. Knowing my tendency to dissolve into a puddle of tears when I mix emotion with speech, I decided to tell him how I felt in a card.

"Daddy," it began, and I immediately saw that familiar face Dad makes when he's getting choked up—the tears glistening in the corners of his eyes, the visible gulp when he swallows. "As I begin this journey on my own, I want you to know that it's because of you that I feel prepared." Then I went on to list all of the major life lessons I've heard from him since I was a little girl.

By now the tears were flowing freely as he read his own words I had written back to him. It's the wisdom he has passed down, and I rely on it for my decision-making every single day.

By the time he'd finished reading, the staff at the restaurant was bringing out buckets and mops to wipe up all the tears. It was such a thrill for me to be able to reassure him that all his years of teaching, prompting, pushing, pulling, and non-stop cheerleading had paid off.

The next morning, I stopped by for one last hug, kiss, and "be careful on the highway" pep talk from Dad. Neither of us wanted the moment to end, but after another round of tears, Dad finally said, "Go! Get out of here; I can't handle any more crying!"

At long last Nashville-bound, following the highway through the mist I couldn't seem to get out of my eyes, all I could think about was the impact Dad has had on my life.

One night I sat down to write a song about my experience of leaving home. The words and emotion came pouring out, giving birth to a song called "Taking You With Me." Everywhere I've sung it, it's the one number that grabs the audience — whether it's a single listener or a roomful of people.

But it's really just a glimpse into my heart where you'll see reflected my father's influence. It follows me wherever I go.

Dad, I am so grateful for the priceless wisdom you have passed on to me. From the NBA basketball courts to the Nashville recording studios, I will carry you in my heart for the rest of my life. I dedicate this song to you:

There's a cardboard box in the corner of my room
Reminding me of all that's left to do
I've packed for days and I'm all worn out
I've cried my tears and faced my doubts
And I've got my dreams firmly in view
How do I pack all these memories?
I know it's time, but I look at you and it's so hard to leave
I'm taking you with me, no matter where I go or what I do
I'm taking you with me, every day I'll think of
          all that we've been through
Because of you I've grown into the woman that I am
And I'm strong enough to make it on my own
But I'm taking you with me
You're always there for me to call

When tears come and my heart feels raw
You show me all the good in things
Love me through my suffering
And your arms are there to catch me when I fall
How do I say thanks for everything?
I'll hold you close one more time
Then turn and spread my wings
I'm taking you with me, no matter where I go or what I do
I'm taking you with me, every day I'll think of
            all that we've been through
Because of you I've grown into the woman that I am
And I'm strong enough to make it on my own
But I'm taking you with me
All the lessons that you taught me are what
            I'll live by every day
These are the things I'll take away, take away
I'm taking you with me, no matter where I go or what I do
Because of you I've grown into the woman that I am
And I'm strong enough to make it on my own
But I'm taking you with me
I'm taking you with me

~Karyn Williams, Songwriter and Singer, Nashville, TN

Meet the Contributors!
About the Authors
Acknowledgments
About Chicken Soup
Share with Us

Meet the Contributors!

Shawn Allen received his A.A.S. from Lewis and Clark Community College in 1987. He volunteers his time to coach the boys' varsity basketball team at MVCS in Alton, IL. Shawn enjoys sports, working with youth and spending time with his wife and four children. Please e-mail Shawn at Shawnallen6@juno.com.

Nick Anderson joined the Orlando Magic's community relations department as community ambassador during the summer of 2006. Anderson, who was a staple in the Orlando community as a player for ten seasons (1989-99), takes part in a variety of community outreach efforts. Out of the University of Illinois, Anderson was the Magic's first-ever NBA Draft selection.

Dwight Bain is an author, counselor, mediator and coach who helps people manage major change. He is a professional member of the National Speakers Association and has given over 1,500 motivational messages to groups on achieving greater success both personally and professionally. Contact him at www.DwightBain.com.

Marc Balara received his Bachelor of Science degree in 1984 and MBA in 1989 from St. Joseph's University in Philadelphia. He is the Director, Visual Branding for Unilever in North Jersey. Marc's inspiration is his wife Donna and their three kids, Victoria, Alexandra and Duncan. He loves coaching basketball.

Mike Barrett is retired from V.F. Corp (apparel), living a quiet life with his wife, Carolyn and best friend and dog, Bennie.

Lloyd Batts received his Master's of Education from Governors State

University in 1995. He is the Dean of Students at a Chicago high school. Lloyd still enjoys playing basketball on a regular basis and now follows his son Lloyd Jr.'s high school basketball games. He also has a daughter, Davina, who is about to graduate from college.

Furman Bisher was born in Denton, NC, spent three years in Navy Air Corps, a sports editor of *Charlotte News, Atlanta Constitution* and *Atlanta Journal*, writer of 1,500 magazine articles, twelve books, a bunch of halls of fame and honorary doctorate of letters from Furman University.

Gwynne Bloomfield-Pike worked for the NY Knicks from 1969-1978. After the Knicks she went to work for Broadway Theatre owners, where she still is working. Gwynne and her husband Gavin live in Port Washington, NY. Her greatest pleasures in life (besides her husband) are her three nieces and nephew, and her dog Wellington.

Betsy Blose is beginning her seventh year as Head Women's Basketball Coach at UNC Asheville in Asheville, NC and her twenty-fifth year in the basketball coaching profession. Betsy is one of seven daughters of the late William G. Blose and Ellen Blose. Betsy grew up outside Harrisonburg, VA with her six sisters and parents on a dairy farm.

Damon Blust began his career in sports entertainment in 1997 as a member of the Bud Light Daredevils. In 1999 Damon pursued a career as a mascot after signing with the Harlem Globetrotters. He has performed as the Boston Celtics mascot since 2003. Damon is a sports enthusiast and plans to write an inspirational children's book. Please e-mail him at airlucky@comcast.net.

Robert Boudwin is a University of Delaware graduate and professional mascot. Robert has coached hundreds, performed worldwide, written children's books, and produced critically acclaimed school shows. Boudwin was a 2006 inductee into the Mascot Hall of Fame.

He resides in Houston with his wife, Susie, an NBA dance coach. E-mail Robert at clutch@rocketball.com.

Nicole Musselman Boykin is owner of Koch, a textile, clothing and handbag design firm. Nicole is a graduate of Southern Methodist University. She is a wife and mother of a three-year-old son, Henry. In addition to designing textiles she is currently working on writing books for children. Please e-mail her at NKMB@sbcglobal.net.

Coach **Doug Branson** graduated with his Bachelor of Science degree from Troy University in 1997. He obtained his Masters of Public Administration from Columbus State University in 2004. Doug loves spending time with his wife Toni and their three children: Virginia, Katherine, and Doug III.

Lynn Bria is entering her first season as Head Women's Basketball Coach at Stetson University. Bria's strong faith guided her when her brother passed away in a 1995 car accident. She is the youngest of nine children — she jokes that her parents couldn't afford to own a baseball team so they grew their own!

Caron Butler is an NBA All-Star and starts at small forward for the Washington Wizards. Born and raised in Racine, Wisconsin, he suffered through a rough childhood; he was arrested fifteen times before the age of fifteen. As a high school basketball player, he was successful enough to receive a scholarship to play at UConn for Coach Jim Calhoun.

Skip Caray graduated from the University of Missouri School of Journalism in 1961, and has been a sports broadcaster ever since. Skip has broadcast professional basketball, football, baseball, hockey and boxing as well as college and high school basketball, football and baseball on both television and radio. For thirty-three years, Skip was a broadcaster for Atlanta Braves baseball. He passed away in the summer of 2008 after a long illness.

Van Chancellor is the Louisiana State University Women's Basketball Coach. Chancellor served for ten years as Head Coach of the Houston Comets from 1997-2006. During that time, Chancellor was named the WNBA Coach of the Year three times (1997, 1998, 1999) and he led the Comets to the league's first four titles (1997-2000). He was enshrined as a member of the Naismith Memorial Basketball Hall of Fame in September 2007.

Tricia Cullop graduated from Purdue University in 1993 with a Bachelor of Liberal Arts degree. She was an assistant coach at Radford University, Long Beach State University, and Xavier University before being named Head Women's Basketball Coach at the University of Evansville in 2000. Tricia remained at UE until 2008 when she was named Head Women's Basketball Coach at the University of Toledo.

Charles "Chuck" Jerome Daly is a former American Basketball Head Coach. He is famous for coaching the Detroit Pistons for nine years, winning consecutive NBA championships in 1989 and 1990, and for coaching the gold medal-winning basketball Dream Team in the 1992 Summer Olympics. During his fourteen-year NBA career, Daly has also coached the Cleveland Cavaliers, New Jersey Nets and Orlando Magic. He was inducted into the Basketball Hall of Fame on May 9, 1994.

Joe Dean, Jr. begins his tenth year as the Athletics Director at Birmingham-Southern College. Dean is directing BSC's move into its four-year transitional phase of NCAA Division III competition and membership in the Southern Collegiate Athletic Conference. Highlights of Dean's seventeen-year college coaching career includes an NCAA Championship in 1978 at UK, two NAIA National Tournament appearances and Coach of the Year honors, three times, at Birmingham-Southern, and a Division I head coaching position at the University of Central Florida. In 1994, Dean was selected to the Birmingham-Southern Sports Hall of Fame.

John DiPietro is a graduate of Assumption College in Worcester, Massachusetts. He is a marketer, national public speaker and author of *You Don't Have to Be Perfect to Be Great*. He enjoys traveling throughout the United States with his wife in their RV. John can be reached via e-mail at john@johndipietro.com. His website is www.perfecttogreat.com.

Matt Doherty is the head basketball coach at SMU. He formerly served as head coach at Notre Dame as well as at his alma mater, the University of North Carolina. Matt was an outstanding player at UNC for the legendary coach, Dean Smith, and was a teammate of the great Michael Jordan.

As Chief Operating Officer of the 49ers, **Andy Dolich** is responsible for the day to day business operations. He's logged over three decades of experience in the professional sports industry and held executive positions in the MLB, NHL, and NBA, most recently as President of Business Operations for the Memphis Grizzlies and FedEx Forum arena. Dolich serves on numerous sports industry and community-invested organizations.

Kip Drown received his Bachelor of Science in Health and Physical Education from Missouri State University in 1977 and his Masters of Science in Education (Secondary School Administration) from Missouri State University in 1981. Kip has taught and coached for thirty years in four different states and is currently the Head Women's Basketball Coach at Colorado State University-Pueblo. He enjoys traveling, reading, and is a die-hard St. Louis Cardinals baseball fan.

Ann Elizabeth Meyers Drysdale is a retired basketball player. She is a distinguished figure in the history of women's basketball and sports journalism. A standout player in high school, college, the Olympic Games, international tournaments, and the professional levels, she is one of the most talented women to ever have played the game. Meyers was the first player to be part of the U.S. National Team while still in high school. She was the first woman to be signed to a four-year athletic scholarship for college, at UCLA.

Tony Duckworth received his Bachelor of Science at Bob Jones University (1990) and Masters of Education from University of Tennessee-Chattanooga (1994). He coached men's college basketball for fifteen years, and is currently the Director of Athletics at Maryville University-St. Louis. Tony enjoys spending time with his wife and two boys while having a love for the outdoors. He can be reached for public speaking engagements via e-mail at tduckworth@maryville.edu.

Fran Dunphy, one of the all-time winningest coaches in Philadelphia Big 5 history, is in his second year at the helm of the Temple University men's basketball program. One of the most respected coaches in the nation, Dunphy, who owns a 322-181 overall record, has personified success over his coaching career. Dunphy and his wife, Ree, reside in Villanova, PA, with their son, J.P.

Jeff Eisen is the director of athletics at Mount Olive College. He has also worked at Saint Francis University, University of Detroit Mercy, and University of Evansville. He received an M.S. (Sports Administration) from St. Thomas University, J.D. from the University of Michigan Law School, and B.A. from Marietta College.

Britt Faulstick is the Associate Sports Information Director at Drexel University. He has been working with Drexel Women's Basketball since 2004. Britt is a 2003 graduate of Syracuse University where he earned his Bachelor of Arts degrees in newspaper journalism and political science. He earned his master's degree in public communication from Drexel University in 2006. Britt lives in Philadelphia, PA. He enjoys reading and writing, playing recreational sports and attending sporting events.

Houston Fancher is currently the Head Basketball Coach at Appalachian State University. He was named the 2003 Southern

Conference coach of the year. He received his BS from MTSU and his Masters in Educational Administration from LMU. His wife Cathy is a professor at ASU and they have two sons, Hayden and Ethan.

John Feinstein is the author of the bestsellers *A Civil War, A Good Walk Spoiled, A Season on the Brink, Hard Courts*, and many others. He writes regularly for *Inside Sports, Golf Magazine, Tennis Magazine*, and *Basketball America*. He is also a commentator for National Public Radio and ESPN. A graduate of Duke University, he lives in Bethesda, Maryland, and Shelter Island, New York, with his wife and children.

Adonal David Foyle (born March 9, 1975, in Canouan, St. Vincent and the Grenadines) is a Vincentian-American professional basketball player currently playing for the Orlando Magic. He was selected by the Golden State Warriors with the eighth overall selection of the 1997 NBA Draft. He played ten seasons with the team until the team bought out his contract on August 13, 2007. He was the Warriors' longest-tenured player.

John Gabriel was inducted into Kutztown University's Athletics Hall of Fame in 2005. He has recently taken a job as the Director of Scouting for the New York Knicks. Previously, he worked as an advisor for Florida Hospital, designing an executive retreat program. He is happily married to his wife Dorothy and they have three children ages eight, twelve and sixteen. John can be reached via e-mail at john@johngabe.com.

Ronald Gallimore received his Bachelor of Arts degree from UNLV in 1988. He has been a Strength and Conditioning Coach since 1985. He coached at UNLV, the Seattle Supersonics and just completed his eleventh year with the Portland Trailblazers. Bob and his wife LeeAnn enjoy spending time with their family.

Bob Ghiloni is the Men's Basketball Coach at Dennison University in Granville, Ohio. He has degrees from Ohio State University and The University of Dayton and has been teaching and coaching for twenty-eight years. Ghiloni and his wife, Molly, have two daughters, Danielle and Andrea.

Michelle (Barlau) Goodman lives in Minneapolis with her husband Ben and young daughter Clara. She teaches sixth grade mathematics in Lakeville, MN. She still plays basketball weekly with her college teammates. She also enjoys cooking, reading, gardening, and being with family and friends. She can be reached via e-mail at michellegoodman11@hotmail.com.

Jim Gorman has been married to his wife, Beverly, for twenty-five years and they have four children, Sara, Brian, Jeff, and Greg. They live outside Baltimore in Lutherville, MD. He is currently the Vice-President of Sales for the LifeCell Corporation and also serves as a volunteer Chairman for Metro Maryland Youth for Christ. Hobbies include golf and coaching basketball.

Gary Hahn has been the radio play-by-play voice of NC State football and basketball since 1990. He has also announced games for the University of Louisville, Ohio State University and the University of Alabama. Hahn is a 1974 graduate of Butler University and resides in Raleigh, NC.

Pat Hanna received a Bachelor's Degree in journalism from West Virginia University in 1974. He currently is regional editor at *The Register-Herald* in Beckley, WV. He previously worked at newspapers in Winston-Salem, NC, and Wheeling, WV.

Jack Harrington captained the first Boston College team to receive a NCAA Tournament Invitation (1958). He later served as an officer in the Navy Seal teams. He is an Executive Director with Oppenheimer & Co.

Vanessa Hayden-Johnson received her Bachelor's Degree from the

College of Agriculture in Family Youth in Community Sciences from the University of Florida in 2004. She played basketball while at Florida and is currently playing professionally in the WNBA with the Minnesota Lynx. Vanessa enjoys spending time with her daughter Zion Briana, reading, and spending time with her family.

Chris Hebb is a graduate of the University of Victoria with an Honors B.A. in Linguistics. While at University, he enjoyed a five-year varsity career on the Vikings basketball team, culminating in a Canadian championship in 1979-80. Chris is currently employed with Maple Leaf Sports and Entertainment. In his spare time, Chris likes to play golf, watch basketball and spend time with his family.

Brian Scott Hesington has worked in sports entertainment since 1994 when he landed the role as the mascot of the University of Arkansas. Since then, he has worked for multiple professional sports teams. He currently works with Stuff, the mascot for the Orlando Magic. Please e-mail your comments to shesington@hotmail.com.

Grant Hill is a professional basketball player currently playing for the NBA's Phoenix Suns. As a collegiate and professional star, Hill was considered one of the best all-around players in the game, often leading his team in points, rebounds and assists.

Dave Hixon has been Head Men's Basketball Coach for Amherst College for thirty-one seasons. He won the National Championship in 2007 and National Runners Up in 2008. His team has been in the Final Four for the past four out of five years. Dave resides with his wife, Mandy, and two sons, Matthew and Michael. He can be reached via e-mail at ddhixon@amherst.edu.

Dylan Howard received his Bachelor of Science degree from the University of Alabama-Birmingham (1992) and Master of Education in Sports Recreation and Management from Hardin Simmons University (2005). Nominated for Who's Who among Graduate

Students, he currently is the Head Men's Basketball Coach at Hardin Simmons University.

Stephen Howard graduated with a Bachelor of Arts in journalism from the University of North Texas in 2004, and is now a Sports Information Director at his alma mater. Sports are his passion, followed closely by a good piece of non-fiction and a homebrew. He can be reached via e-mail at stephen.howard@unt.edu.

Richie Hughes has more than twenty years of experience in Education, Athletics and Ministry. The former State Champion High School Coach has had an impact on young people and adults. As a Pastor/Author, Hughes has had the opportunity to minister to thousands of people on a weekly basis. To schedule Richie Hughes, please visit www.richiehughes.com.

Two-time Mid-Continent Conference Coach of the Year, **Ron Hunter** returns to the IUPUI bench for his fourteenth season in 2007-08. Last November, Hunter signed a three-year contract extension, keeping him on the sidelines through the 2012-13 seasons. Hunter is also one of seven head coaches currently serving on the Division I Basketball Academic Enhancement Group, as appointed by NCAA President Myles Brand.

Kenneth Hussar is a comedian who has provided laughs for over 4,000 audiences. He is a retired elementary teacher, newspaper columnist, and Strasburg Railroad Brakeman. His wife, Carolyn and he live in Lancaster, PA. Contact Ken via e-mail at ridingsway@netzero.net for information.

Phil Jasner won the Curt Gowdy Award for print journalism from the Naismith Memorial Basketball Hall of Fame in 2004. He was named Pennsylvania Sports Writer of the Year in 1999 and 2007. He has covered the 76ers and the NBA for twenty-nine seasons for the *Philadelphia Daily News*.

Maryalyce Jeremiah is the Head Women's Basketball Coach at Cal State University, Fullerton. As the all time winningest coach at the University, she ranks nationally among the top fifty in wins in NCAA Division I. Dr. Jeremiah has authored two books on coaching, has been the recipient of the Carol Eckman Award given to the coach nationally who displays ethics and sportsmanship in coaching, and is a member of the Ohio Basketball Hall of Fame and Museum.

Tony Jimenez, who resides in Wichita, KS, has written about junior college basketball nationally longer than anyone in the USA. He is a regular contributor to the *Sporting News*, a columnist for *Basketball Times* and authors *JC Reports*, an informational/recruiting service for two-year school players. E-mail him at tjderby@cox.net.

Jim Johnson and **Mike Latona** are from Rochester, NY, where Jim has won 287 career high-school games and Mike has earned seven first-place national writing awards. They are co-authoring the book *The Miracle of J-Mac*. Contact Jim via his website, *www.coachjimjohnson.com*, or e-mail Mike at mlatona@catholiccourier.com.

Sheila C. Johnson is President and Managing Partner of the WNBA's Washington Mystics and the only African-American woman to have ownership in three professional sports teams including the NBA's Washington Wizards and the NHL's Washington Capitals. She is CEO of Salamander Hospitality, founding partner of Black Entertainment Television, a film producer, and global ambassador for CARE.

Not only was **Bobby Jones** one of the most brilliant defenders ever to wear an NBA uniform, but he was also one of the most virtuous. It was Jones's stellar defensive play, along with his other specialties, that made him a standout sixth man. In 2003, Jones co-founded a Charlotte, North Carolina-based religiously affiliated non-profit, 2Xsalt, which supports underprivileged youth through sports.

Gordie Jones is the former sports columnist for *The Morning Call*, in

Allentown, PA. He lives in Lititz, PA, with his wife, Barbara, and son, Ryan.

Jim Jones, Jr. is an Account Executive for Biosite Inc. He has a wonderful family, and he enjoys watching his son, Rob, play basketball for the University of San Diego.

Ted Jones resides in Winter Springs, FL with his wife Meghan and three children. He serves as a reading teacher and assistant basketball coach at Winter Springs High School. Ted is the author of the 2007 basketball book, *Springing Forward*. Ted can be contacted via e-mail at springingforward@yahoo.com.

Cyndi Justice received her Bachelor of Science from Virginia Tech in 1992. She is an Assistant Women's Basketball Coach at Bridgewater College (Virginia). She enjoys sports, reading, and crafts. She would someday like to write children's books.

Matthew Keller graduated from the University of Florida in May of 2005, where he earned a Bachelor's degree in Psychology. After college Matthew decided to follow his passion for sports and is now the Special Events/Marketing Coordinator for the Orlando Magic.

Steve Kirschner is the Associate Athletic Director for Athletic Communications at the University of North Carolina. He is in his 20th year at UNC and 25th in sports information. He has worked with the Tar Heel basketball program since 1989 and has attended eight Final Fours including the 1993 and 2005 national championship seasons.

Greg Kite and his wife, Jenny, reside in Orlando where they are parents to ten children. Greg is the "old man who lives in a shoe." Before his days in "the shoe" he played professional basketball in the NBA for twelve years and was a member of the 1984 and 1986 World

Champion Boston Celtics. Greg is now working as an Investment Adviser.

Mike Krzyzewski is the Head Coach for both Duke Basketball and the United States National Team. Krzyzewski—fans worldwide know the three-time national champion as "Coach K"—is entering his twenty-eighth season at Duke, has led the Blue Devils to numerous winning seasons, coached players who have produced superb graduation rates and crafted a tremendous on-court legacy.

Jim Les is the Head Men's Basketball Coach at Bradley University. He was picked in the third round (seventieth pick overall) of the 1986 NBA Draft out of Bradley University. When he left college in 1986, he had compiled the second most assists in NCAA history. Les played seven seasons in the NBA, from 1988 to 1995 for four franchises.

Doug Lesmerises first wrote about the DelleDonne family while working for *The News Journal* in Wilmington, Del. A previous contributor to *Chicken Soup for the Baseball Fan's Soul*, he now writes for the *Cleveland Plain Dealer*. He lives in Westerville, OH, with his wife, Katie, and daughters Kyra and Daria.

Robert (Bob) Earl "Butterbean" Love (born December 8, 1942, in Bastrop, LA) is a retired American professional basketball player who spent the prime of his career with the Chicago Bulls. A versatile forward who could shoot with either his left or right hand, Love now works as the Bulls' Director of Community Affairs.

Bart Lundy is the Head Men's Basketball Coach at High Point University in High Point, North Carolina. At age thirty-six, Lundy is one of the youngest Division I head coaches in the country. His career record of 202-106 (.657) ranks him among the national leaders for active coaches in overall winning percentage. In 2004, he was named the National Rookie Coach of the Year in Division I men's basketball.

Nancy Martinz is a Supervisory Law Enforcement Park Ranger at Mount Rushmore. She dedicates her time to supporting her boys, Cody and Blake, who love basketball. Cody started playing when he was eighteen months old and wants to someday play in the NBA. Contact her via e-mail at martinz@gwtc.net for speaking engagements.

A veteran of radio and television for over thirty-five years, **Mac McDonald** has been the play by play voice for the University of Virginia and Wake Forest. A five-time Sportscaster of the Year, Mac hosts his own charity golf tournament to benefit the UVA Children's Hospital. Mac is now self-employed and is authoring his first book.

Gil McGregor is an original member of the Hornets broadcast team and begins his twentieth year behind the microphone. McGregor currently serves as an analyst for all Hornets telecasts on Cox Sports Television. McGregor is also an analyst of Atlantic Coast Conference Basketball telecasts with Jefferson Pilot/Raycom Sports. His other broadcast experience includes the NCAA Tournament on ESPN, MEAC Basketball telecasts on ESPN2, CIAA Basketball and Football and analyst for Southern University Jaguar basketball on Cox.

Bob Medina received his Bachelor of Arts degree from UNLV in 1988. He has been a Strength and Conditioning Coach since 1985. He coached at UNLV, Seattle Supersonics and just completed his eleventh year with the Portland Trailblazers. Bob and his wife LeeAnn enjoy spending time with their family.

Dr. Dwayne Mercer had been the pastor at First Baptist Church, Oviedo, FL, for fifteen years with now over 2,500 in attendance. He has been a contributing author to various newspapers, magazines and books. Dr. Mercer hosts the nationally televised program "The Winning Edge." He enjoys golf and spending time with his wife, Pam.

Tom Monahan lives in Nashua, NH with Jill, his wife of thirty-three years, and has three children. Although Tom's primary business has been real estate development, he recently acquired ownership of three radio stations that service Manchester and Nashua, NH with sports and local talk. Tom has been very successful and gives back to the community with his membership on numerous civic and charitable boards and organizations.

Under coach **Brian Morehouse** the Flying Dutch over the past decade are 288-56 (84%), claimed seven MIAA titles, made seven trips to the NCAA tournament, and won the Division III national championship in 2006. Coach Morehouse was chosen the 2005-06 Division III national coach of the year by the Women's Basketball Coaches Association (WBCA) and DIII News. Contact him via e-mail at morehouse@hope.edu.

John David Morris is a 1975 graduate of Ohio State, a twenty-year member of People of Faith Church, and Orlando area resident. He served for twelve years as Chairman for the congregation's Pastor's Masters Tournament Fundraiser. He and Linn, his wife of thirty-four years, have three sons — Eric, Tim, and Bryan.

William "Speedy" Morris is a retired college basketball coach. He was Head Coach at La Salle University from 1986 to 2001. He led the Explorers to four NCAA tournament appearances. He currently runs a basketball camp at Saint Joseph's Prep High School.

Marc Narducci has been a sportswriter for *The Philadelphia Inquirer* since 1983. A graduate of New Jersey's Glassboro State College (now Rowan University) he has covered high school, college and professional sports. Among the events he has covered are three NBA all-star games and one Super Bowl. Marc can be reached via e-mail at mnarducci@live.com.

Donnie Nelson is the General Manager and President of Basketball Operations for the Dallas Mavericks, an NBA team. He is the son of

Don Nelson, the current Head Coach of the Golden State Warriors. In a 2007 *Sports Illustrated* article ranking the NBA's personnel bosses from 1-30, Donnie was ranked #2. Donnie Nelson is involved in every aspect of the Mavericks' basketball operations. Nelson, who has twenty-two years of NBA experience, came to Dallas on Jan. 2, 1998, after three seasons as Assistant Coach with Phoenix.

David Nichols, retired from the superior court bench in 2005 and lives in Northwest Washington on the shores of Lake Whatcom. He has an intense interest in art, and now in retirement he devotes full time to his passion. Visit David at http://www.davenicholsart.com.

Dickey Nutt received his Masters of Education at Oklahoma State University. After thirteen years he resigned as Head Men's Basketball Coach at Arkansas State University. Dickey enjoys spending time with his wife Cathy and three children. Dickey spends most of his time now traveling and speaking to numerous business groups around the country on motivation and becoming the best you can be. He plans to either continue coaching or eventually get into athletic administration.

Ed O'Bannon is currently living in Henderson, NV, with his lovely wife Rosa and their three children, Aaron, Jazmin, and Ed. Jr. When he is not attending one of their many sporting events, you can usually find him at Findley Toyota, where he is a Sales Manager. If you are looking for a great car or just want to say hello, please e-mail him at eddieob31@cox.net.

Joe O'Toole: Retired Athletic Trainer after twenty-eight years with the Atlanta Hawks, Athletic Trainer University of Wisconsin, and State University of New York at Cortland, BS, Physical Education, Mayo Clinic, Physical Therapy, Indiana University, MS, and Athletic Training.

Luiza R. Osborne is currently attending Humboldt State University in Arcata, CA. She plays point guard on the women's team, even though she consistently asks to play center. As she's only 5'4" the coaches always readily refuse. She enjoys reading, playing cards, writing short stories, and of course playing basketball. She currently lives in Los Angeles with her older sister; unless she's at school where she lives in a large box with her teammate/best friend. Please e-mail her at luoz14@aol.com.

Chris Paul is an NBA All-Star and starts at point guard for the New Orleans Hornets. A Winston-Salem, NC native, Paul chose to stay close to home for college and starred at Wake Forest University where he went on to become a two-time All-American. Paul earned an Olympic gold medal as a member of the 2008 United States Men's Basketball Team.

Bob Pettit played eleven seasons in the NBA, all with the Milwaukee/St. Louis Hawks (1954-1965). He was the first recipient of the NBA's Most Valuable Player Award. He was elected to the Naismith Memorial Basketball Hall of Fame in 1970, and was named to the NBA 50th Anniversary All-Time Team in 1996.

Bobby Pinson is a former basketball player at Furman University in Greenville, South Carolina. He has lived his entire adult life in nearby Spartanburg, where he and his wife, Dixie, raised three daughters. Pinson spent many years in the oil transportation business and remains a community leader in Spartanburg County.

John Platz has been an announcer on Stanford University basketball radio broadcasts since 1988. A letterman guard on Cardinal teams in the early 1980s, Platz earned his undergraduate and law degrees from Stanford, and is currently Senior Counsel at Cisco Systems. His feature writing has appeared in *Stanford Magazine*.

Gregg Popovich has led the Spurs to four NBA Championships in his eleven seasons as the team's Head Coach. He is involved in several charities in the San Antonio area including the San Antonio Food Bank, Roy Maas' Youth Alternatives and the Kids Sports Network. Gregg and his wife, Erin, have been blessed with two children, Micky and Jill.

Jeff Price has served as the Head Basketball Coach at Georgia Southern University for the past nine years and has been a college basketball coach for twenty-seven years at various levels. He enjoys spending free time with his wife Jody, son Jaxson and daughter Abby.

Richard "Dick" M. Rea received his Bachelor of Science from Butler University in 1981. He's worked in TV news as a sports reporter/anchor/producer in Indianapolis for more than twenty-five years. Dick enjoys spending time with his wife, two sons, and a Chinese Sharpei. Contact him via e-mail at dick@reacompany.com.

Pat Riley is a former NBA Head Coach and current Team President of the Miami Heat. Widely regarded as one of the greatest NBA coaches of all time, Riley has served as Head Coach of five championship teams and Assistant Coach to another. He most recently won the 2006 NBA Championship with the Miami Heat.

John Rudometkin takes pleasure in being out in nature: traveling, fly fishing, and organic gardening. He also enjoys leading a weekly Bible study group. John has been married to his high school sweetheart, Carolyn, for forty-seven years and they have three sons, one daughter-in-law, and two grandsons. He can be reached via e-mail at jrudo44@gmail.com.

Donna Ruiz is the Vice President of Human Resources for the NBA's Sacramento Kings and the WNBA's Sacramento Monarchs. She graduated with honors from the University of California, Sacramento with a BA in Communications. Donna enjoys spending time with her husband and their children, sports, photography, movies and reading.

Steve Scalzi is a 2006 graduate of Boston College. His tenure as Student Assistant with BC basketball coincided with the winningest four-year period in the program's history. After one NIT and three NCAA tournament appearances, Steve joined the coaching staff of Northeastern University in 2006 where he became the youngest Director of Basketball Operations in the Colonial Athletic Association. Steve is engaged to his high school sweetheart and currently working towards his MBA. He can be reached via e-mail at s.scalzi@neu.edu.

Dolph Schayes received his Bachelor of Engineering from NYW in 1948. He played basketball for sixteen years in the NBA with the Syracuse Nationals and the Philadelphia 76ers. Dolph coached the 76ers for four years and the Buffalo Braves for one year. He enjoys traveling, swimming, reading and spending time with his family. Dolph currently manages apartments in the Syracuse area.

Jerry Schemmel has been the radio play-by-play announcer for the Denver Nuggets since 1992. On July 19, 1989, he survived the crash of United Airlines Flight 232 in Iowa. 112 of the 296 passengers died in the tragedy.

Steve Schultz is the Men's Basketball Coach at Fountain Valley High School located in Southern California. He teaches English, Philosophy, and leadership. Steve is the author of the book, *Anything and All Things... The Anthem of a Championship Life*. Contact him via e-mail at steve_schultz@hotmail.com.

Clayton Sheldon is the Director of Purchasing at Widener University in Philadelphia. He is also involved in community work and serves as a board member for the Salvation Army. His three beautiful granddaughters are the lights of his life and he flies to the West Coast as often as possible to visit with them.

Stephanie Sidney has had the privilege of working for the San Antonio Spurs for the past two years. She loves reading, cooking, spending time with her family and traveling. Please e-mail her at stephmsidney@yahoo.com.

Sam Smith is a freelance basketball writer and contributor to radio and television programs. He worked for twenty-nine years at the *Chicago Tribune*, where he was the basketball writer. He is the author of the bestseller *The Jordan Rules* and *Second Coming: The Strange Odyssey of Michael Jordan*.

Tom Smith is the Head Athletic Trainer for the Orlando Magic. He was first exposed to the international game of basketball while living in Ivory Coast West Africa. He has traveled with basketball teams to the Philippines and China. Tom and his wife Lisa have three children, Grant, Kailee Jo, and Jackson.

Tarek O. Souryal MD is a leading orthopedic surgeon in the field of sports medicine. He is the Head Team Physician for the Dallas Mavericks of the NBA. He also served as the Head Physician for the Dallas Texans of the Arena Football League, the Dallas Burn of MLS, the Dallas Freeze of the Central Hockey League and Wilmer-Hutchins High School. Dr. Souryal is the Medical Director at Texas Sports Medicine and former Director of the Sports Injury Clinic at S.M.U. Dr. Souryal is known internationally for his work on ACL injuries and ACL Surgery. He is married and has three children.

Tom Sterner has coached basketball for thirty years at every level: high school, college and pro. Most of his NBA career was spent with the Orlando Magic. He has a Masters of Education in Sports Administration from Temple University. He can be reached via e-mail at malorie630@aol.com.

No one has scored more points in Kansas High School basketball history—male or female—than **Jackie Marie Stiles**, the pride of the Claflin Wildcats. Jackie has carried her love for basketball into the next stage of her career by starting her own company J. Stiles

Total Training. She provides motivational speeches, basketball clinics/ camps, private basketball lessons, sports commentary and personal training. Please contact her via e-mail at stiles.jackie@gmail.com.

Dee Stokes has been involved with collegiate basketball for twenty years as a player and coach. She has spent many years rebuilding programs and is currently rebuilding the women's basketball program at Winston-Salem State University. Coach Stokes takes pride in building relationships with players and watching them grow as people.

Rachel Styles was affiliated with the Atlanta Hawks from 1968 to 1997, starting out as an usher at the Georgia Tech Coliseum where the Hawks played their games while the Omni Coliseum was being built. She worked at the Omni Coliseum from 1972-1997 as House Manager for all the events.

Richard Sutter has been at Westfield State for ten years and has been coaching since 1980. Sutter has twice been named MASCAC Coach of the Year and the team won the league title in 2006. Sutter assisted Coach Bruen at Colgate and also worked with Coach Curran of Molloy High School.

John Valore teaches physical education at Cherry Hill High School East in Cherry Hill, NJ. Valore is also the head coach for the boys' basketball team, which is consistently ranked year after year in the Top Ten in South Jersey. Valore is also a member of the South Jersey Hall of Fame.

Charlie Villanueva, now with the Milwaukee Bucks, was selected 7th overall in the 2005 NBA draft by the Toronto Raptors. Villanueva's most notable highlight was recorded when he set a career high and a franchise rookie record with forty-eight points in a game; the fourth highest performance ever by a rookie. Villanueva suffers from an autoimmune skin condition called alopecia areata which affects over five million North Americans. For more information, please visit www.cv3.com.

Jonathan Wallace played point guard for the Georgetown University's men's basketball team from 2004-08. A government major, Wallace was accepted to Georgetown University Law Center during his senior season.

Scott Wedman is a former NBA All-Star. He was drafted by Kansas City-Omaha Kings in the first round in the 1974 NBA Draft. Wedman played for the Kings, Cleveland Cavaliers and Boston Celtics during his thirteen-year career.

Bobby Williams is currently the Farm Director for the Washington Nationals Major League Baseball team. He has spent nine years in professional baseball after attending Rollins College and Georgia Southern University. Bobby and his wife, Mary Lynn, were married in November, 2008. They currently reside in Washington, DC and Sarasota, FL.

Karyn Williams, eldest daughter of NBA executive Pat Williams, grew up in an international family of nineteen children. She graduated from the University of Florida where she held the title Miss UF, 2000. Karyn lives in Nashville, TN, where she is building a career as a singer, writer, and author. Booking information: www.myspace.com/karynwilliams.

Dan Wood has served as Executive Director of the National Christian College Athletic Association (NCCAA) since May 2000. He coached and taught at Oklahoma Wesleyan University and Indiana Wesleyan University from 1987-1999. He is active in presenting the NCCAA's Game Plan 4 Life Character Program and would welcome invitations to present to churches, youth associations, home school groups and other youth agencies. He and his wife Kelly have two children, Courtney and Grant. Dan can be reached via e-mail at dwood@thenccaa.org.

Stephanie Zonars is a Certified Life Coach, passionate about helping women in sports win in life. She has served with Athletes in Action for seventeen years and is the author of *Timeout: Moments with God for Winning in Life*, a thirty-day devotional. Please contact her via e-mail at coach@lifebeyondsport.com or visit www.lifebeyondsport.com.

Who Is
Jack Canfield?

Jack Canfield is the co-creator and editor of the Chicken Soup for the Soul series, which Time magazine has called "the publishing phenomenon of the decade." Jack is also the co-author of eight other bestselling books including *The Success Principles™: How to Get from Where You Are to Where You Want to Be*, *Dare to Win*, *The Aladdin Factor*, *You've Got to Read This Book*, and *The Power of Focus: How to Hit Your Business and Personal and Financial Targets with Absolute Certainty*.

Jack is the CEO of the Canfield Training Group in Santa Barbara, California, and founder of the Foundation for Self-Esteem in Culver City, California. He has conducted intensive personal and professional development seminars on the principles of success for over a million people in twenty-three countries. Jack is a dynamic keynote speaker and he has spoken to hundreds of thousands of others at more than 1,000 corporations, universities, professional conferences and conventions, and has been seen by millions more on national television shows such as *The Today Show*, *Fox and Friends*, *Inside Edition*, *Hard Copy*, CNN's *Talk Back Live*, *20/20*, *Eye to Eye*, and the *NBC Nightly News* and the *CBS Evening News*.

Jack is the recipient of many awards and honors, including three honorary doctorates and a Guinness World Records Certificate for having seven books from the *Chicken Soup for the Soul* series appearing on the New York Times bestseller list on May 24, 1998.

You can reach Jack at:

Jack Canfield
The Canfield Companies
P. O. Box 30880 • Santa Barbara, CA 93130
phone: 805-563-2935 • fax: 805-563-2945
www.jackcanfield.com

Who Is
Mark Victor Hansen?

Mark Victor Hansen is the co-founder of Chicken Soup for the Soul, along with Jack Canfield. He is also a sought-after keynote speaker, bestselling author, and marketing maven. For more than thirty years, Mark's powerful messages of possibility, opportunity, and action have created powerful change in thousands of organizations and millions of individuals worldwide.

Mark's credentials include a lifetime of entrepreneurial success. He is a prolific writer with many bestselling books, such as *The One Minute Millionaire*, *Cracking the Millionaire Code*, *How to Make the Rest of Your Life the Best of Your Life*, *The Power of Focus*, *The Aladdin Factor*, and *Dare to Win*, in addition to the Chicken Soup for the Soul series. Mark has had a profound influence in the field of human potential through his library of audios, videos, and articles in the areas of big thinking, sales achievement, wealth building, publishing success, and personal and professional development. Mark is also the founder of the MEGA Seminar Series.

He has appeared on *Oprah*, CNN, and *The Today Show*. He has been quoted in *Time*, *U.S. News & World Report*, *USA Today*, *The New York Times*, and *Entrepreneur* and has given countless radio interviews, assuring our planet's people that "You can easily create the life you deserve."

Mark is the recipient of numerous awards that honor his entrepreneurial spirit, philanthropic heart, and business acumen. He is a lifetime member of the Horatio Alger Association of Distinguished Americans, an organization that honored Mark with the prestigious Horatio Alger Award for his extraordinary life achievements.

You can reach Mark at:

Mark Victor Hansen & Associates, Inc.
P. O. Box 7665 • Newport Beach, CA 92658
phone: 949-764-2640 • fax: 949-722-6912
www.markvictorhansen.com

Who Is
Pat Williams?

As one of America's top motivational, inspirational, and humorous speakers, Pat has addressed employees from many of the Fortune 500 companies. Pat is also the author of more than fifty books, his most recent title being *Chicken Soup for the Soul: Inside Basketball.*

Since 1968, Pat has been the general manager of NBA teams in Chicago, Atlanta, Philadelphia and Orlando. In 1996, Pat was named as one of the fifty most influential people in NBA history by Beckett Sports, a national publication.

Pat and his wife, Ruth, are the parents of nineteen children, including fourteen adopted from four nations, and have seven grand-children. Pat and his family have been featured in *Sports Illustrated, Readers Digest, Good Housekeeping, Family Circle* and *The Wall Street Journal.*

You can contact Pat Williams at:

Pat Williams
c/o Orlando Magic
8701 Maitland Summit Boulevard
Orlando, FL 32810
407-916-2404
pwilliams@orlandomagic.com
www.PatWilliamsMotivate.com

If you would like to set up a speaking engagement for Pat Williams, please call Andrew Herdliska at 407-916-2401 or e-mail him at aherdliska@orlandomagic.com.

Thank You!

With deep appreciation I acknowledge the support and guidance of the following people who helped make this book possible:

Special thanks to Alex Martins, Bob Vander Weide and Rich DeVos of the Orlando Magic.

Thanks also to my writing partner Ken Hussar for his superb contributions in shaping this manuscript.

Hats off to three dependable associates—my assistant Latria Graham, my trusted and valuable colleague Andrew Herdliska, and my ace typist Fran Thomas. I particularly salute Andrew, who went way beyond the call of duty on this enormous project.

Hearty thanks also go to my friends at Chicken Soup for the Soul Publishing LLC. Thank you all for believing that we had something important to share and for providing the support and the forum to say it. We offer thanks to our editors, Publisher Amy Newmark and Assistant Publisher D'ette Corona, for their assistance, guidance and advice.

We owe a very special thanks to our Creative Director and book producer, Brian Taylor at Pneuma Books, for his brilliant vision for our cover and interior. Finally, none of this would be possible without the business and creative leadership of Chicken Soup for the Soul Publishing's CEO, Bill Rouhana, and President, Bob Jacobs.

And finally, special thanks and appreciation go to my wonderful and supportive family. They are truly the backbone of my life.

~Pat Williams

Chicken Soup for the Soul

Improving Your Life Every Day

Real people sharing real stories—for fifteen years. Now, Chicken Soup for the Soul has gone beyond the bookstore to become a world leader in life improvement. Through books, movies, DVDs, online resources and other partnerships, we bring hope, courage, inspiration and love to hundreds of millions of people around the world. Chicken Soup for the Soul's writers and readers belong to a one-of-a-kind global community, sharing advice, support, guidance, comfort, and knowledge.

Chicken Soup for the Soul stories have been translated into more than forty languages and can be found in more than one hundred countries. Every day, millions of people experience a Chicken Soup for the Soul story in a book, magazine, newspaper or online. As we share our life experiences through these stories, we offer hope, comfort and inspiration to one another. The stories travel from person to person, and from country to country, helping to improve lives everywhere.

Share with Us

We all have had Chicken Soup for the Soul moments in our lives. If you would like to share your story or poem with millions of people around the world, go to www.chickensoup.com and click on "Submit Your Story." You may be able to help another reader, and become a published author at the same time. Some of our past contributors have launched writing and speaking careers from the publication of their stories in our books!

Your stories have the best chance of being used if you submit them through our website, at

www.chickensoup.com

If you do not have access to the Internet, you may submit your stories by mail or by facsimile. Please do not send us any book manuscripts, unless through a literary agent, as these will be automatically discarded.

Chicken Soup for the Soul
P.O. Box 700
Cos Cob, CT 06807-0700
Fax 203-861-7194

The Golf Book

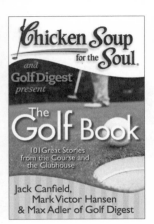

Chicken Soup and Golf Digest magazine's Max Adler and team have put together a great collection of personal stories that will inspire, amuse, and surprise golfers. Celebrity golfers, weekend golfers, beginners, and pros all share the best stories they've told at the 19th hole about good times on and off the course. Chicken Soup's golf books have always been very successful — with the addition of Golf Digest's industry connections, this book should hit a hole in one.

Tales of Golf & Sport

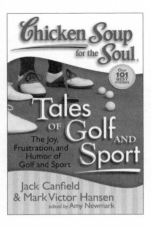

Golfers are a special breed. They endure bad weather, early wake up calls, great expense, and "interesting" clothing to engage in their favorite sport. This book contains Chicken Soup's 101 best stories about golfers, golfing, and other sports. Chicken Soup's approach to sports books has always been unique — professional and amateur athletes contribute stories from the heart, yielding a book about the human side of golf and other sports, not a how-to book.

The Wisdom of Dads

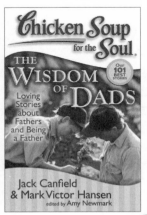

Children view their fathers with awe from the day they are born. Fathers are big and strong and seem to know everything, except for a few teenage years when fathers are perceived to know nothing! This book represents a new theme for Chicken Soup — 101 stories selected from 35 past books, written by sons and daughters about their fathers, and by fathers relating stories about their children.

Golf and Dads!

Loving Our Dogs

We are all crazy about our dogs and can't read enough about them, whether they're misbehaving and giving us big, innocent looks, or loyally standing by us in times of need. This new book from Chicken Soup for the Soul contains the 101 best dog stories from the company's extensive library. Readers will revel in the heartwarming, amusing, inspirational, and occasionally tearful stories about our best friends and faithful companions — our dogs.

Teens Talk High School

This book focuses on issues specific to high school age kids, ages fourteen to eighteen — sports and clubs, religion and faith, driving, curfews, growing up, self-image and self-acceptance, dating and sex, family relationships, friends, divorce, illness, death, pregnancy, drinking, failure, and preparing for life after high school. High school students will find comfort and inspiration in the words of this book, referring to it through all four years of their high school experience, like a portable support group.

Teens Talk Middle School

This "support group in a book" is specifically geared to middle school students ages eleven to fourteen — the ones still worrying about puberty, cliques, discovering the opposite sex, and figuring out who they are. Stories cover regrets and lessons learned, love and "like," popularity, friendship, tough issues such as divorce, illness, and death, failure and rising above it, embarrassing moments, bullying, and finding something you're passionate about.

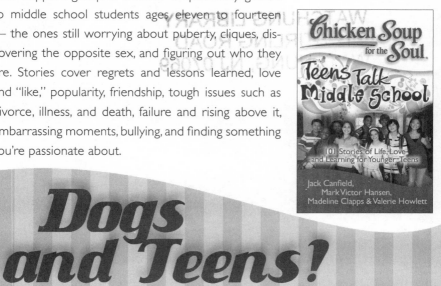

Dogs and Teens!

www.chickensoup.com